Real-Time Risk

Real-Time Risk

*What Investors Should Know About
FinTech, High-Frequency Trading,
and Flash Crashes*

IRENE ALDRIDGE AND
STEVE KRAWCIW

WILEY

For general information on our other products and services or for technical support, please contact our Customer Care Department within the United States at (800) 762-2974, outside the United States at (317) 572-3993 or fax (317) 572-4002.

Wiley publishes in a variety of print and electronic formats and by print-on-demand. Some material included with standard print versions of this book may not be included in e-books or in print-on-demand. If this book refers to media such as a CD or DVD that is not included in the version you purchased, you may download this material at http://booksupport.wiley.com. For more information about Wiley products, visit www.wiley.com.

Library of Congress Cataloging-in-Publication Data is available:

ISBN 9781119318965 (Hardcover)
ISBN 9781119319061 (ePDF)
ISBN 9781119319047 (ePub)

Cover Design: Wiley
Cover Image: © PM Images/Getty Images

Printed in the United States of America

10 9 8 7 6 5 4 3 2 1

To Henry and Rosalind

Contents

Acknowledgments   xi

CHAPTER 1
Silicon Valley Is Coming!   1
    Everyone Is into Fintech   3
    The Millennials Are Coming   7
    Social Media   9
    Mobile   10
    Cheaper and Faster Technology   13
    Cloud Computing   14
    Blockchain   15
    Fast Analytics   15
    In the End, It's All About Real-Time Data Analytics   18
    End of Chapter Questions   19

CHAPTER 2
This Ain't Your Grandma's Data   21
    Data   21
    The Risk of Data   23
    Technology   27
    Blockchain   30
    What Elements Are Common to All Blockchains?   31
    Conclusions   39
    End of Chapter Questions   39

CHAPTER 3
Dark Pools, Exchanges, and Market Structure   41
    The New Market Hours   51
    Where Do My Orders Go?   52
    Executing Large Orders   54
    Transaction Costs and Transparency   56
    Conclusions   57
    End of Chapter Questions   57

CHAPTER 4

Who Is Front-Running You?   **59**

Spoofing, Flaky Liquidity, and HFT   64
Order-Based Negotiations   78
Conclusions   80
End of Chapter Questions   81

CHAPTER 5

High-Frequency Trading in Your Backyard   **83**

Implications of Aggressive HFT   89
Aggressive High-Frequency Trading in Equities   96
Aggressive HFT in US Treasuries   98
Aggressive HFT in Commodities   99
Aggressive HFT in Foreign Exchange   101
Conclusions   102
End of Chapter Questions   102

CHAPTER 6

Flash Crashes   **103**

What Happens During Flash Crashes?   104
Detecting Flash-Crash Prone Market Conditions   116
Are HFTs Responsible for Flash Crashes?   124
Conclusions   126
End of Chapter Questions   127

CHAPTER 7

The Analysis of News   **129**

The Delivery of News   130
Preannouncement Risk   139
Data, Methodology, and Hypotheses   143
Conclusions   154
End of Chapter Questions   154

CHAPTER 8

Social Media and the Internet of Things   **155**

Social Media and News   160
The Internet of Things   165
Conclusions   169
End of Chapter Questions   170

CHAPTER 9
Market Volatility in the Age of Fintech   **171**
    Too Much Data, Too Little Time—Welcome, Predictive
      Analytics   174
    Want to Lessen Volatility of Financial Markets? Express
      Your Thoughts Online!   175
    Market Microstructure Is the New Factor in Portfolio
      Optimization   176
    Yes, You Can Predict $T + 1$ Volatility   178
    Market Microstructure as a Factor? You Bet.   179
    Case Study: Improving Execution in Currencies   183
    For Longer-Term Investors, Incorporate Microstructure
      into the Rebalancing Decision   184
    Conclusions   185
    End of Chapter Questions   185

CHAPTER 10
Why Venture Capitalists Are Betting on Fintech to Manage Risks   **187**
    Opportunities for Disruption Are Present, and They May
      Not Be What They Seem   189
    Data and Analytics in Fintech   191
    Fintech as an Asset Class   192
    Where Do You Find Fintech?   194
    Fintech Success Factors   194
    The Investment Case for Fintech   196
    How Do Fintech Firms Make Money?   198
    Fintech and Regulation   198
    Conclusions   200
    End of Chapter Questions   200

Authors' Biographies   **201**

Index   **203**

Acknowledgments

We would like to thank our intrepid editor Bill Falloon, and the great production team: Judy Howarth, Cheryl Ferguson, Sharmila Srinivasan, and Michael Henton for great cover design.

CHAPTER 1

Silicon Valley Is Coming!

Knock-knock.

—Who is there?

—Bot.

—Bot who?

—Bot and sold, it's a stat-arb world.

Do you wonder why the markets have changed so much? Where's it all heading? How will it affect you? You are not alone. Today's markets are very different from what they used to be. Technological advances morphed computers and infrastructure. Changes in regulation allowed dozens of exchanges to coexist side by side. The global nature of business has ushered in round-the-clock deal making. All of this has created stratospheric volumes of data. The risks that come along with automated trading in real-time are numerous. Now, the inferences from these data allow us to go to previously untapped depths of markets and discover problems and solutions that could not even be imagined 20 years ago.

Do you remember Bloomberg terminals? If so, you are reading this book not so long after it was written. JP Morgan's January 2016 announcement "to pull the plug" on thousands and thousands of Bloomberg terminals is a leading example of the sweeping disruption facing investment managers. Billion-dollar hedge fund Citadel followed suit on August 16, 2016, by announcing that it was taking on Symphony messaging as Bloomberg's replacement. Symphony, who? Many still struggle to wrap their head around the situation, with social media platforms like LinkedIn buzzing with discussions about pulling the plug on traditional sources of market data. Yet, here is fact: The competition is not sleeping, but working hard. And now, the competition is so strong that Bloomberg, Thomson Reuters, and others may end up in significant financial peril if they ignore fintech. Is your company also oblivious to changes in innovation?

The unfortunate truth is that many established firms are completely unprepared for the fast train of innovation currently passing them by. Old, manual procedures may have been fine in the past, but with innovation sweeping through, risk management executives have to be ready to see established operating models and platforms go out the door as newer, untried approaches take their place.

Consider the investment advisory industry. Reliance on charming brokers to seduce ever-dwindling pools of clients into paying for their commissions and overhead expenses remains the business model for some firms. At the same time, a number of well-established startups deliver cutting-edge portfolio-management advice to investors right over the Internet, with some charging as little as $9.95 per month.

TRADING FLOOR SUPERVISOR

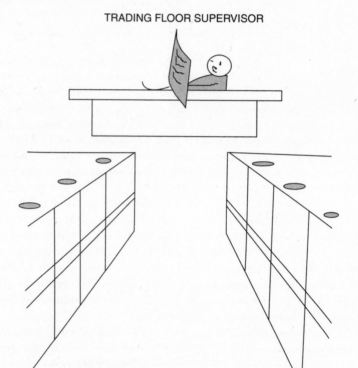

Global banks like Barclay's and Credit Suisse have exited the US wealth management arena while at the same time hundreds of millions of dollars in venture funding have been channeled to fintech startups working to streamline financial advice and beyond.

The bet has been wagered that new innovative and cost-efficient business models are here to stay. Innovation can take the form of a completely new approach to conducting business or through advances in the information used for the existing way of conducting business. As an illustration, while many finance professionals are still debating market structure and whether a new exchange will help people avoid high-frequency traders, companies like AbleMarkets deliver a streaming map of high-frequency trading activity directly to subscribers' desktops, leaving nothing to chance and helping to significantly improve trading performance across all markets. Similar innovations are going on in insurance, risk management, and other aspects of financial services, and firms that are not up to par on what's going on are at a significant risk of failure.

EVERYONE IS INTO FINTECH

Have you ever missed opportunities in the markets because you felt you were disrupted? We have been in a unique and fortunate position to be immersed in the heart of fintech innovation and to observe first-hand the extent of what is becoming a true disruption to businesses that, in turn, disrupted financial markets in the late 1970s and 1980s. Think of this as Finance 3.0. The possibilities are endless, and the new players are already embedded in most facets of traditional finance. These new players are not boiler rooms—most founders have advanced degrees and the most recent scientific innovations at their fingertips.

According to the Conference Board, investment in financial technology, trendily abbreviated into fintech, grew by 201 percent in 2014 around the world. In comparison, overall venture capital investments have only grown by 63 percent. The digital revolution is well underway for banks, asset managers, and customers. The impact on the financial institutions from the many startups that are trying unproven ideas is beginning to crystallize. Venture capitalists are betting that the once-stodgy financial industry is about to experience a considerable transformation.

The pace of change for the financial world is speeding up, and startups and venture capitalists are hardly alone in the fintech craze. Apple, Amazon, and Google, among others, have already launched financial services platforms. They have aimed at niches where they can establish a strong position. Threatened by these new entrants, traditional financial stalwarts are hearing the pitch: Adapt to the new environment or perish.

Banks are launching their own internal funds and hiring significant numbers of developers for internal builds. Why now? In his latest annual letter to shareholders, Jamie Dimon, CEO of JPMorgan Chase, wrote that "Silicon Valley is coming." While this statement went unnoticed by the news, it reflects the torrent of venture capital flowing into fintech. Estimates by the *Economist,* shown in Figure 1.1, suggest that 2014 was the watershed year for fintech startups.

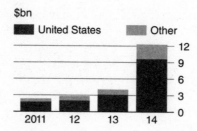

FIGURE 1.1 Global fintech investment
Source: Economist, May 19, 2015.

The Current State of Big Data Finance

What is big data finance? For many financial practitioners, *big data* is still just a buzzword, and *finance* is business as usual. However, looking at the hottest-financed areas of business, one uncovers particular trends that move beyond buzz into billion-dollar investments. According to Informilo.com, for instance, the fastest-growing areas of big data in finance in 2015 were:

- Payment services
- Online loans
- Automated investing
- Data analytics

Each of these areas, in turn, translates into automation. The payment services businesses, such as TransferWise, harness technology to commoditize counterparty risk computations. *Counterparty risk* is a risk of payment default by a money-sending party. Some 20 years ago, counterparty risk was managed by human traders, and all settlements took at least three business days to complete, as multiple levels of verification and extensive paper trails were required to ensure that transactions indeed took place as reported. Fast-forward to today, and ultra-fast technology enables transfer and confirmation of payments in just a few seconds, fueling a growing market for cashless transactions.

Similarly, the loan markets used to demand labor-intensive operations. Just 10 years ago, the creditworthiness of a bank's business borrowers were often judged during a round of golf and drinks with the company's executives. Of course, quantitative credit-rating models such as the one by Edward Altman of New York University have proved invariably superior for predicting defaults over most human experts, enabling faster online loan approvals. Online loan firms now harness these quantitative

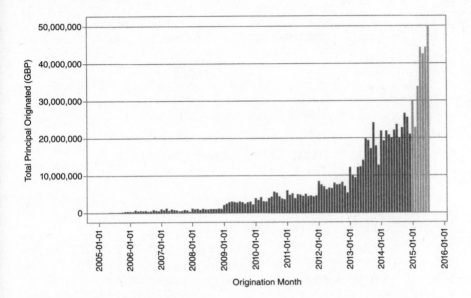

FIGURE 1.2 Zopa originations by month
Source: p2p-banking.com

credit-modeling approaches to produce fast, reliable estimates of credit risk and to determine the appropriate loan pricing.

Can anyone issue loans over the Internet or facilitate payments? According to recent industry reports, yes, the founders of many loan startups that originated during the credit squeeze of 2009—have little prior background in lending.

The key issues in lending are (1) having capital to lend, and (2) estimating credit risk of the borrowers correctly. The pricing of the loan service, *interest,* is then a function of the credit rating. If and when a borrower defaults, the loan should be optimally paid out from the interest. More generally, the average loan interest should exceed the average loan amount outstanding in order for the lender to make money.

The lending business is central to banking, and banks have had a near monopoly over the lending business for a very long time. New approaches to lending have emerged that compete with banks. Banks fund loans with deposits, whereas peer-to-peer lending is funded by investors. The leading players in this new approach to lending are the LendingClub and Prosper in the United States and Funding Circle and Zopa in the United Kingdom. In 2015, Zopa passed the Great Britain pound (GBP) 1 billion mark. Zopa's growth is shown in Figure 1.2.

With peer-to-peer lenders prospering with their new model, not only have banks noticed, but in some cases, started to acquire the upstart companies. SunTrust Bank acquired FirstAgain in 2012, later rebranding it LightStream.

New technologies are making their presence felt in wealth management as well. The topics of the robo-advising and a broad group of analytics are the most diverse and least exact. Robo-advising takes over the job of traditional portfolio management. The idea behind robo-advising is that a computer, programmed with algorithms, is capable of delivering portfolio-optimized solutions faster, cheaper, and at least as good as its human counterparts, portfolio managers. Given a selected input of parameters to determine the customer's risk aversion and other preferences (say, the customer's life stage and philosophical aversion to selected stocks), the computer then outputs an investing plan that is optimal at that moment.

Automation of investment advice enables fast market-risk estimation and the associated custom portfolio management. For example, investors of all stripes can now choose to forgo expensive money managers in favor of investing platforms such as Motif Investing. For as little as $9.95, investors can buy baskets of ETFs preselected on the basis of particular themes. Companies such as AbleMarkets.com offer real-time risk evaluation of markets, aiding the judgment of market-making and execution traders with real-time inferences from the market data, including the proportion of high-frequency traders and institutional investors present in the markets at any given time.

Not only are the changes aimed at managing the portfolios of the retail investor but also in the way companies are raising capital from these same investors. Crowdfunding has become a popular way for ideas to turn into projects with real funding. Kickstarter is one of the more popular sites.

And companies like Acuity Trading, Selerity, and iSentium are trying to harness data from platforms like Twitter to give an indication of investor "sentiment," which, in turn, gives them an idea of which way to trade.

The information-driven revolution is changing more than the investing habits of individuals. Institutional investors are increasingly subscribing to big data information sources, the more uncommon or uncorrelated is the data source, the more valuable it is. Each data source then drives a small profit in market allocations, and, when combined, all of the data sources deliver meaningful profitability to the data acquirers. This uncommon-information model of institutional investing has become known as Smart Beta or the Two Sigma model, after the hedge fund that grew 400% in just three years after the model adoption.

Underlying all these developments are the advances in scalable architecture and data management. Ultra-fast computation and data processing are critical enablers of other innovative forms of financial research and investing. Several companies have lately generated multibillion-dollar valuations by providing analytics in the software-as-a-service (SaaS, pronounced "sass"). For instance, Kensho is delivering the power of human-language queries in customers' data, which have been rolled out across Goldman Sachs.

Risk managers face a daunting challenge. Finding a risk event is the needle in a haystack. With automation and big data, the haystack becomes a mountain, and that mountain is virtual. The potential to catch issues could never have been stronger, but the ways of doing so are drastically novel.

THE MILLENNIALS ARE COMING

Why is technology transforming financial services now? Where was it 20 years ago, when computers and the Internet already existed? The short answer is the millennials, a generation of young people loyal to their smart phones and technology platforms and caring little for other brands, such as those of banks. With this generation of people now in the workforce, the choices that this group of 84 million make can provide the momentum to carry change. The millennials, born between 1980 and 2000, are expected to hold $7 trillion in liquid assets by 2020.

Recent findings in the Millennial Disruption Index (MDI) paint a startling portrait of preferences so different from older generations and so aligned with corporate digital heavyweights that financial services may change further dramatically. For example, according to the MDI study, one in three millennials will switch banks in the next 90 days. Additionally, over 50 percent of the 10,000+ respondents consider all banks to share the same value proposition. In other words, millennials don't see any difference among financial institutions. With over 70 percent of respondents saying, *"They would be more excited about a new offering in financial services from Google, Amazon, Apple, Paypal, or Square than from their own nationwide bank,"* it is clear that change is before us. Such findings open the door for brands like Google to enter the market and build a stable business with the millennials before bringing in older generations.

Traditional banks are feeling the threats of new entrants. Apple, Google, and Amazon are now all actively participating in the financial services industry. Whether through payments, cloud infrastructure, or investments into other fintech companies, firms considered technology leaders are focusing on financial services. The technology giants have even created their own lobbying group to avoid getting mired in regulatory red tape encasing banks. (See "An Excerpt about the Silicon Valley Lobbying Entity.")

AN EXCERPT ABOUT THE SILICON VALLEY LOBBYING ENTITY

Leading Silicon Valley players are so intent on entering financial services that they have launched a collaborative advocacy group to push Washington to create rules that are friendly to new technologies for financial services. The group, known as Financial Innovation Now, comprises founding members Google, Apple, Amazon, PayPal, and Intuit.

"These five companies are coming together because innovation is coming to financial services," Brian Peters, the group's executive director, told BuzzFeed News. "And they believe that technological transformation will make these services more accessible, more affordable, and more secure."

Whether through products like Google Wallet, Amazon Payments, and Apple Pay, acquisitions like PayPal's purchase of mobile payment startup Venmo, or investments like Google's in peer-to-peer lending outfit Lending Club, the group's founding companies all have a stake in the evolving industry and its regulation.

"The goal here is to serve as the voice of technology and innovators," Peters said. "Because honestly the banking policy conversations in Washington have not had that voice historically."

Source: Buzzfeed, Nov. 3, 2015.

How can this affect you? For years, financial services companies focused their investments on meeting regulatory changes or incremental improvements—automation, workflow, and so on. The essential business model went untouched. What's changing now is that new startups are bringing a Silicon Valley approach, and they are entering financial services with bold new business ideas.

The same message resonates for most investors: institutional or retail, global macro or small-cap, trading in the dark pools or lit exchanges. The sudden demand for new technology concerns all aspects of the financial ecosystem. At least some of the demand is based on the idea that operating models need to become leaner to offer services at lower price points, utilize a labor force based all over the world, and compete with new players. While slimming their offerings makes banks less prominent, it may enable them to face the challenge of new well-heeled Silicon Valley entrants as they get into the business of financial services.

How do you protect your company in an environment of disruptive change? How do you anticipate shocks to the markets precipitated by new dynamics at play? How do you ensure you know your customer when more and more of your company's process are moving to new platforms? These are some of the questions we explore in the following chapters.

How is the current environment different from the one, say, just 10 years ago? Today, many companies have adopted the *Digital One* company strategy with the idea to integrate social media, mobile technology, cheap computing power, fast analytics, and cloud data storage.

SOCIAL MEDIA

Social media alone creates change, and not just because of all the new tools connecting billions of individuals worldwide. People use social networks to gain immediate access to information that is important to them. The increased independence that people feel when they can access their networks whenever and wherever they want makes these networks a treasured part of the way they spend their day.

For investors, social media may mean wide access to a variety of information on the go. On the train and feel like learning the business model of some obscure public company? Not an issue. At the airport, but thought of investing in a specific municipal bond and need more information on the jurisdiction? Here it is. A successful fintech business has a social network that reaches investors both proactively and responsively. By offering a social experience, the business can provide traditional services in a setting that is consistent with the social network's way of navigating. Analyzing a customer's use of the social network allows a company to respond to clients in a tailored fashion, offering messages and ideas that are consistent with what the customer wants.

The implications of social media, however, go far beyond the communication and customer service experience a business can have with prospects and clients. Unlike news, social media is a powerful user-generated forum where ideas collide, opinions are formed, and beliefs are floated, often completely under the radar of traditional media. The participants who offer the opinions often join in anonymously, concealing their identity in a degree of masquerade where they feel comfortable to disclose their thoughts honestly and passionately. The same degree of honesty is often impossible in our politically correct daily interactions, even with the nearest friends behind closed doors. The chatroom-formed opinions then often trickle into the stock markets as people trade on their beliefs, putting their money where their mouths are.

Harvesting and interpreting social media content has thus been a boon for a range of financial businesses. Machine-collected sentiment on specific stocks has been shown to predict intraday volatility and future returns. The AbleMarkets Social Media Index, for example, has consistently predicted short-term volatility over the past six years, and is used by investors, execution traders, and risk management professionals.

Is all social media content created equal? As you have guessed it, this is very far from being the case. With proliferation of automatic social media tools, for instance, a lot of the content comprises "reposts" and "retweets" of information found elsewhere. This duplication of materials sometimes is worthwhile and reflects the copying party's agreement or endorsement of the original content. In many instances, however, duplicate content appears to be streamed simply to fill the informational void of a given social media participant's stream.

Another social media hazard is fake news. This may come in the form of individuals' posts or, much worse, via fraudulent posts on hijacked accounts of other users. A classic in the latter category was a Twitter post on the Associated Press account informing followers of an explosion at the White House on April 23, 2013.

Separating the wheat from the chaff in the social media space is not a job for dilettantes, and requires advanced machine-learning algorithms. In today's market environment, where the profit margins are thin and every bit of information is valuable, correct inferences are critical and experience in dealing with various circumstances is worth a lot.

MOBILE

How is mobile affecting your business? The prevalence of mobile devices has already driven business of all shapes and sizes to offer their services through an online channel. Why are people choosing to transact over the mobile channel? Accessing a service at a convenient time without any concern of intrusions during the experience is a very powerful use case. There are no lines, no puddles to navigate on the way to the service, and the customer can jump between the transaction and doing something else as needed.

Furthermore, mobile takes instant gratification to a new level. Are you sitting on the beach, yet have a sudden urge to send money back to your parents in Canada? TransferWise will take your order right there and then.

Need to apply for a loan at the same time? No problem—100 or so new apps will be at the ready to process your information and issue preapproval in a matter of minutes, if not seconds.

The ability to fulfill your latest craze or wish anywhere at any time is clearly driving much of market innovation. In response to people's 24/7 newly found ability to demand financial services, companies like the Chicago Mercantile Exchange (CME) now offer around-the-clock trading in selected futures. Whenever you want it, you can bet your money on the latest thought or piece of research.

Adding to the real-time 24/7 availability of services is the proliferation of smart watches. Whereas "traditional" mobile devices may be securely packed out of site, say, in your back pocket, the wrist gadget is much harder to ignore. And the millennials reportedly love it. In response, the development of smartwatch applications devoted exclusively to all things financial has exploded. According to Benzinga, there are at least 22 fintech apps coming to Apple Inc.'s smartwatch (see "Financial Services Applications Being Developed for the Apple Smartwatch"). And there is no mention of Bloomberg or Thomson Reuters on this list. Are they wise to stay away from the smartwatch, or will someone else just step in and replace them altogether?

FINANCIAL SERVICES APPLICATIONS BEING DEVELOPED FOR THE APPLE SMARTWATCH

1. *Scutify.* Scutify (a financial social network) was the first fintech company to confirm to Benzinga that it was developing an app for Apple Watch.

   "Anyone that's an investor [will] want to be able to check stock quotes and interface with their portfolio and see if the portfolio is up or down and what it's doing for the day," Cody Willard, chairman of Scutify, told Benzinga. When asked why Scutify was so eager to jump on the Apple Watch bandwagon, Willard recalled the words of a hockey legend that was famously quoted by Apple co-founder Steve Jobs.

   "You want to be as, Wayne Gretzky famously said, skating to where the puck is going, not to where it is," said Willard. "We've got to move forward if we're moving to a wearables culture."

2. *NewsHedge*. NewsHedge, a Chicago-based fintech startup that develops software solutions for the global financial community, is working on an app for multiple smartwatches.

3. *Prism*. Consumers want a simple way to pay bills. Prism, a startup devoted to addressing this issue, has developed an Apple Watch companion app for use with its iPhone app.

4. *Unspent*. Unspent, an app that allows users to track their spending and set up budgets for multiple spending types, is coming to Apple Watch.

5. *Fidelity*. Fidelity is building an app for Apple Watch that will give its customers a "distinctive overview of global markets and alerts on stocks and investments in real-time right on their wrist."

6. *iBank*. iBank will provide some of the same features as Unspent—plus a whole lot more.

7. *MoneyWiz 2*. MoneyWiz is bringing its latest app to Apple's highly anticipated smartwatch. The app will allow users to check account balances and create expenses/incomes on the go. Users will also be able to change the theme to match the look of their watch.

8. *Citibank*. Citigroup Inc. has developed an Apple Watch app that will allow customers to check their account details and locate the nearest ATMs, among other features.

9. *E*TRADE*. E*TRADE plans to have an app available in time for the Apple Watch's domestic debut on April 24. Finance Magnates detailed the app, which will allow users to "follow the markets and their own portfolios." Users will not be able to enter trades, however.

10. *IG Group Holdings*. In a separate story, *Finance Magnates* reported that IG Group Holdings Plc was the first company to announce an actual trading application for the Apple Watch.

11. *Chronicle*. Some people need help remembering when it's time to pay their bills. Chronicle hopes to meet their needs.

12. *Redfin*. Scheduled to debut at launch, the Redfin home buying app will allow users to find nearby homes that are for sale, view photos and statistics (prices, square footage, etc.) and info with friends and family, among other features.

13. *Trulia*. According to *Time*, Trulia will also bring real estate listings to the Apple Watch.

14. *BillGuard*. Lots of apps allow users to track their spending—this one also lets them know when a fraudulent charge has been made. According to *Time*, BillGuard (which is already on iOS and Android) will provide those features to Apple Watch users.

15. *Discover*. *Time* also reported that Discover Financial Services is making an app that will allow Discover cardholders to check available credit, bank balances and other tidbits.

16. *BankMobile*. According to *Bank Innovation*, BankMobile is among the startups that are interested in Apple's new smartwatch. The company, which claims to be the only banking service in America with "absolutely no fees," is reportedly working on an Apple Watch app.

17. *DAB Bank*. *Bank Innovation* also reported that German company DAB Bank is developing an Apple Watch app.

18. *PortfolioWatch*. PortfolioWatch is one of the few apps that actually requires users to pay a couple bucks. Buy the iPhone/iPad version today and get the Apple Watch version for free when it becomes available.

19. *24me*. There has been a lot of talk about the Apple Watch's various health and fitness features, but few have talked about its ability to act as a personal assistant. 24me could change that. Best of all, users can add info from their favorite financial service providers.

20. *Pennies*. Another personal budgeting app, Pennies is available for the iPhone and is being developed for the Apple Watch.

21. *Call Levels*. Call Levels announced this week that it is bringing its real-time financial monitoring and notification service to Apple's smartwatch.

22. *Mint*. Mint was one of the first apps confirmed for the Apple Watch. The company describes it as a "companion to the Mint iPhone experience."

CHEAPER AND FASTER TECHNOLOGY

What would it mean to you if your technology costs dropped? Over the past 30 years, the costs of computing have been falling steadily and, sometimes, exponentially. Some 30 years ago, a computer of decent processing power cost as much as US$20 million and was so big that it required its own highly air-conditioned room. Today, a machine with comparable specifications can be picked up at a local Best Buy for about $200, and it is about the size of a high school yearbook. The decline in the costs of computer technology has been driven by several factors:

1. Broadly-based demand for fast, superior computing by retail users, such as video gamers, has created a business case for a larger-scale manufacturing of computers, reducing costs.
2. Investments in research and development by Silicon Valley consumer-oriented companies, such as Google and Apple, have resulted in faster, leaner, and more affordable solutions.
3. Overseas investments by countries such as Singapore enabled foreign production of top-quality components at a fraction of the cost, reducing overall ticket prices of machines.

Lower costs have permeated every aspect of computing from data storage to analytic power, allowing innovations such as cloud computing to flourish.

CLOUD COMPUTING

The term *cloud* refers to a collection of computers, each with its separate processing and storage engines, which are interconnected and operate with a single interface. The interface is a complex computer program with built-in intelligence to automatically distribute the workload and the storage capacity among the participating machines. The cloud enables companies to reduce their data storage and processing costs by outsourcing at least some of their infrastructure and data storage.

A great example of a successful cloud deployment is Tradier.

> *According to Forbes, Tradier offers a brokerage-account management system, a trading engine, and some market data. It then hands them off to application developers who can launch their own trading platforms, mobile apps, algorithmic trading systems, or other customized features for their customers, who are traders and investors who want to play the markets their own way. Account settings and market data are based in the cloud, so customers can log in to, and trade from, any of Tradier's developer partners.*
>
> *As Dan Raju, the CEO of Charlotte, N.C.–based Tradier, explains it, "Tradier has decoupled the individual brokerage account from the front-end investing experience." Raju believes that his firm is offering a democratic platform that gives everyone*

access to the same cloud-based engine that powers retail trading. He thinks of the developers as delivering "that most innovative last mile" to the trader, while the nuts and bolts of account management, tax reporting, funding, and so on are handled by Tradier.

BLOCKCHAIN

Blockchain, a technology underlying Bitcoin and gaining an increasingly wider acceptance in financial settlement, is an example of a cutting-edge technology made possible by the cloud. The key idea underlying blockchain is an algorithm allowing users to simultaneously update the cloud database while maintaining the database's integrity, all in real time. Applied to financial trading, blockchain enables brokers and other institutions that handle their orders and money to reconcile their ledgers in real time. In other words, blockchain shortens the settlement procedures from $T + 3$ and $T + 1$ (still a standard in many financial instruments today) to real time. Shorter settlement times, in turn, allow for real-time margin calculation and lower margin-related risks. These developments, once adopted, will lead to even more real-time trading.

This won't happen overnight. The complexities involved in moving all trading toward real time are nontrivial. Topics like margin, securities lending, and over-the-counter (OTC) trading introduce time-consuming administrative procedures or custom trades that are not perfectly suited to the standardized type of blockchain discussed at this time.

Of course, the value of blockchain extends far beyond financial settlement. It is a tool that allows multiple parties to do business together ensuring reliability and at the same time without the threat of corrupting data. The financial businesses that are likely to be affected by blockchain technology require real-time electronic negotiations, such as over-the-counter trading, loan origination, and any kind of workflow that was historically done slowly due to the high degree of error and the complexity of transactions. In short, before blockchain, many tasks had to be executed by one party at a time to prevent corrupting data. With blockchain, many parties can do tasks at the same time without worrying about possible overwrites, miscommunications, and so on.

FAST ANALYTICS

TransferWise and loan-issuing apps did not emerge as a function of an ability to quickly send requests on the go. Beneath every successful money transfer and loan approval is a complex analysis that determines the risk of each operation.

At the core of all the super-fast information sharing is data analytics. Take, for instance, any near-instantaneous loan approval process. All loans are subject to credit risk—the risk that the loan is not repaid on time, if at all. Typically, the higher the probability that the loan is repaid in full and on schedule, the lower are the interest rates the lender needs to charge the borrower to make the transaction worthwhile. The reverse also holds: The higher is the probability that the borrower defaults, the higher are the rates the lender needs to charge to compensate for the risk of a default. The creditworthiness of the borrower can be forecasted using various factors, of which free cash flow and its relationship to the existing short-term and long-term debt, as well as other factors from Edward Altman's model, are critical. The ability to gather and process the required data points in real time are making the here-and-now loan approvals possible.

In general, risk, to many financial practitioners, has implied a multiday Monte Carlo simulation, something impossible to accomplish in a matter of hours, let alone seconds. Now, with new technologies, über-fast processing of data is not only feasible, it is already in deployment in many applications.

How does data processing accelerate over time? Several applications running atop cloud architecture help dissect vast amounts of data faster than a blink of an eye. MapReduce was a first generation of fast software that allowed data mining extensive volumes of information and helped propel Google Analytics to its current lead. Still, newer, faster applications are here. Spark, an application that also runs on top of a cloud architecture, outperforms MapReduce and delivers lightning-fast inferences through advanced management of computer resources, data allocation, and, ultimately, super-fast computational algorithms rooted in the same technology that allows real-time image and signal processing.

To understand why customers make decisions, companies harness the data available to them. In the past, customer segmentation studies were fixed in a point in time and used a variety of analytical approaches. Why go through this effort? By identifying types of customers who have similar tendencies to make similar decisions, a company can tailor their marketing, products, and investments. But that is the traditional approach.

With all forms of transactional and social data available and with enormously more computing power, companies can predict future behavior of clients almost at the same pace as clients are making their own decisions. For example, where will the aggressive high-frequency traders trade in five minutes? New technologies, such as the one of several offered by AbleMarkets, can answer this question on the fly.

Traditional players need to review their technology spend and consider that while they are making incremental improvements, their clients may be evaluating a leap to an insurgent with a category-killing new app.

Not only are startups working to provide discrete services with the likes of Google but also entire business models are being created to challenge established ways of doing business. For example, robo-investing is a substitute for online brokers as well as full-service brokers and financial planners. The idea has been around for a while; however, in the last five years the momentum has started to grow. According to Corporate Insights, robo-advisers had gathered $20 billion in assets by the end of 2014, which is a small portion of the $24 trillion in retirement assets in the United States. The growth and the high-profile venture capital funding of Betterment and Wealthfront have led players such as Vanguard to launch their own robo-advisers. The growth of these companies is a topic the entire investment management industry is watching and the question becomes will the baby boom generation adopt this form of wealth management in their retirement or is this service geared to the millennials.

The innovation to use predictive technology is not just about consumer habits. Of course, future fintech solutions will churn through transaction history to spot trends and use that information to provide intelligent recommendations on decisions such as what credit card to pay off first, how much to put down on a home, or how to save for a new car. They'll even suggest things like whether it's better to buy or lease a car. However, the majority of changes from predictive analytics will occur at the institutional level, resulting in sweeping organizational and operational changes at most financial services.

For institutional asset managers, predictive analytics assess future volatility, price direction and likely decisions by fund managers. A pioneer in predictive analytics for investment management is AbleMarkets, which brings aggressive high-frequency trading (HFT) transparency to market participants. AbleMarkets estimates, aggregates, and delivers simple daily averages of aggressive HFT so that professionals can improve their prediction of the market's reaction to events, assessments of future volatility, and shorter-term price movement. It is used for portfolio management, volatility trading, market surveillance by hedge funds, pension funds, and banks.

What is different now? Computers are now involved in many economic transactions and can capture data associated with these transactions, which can then be manipulated and analyzed. Conventional statistical and econometric techniques such as regression often work well, but there are issues unique to big data sets that may require different tools. First, the sheer size of the data involved may require more powerful data manipulation tools. Advanced databases and computer languages are required for most large data sets; after all, even the latest version of Excel stops at some one million rows. What if your data set contains five billion records? Second, we may have more potential predictors than appropriate for estimation, so we need to do some kind of variable selection. A popular technique called principal component analysis does just that: it estimates clusters of properties common among the records. Those clusters next become important variables in slicing and dicing the data. Third, large datasets may allow for more flexible relationships than simple linear models. Machine learning techniques such as decision trees, support vector machines, neural nets, deep learning, and so on may allow for more selective ways to model complex relationships.

What are the old-timers, who want to survive and thrive in the new competitive environment, to do? First, one needs to understand the lay of the new land. The borders have been redrawn, the capitals have moved, and Finance 3.0 is simply not the business it used to be.

IN THE END, IT'S ALL ABOUT REAL-TIME DATA ANALYTICS

Much of this book is devoted to the innovation in the growing field of data analytics. In the last 20 years, finance has seen nothing short of an explosion of data. Just 20 some years ago, the only data available to investors comprised five figures reported in the long tables in the newspapers on the following day $(T + 1)$. The data comprised daily open, high, low, close and volume for the previous trading day. No information about the market conditions beyond these numbers was available even within the banks and other market makers: by law, only the latest 21 days of intraday data were required to be handy at most institutions. Data storage was expensive, number crunching took forever, the profit margins were thick enough to avoid any additional data-driven work.

As technology became cheaper and more sophisticated at the same time over the following decades, the market participants began reevaluating the cost–benefit equation of more data. Quant traders and portfolio managers were the first to deploy data analysis to improve financial functions in a semi-algorithmic framework. Using mostly daily data and armed with the latest inferences from physics and other research fields, the quants sought answers to challenges associated with portfolio risk, derivatives pricing, diversification, and other issues. Their findings paved the way to modern exchange-traded funds (ETFs), passively managed, yet actively traded indexes.

As the daily-data field became saturated, researchers turned to intraday data. The late 1990s saw the birth of high-frequency trading and execution algorithms, requiring a higher degree of processing speed. With Regulation Alternative Trading Systems (Reg ATS, 2000), the volume of data increased further as a number of new trading venues and exchanges came online.

Regulation National Market Systems (Reg NMS, 2005) has further driven data storage and processing, by requiring the compilation of market quotes in the government's Security Information Processor (SIP) system and the following redistribution of SIP data back to trading venues. The introduction of SIP has shored up the real-time nature of data on many exchanges and contributed a great deal to the volumes, depth, and sophistication of financial data we observe today. And the regulatory shift is chasing the data advances to their utmost frontiers. For example, the latest regulations about pre- and post-trade analytics coming from MiFiD II and the intraday liquidity risk management from Basel all demand new, faster, ever more powerful data and analytics.

And the data sets are still growing. As new asset classes and new exchanges come online, trading hours extend and trading becomes more and more global, generating volumes of new data. In addition, the world of data outside of financial services has a direct influence on what is going on within the markets, and making use of this data requires storage and real-time processing. Taken in aggregate, the news delivered by companies like Dow Jones, along with the blog posts by random individuals, and even the Internet activity collected by the data behemoths like Google, can all be used to understand and improve upon market movements. And it is all happening right this moment, while you are reading this sentence.

This book is written for investors who are interested in the impact of the latest revolution to affect finance and what that means for their decision making. The book is not heavy on the models, although references are provided, where appropriate. Instead, the book discusses at length the perceived and documented impact these disruptions will have on companies and what that will mean for the markets. With market crashes, interest rate uncertainty, and wars threatening to disrupt the market stability, it is more important than ever to have a balanced data-driven perspective on what is really going on in today's markets.

Have you ever been concerned that the big data revolution and real-time disruption is leaving you and your investment portfolio behind? This book seeks to close the gap in knowledge so that you can be more confident in making investing decisions going forward.

END OF CHAPTER QUESTIONS

1. What is fintech?
2. Why is fintech boom happening now?
3. What are the primary enablers of fintech innovation?
4. What are the hottest areas of fintech innovation?
5. What are the biggest risks of fintech innovation?

CHAPTER 2

This Ain't Your Grandma's Data

—What do bots and intraverts have in common?

—They like to keep their cool.

Real-time risk is the possibility of lost value in an investment that occurs very fast, in real time or near-real time. It is often known as intraday drawdown, or instantaneous or short-term downward volatility; it is closely related to intraday margining. While real-time risk has in principle existed since the beginning of financial time, there was little way to scientifically measure and estimate it. This chapter focuses on the trends that allowed for the development of real-time risk as a discipline.

DATA

A *New York Times* article covering the latest Triple Crown horse race winner, American Pharoah, in early 2016 noted that the horse was identified as having amazing potential when the animal was only one year old. The prediction of success was made by a team of data scientists who estimated the horse's performance by noting the size of the winner's heart, among other characteristics compared with past race winners. On the future potential of the horse, the data scientists advised the owner "to sell the house, but keep the horse." Their prediction paid off—American Pharoah won and made the owner a small fortune. The real victory, however, can be assigned to data science—the researchers' ability to identify the winner ahead of time based on quantitative metrics.

At its core, the data science behind the horse's win is similar to the methods deployed by modern analysts of financial markets. By observing and measuring recurring characteristics and phenomena in the stream of financial digits, data scientists are able to pinpoint winning stocks, predict market crashes, detect market manipulation, and the like.

With time, financial analysis is becoming increasingly precise and data-intensive. This change is driven by ever-plummeting costs of the technology required to crunch data, by ever-expanding data availability, and by the success of data science in financial applications. Big data analyses often drift to the shortest time frames, involving data captured in milliseconds and microseconds. Firms such as Getco, Virtu, and Quantlab have developed their capabilities to analyze data with short-term time frames over the past couple of decades. Not only do institutions benefit from the advantages of short-term financial data analyses, but also smaller investors can reap handsome rewards, as well.

The speed of analysis has changed the data itself. Today, data come in many shapes and sizes. Broadly, data can be thought of as structured versus unstructured. *Structured data* refers to numbers that fit neatly into a database. Structured data have well-defined columns and rows, and are delivered in this deliberate manner. As a result, structured data sets immediately lend themselves to financial analysis, and can be tested as factors in factor models, similar to a market model or an extended capital asset pricing model (CAPM).

Unstructured data is the opposite of structured. It can take many forms such as human speech, diverse web content, and raw market data comprising every single tick of data across the markets. Unstructured data are generally unsuitable to analyses involving traditional financial modeling, and must be first cleaned and structured in order to be useful.

The process of data structuring can be complex, tedious, and above all, uncertain. Fitting loose data into a rigid table almost always results in tossing overboard some "extraneous" data points, which may prove to be extremely valuable in another pair of hands. Extracting meaningful insights is generally not even an exercise in machine learning—it is art as much as it is science, and years, if not decades, of experience are required to produce meaningful inferences beyond basic summaries.

As a result of the complexity embedded in the process of data structuring, structured data is becoming a hot commodity, purchased by hedge funds to improve returns and by industry vendors who want to improve their competitive analysis.

In addition to the structured versus unstructured classification, some researchers like to distinguish between data and information. Strictly speaking, information is only new data. Old data is not news—it is old data. Information arrives in an unpredictable pattern, and can comprise people's opinions, events, and other, potentially noisy, bits. Old data, on the other hand, are neatly stored in often easily-accessible formats and frameworks. Regardless of mnemonics, both information and data are critical in today's markets. Information provides us with inputs into real-time assessments of the market conditions, and the old data allow us to train our assessments on past behavior.

Of course, the past is not predictive of the future; however, some past behaviors of the markets and market participants recur again and again.

Take, for example, exchange-traded funds (ETFs), discussed in detail later in this book. As long as ETFs exist, people will trade around them in a highly consistent fashion. Analyzing this consistency can produce inferences about future behavior. However, the power of any data to create predictions may wane over time or be obliterated altogether.

THE RISK OF DATA

Data analysis in itself is subject to risks that may lead to faulty inferences and bad decisions that follow:

1. The process of analyzing data, regardless of complexity, can go off the rails on several fronts: A small data sample may pick up a pattern that does not recur on a sufficiently long timeline, misleading the researchers of the pattern's power and predictability.
2. Oversampling data may occur when researchers torture the same sample of data over and over to tell them something useful about the markets. Often, the only outcome of such analysis is a misleading forecast.

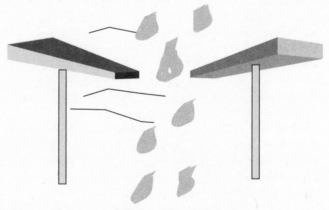

Bzzzz, it's snowing, we lost the data signal...

3. Overreliance on machine learning is another issue plaguing data scientists. Machine learning may mean many things to different people, but it usually refers to algorithmic factorization of data and iterative refinement of models based on their realized predictive power. While it is very tempting to entrust computer scientists and machines to sift through mountains of data in search of a gold nugget of predictability, the reality is that markets are driven by economic models that require deep understanding of not just mathematics and computer science, but also the market participant behavior and existing economic models.

Understanding the often nonlinear economics underlying the markets helps speed up subsequent machine learning by a factor of weeks, if not months or years. How is this possible? Pure machine learning often begins with a so-called spaghetti principle, as in, "Let's throw the spaghetti (market data) against the wall (past market data and other data), and see what sticks." Thorough understanding of economics helps reduce the amount of wall space needed for these experiments, a.k.a the data drivers, considerably, saving time and labor for the data science crew.

4. Duplication of models is a serious problem that presents itself in financial circles. A blogger recently posted that the current career trajectory of financial data modelers follows a pattern: Year 1: Glory, Year 2: Sweat and Tears, and Year 3: a Wild card. In the first year at a new employer, data modelers bring over a proven successful model from the previous place of employment or deploy a model that had been in development for a while and implement it profitably, obtaining a bonus reward. In the second year, the employer's expectations are high with hopes of a repeat performance, but with a second model. Developing this new model requires very hard work—something that only very few people can do, resulting in sweat and tears. In the third year, the workers reap the results of their previous year's labor, and their new models either work, or the workers are sent out to pasture, which most often means to the next fund where they start by implementing the model that was successful in year one at their previous job. In the end, models tend to circulate financial shops several times over, diluting their quality and also creating systemic risks. Suppose a given model has an Achilles' heel that is activated under certain rare market conditions. Due to the large amounts of money invested in the working models across a wide range of financial institutions, the impact of the Achilles' heel may be greatly amplified, resulting in a major market crash or other severe destruction of wealth across the financial markets. And, if the money used to prop up the strategies is borrowed, as is customary with hedge funds, the effect of just one flaw in a single model can be disastrous for the economy as a whole.

Does this sound like an exaggeration? Think back to August 2007, when hundreds of Wall Street firms, including proprietary trading desks at the investment banks, were running the same automated medium-term statistical-arbitrage (stat-arb) strategies popularized by an over-zealous group of quants. That August, in the midst of the quietest two weeks of the year when most people manage to leave for a vacation, these models broke down overnight, resulting in billion-dollar losses across many financial institutions. Rumors circulated that some firms recognized that someone figured out how to destroy the delicate equilibrium of stat-arb strategies and ran the models backward with a huge amount of capital to confuse poorly staffed markets, only to suddenly reverse the course of events and capitalize dramatically on everyone else's failures. Most of the trading firms were trading on heavily borrowed money. It was in vogue at the time to trade on capital that was levered 200 times the actual cash. And the impact was likely the first step leading to the financial crisis of 2009—debt obligations were unmet, valuations destroyed, and panic and confusion seeded in the hearts of previously invincible quant traders.

5. Finally, to err is human, and it is humans who tell computers how to analyze data and to learn from it. As a result, errors creep into models and it can be very difficult and expensive to catch them. One solution to this problem deployed in banks and other large organizations is to vet models or to have validation teams on staff whose sole job is to make sure the original models are sound. The problem with this approach? Besides an outrageous expense, the validation team members have all the incentives to leave for a competitor as soon as they learn a valuable model that they can deploy elsewhere.

Data Storage

As the amount of data has grown exponentially, new, flexible databases have been developed to accommodate the new data frontier. Fast sorting and retrieval are as important as flexibility in data field construction. The previous generation of databases, still in use by many institutions, stored data in long rows of tables with many columns. These so-called row-oriented databases were friendly to humans, as people could easily read the data from a table printout. However, the same databases were relatively slow to search and retrieve specific data items. To retrieve one element of a requested search, most row-oriented databases have to load entire tables, and parse through all the columns, whether relevant to the search or not.

Traditional row-oriented databases are increasingly yielding to column-oriented databases. As their name implies, the column-oriented databases store data in independent columns. Often, each table comprises just one column, loosely joined with other tables by an id, a timestamp of the data, or just the sequential number of each row. Figure 2.1 illustrates the breakdown of a row-oriented database into a column-oriented database.

If each table stores only one piece of information, that data table is hard for humans to examine. Essentially, it lacks the context we expect from an information table: Where is the supplemental data that tethers these numbers to the world around us? For machines, however, single-column tables are a

Index	Timestamp	Bid
256	46522817	17.26
257	46522819	17.27
258	46522910	17.26

46522817
46522819
46522910

17.26
17.27
17.26

FIGURE 2.1 Breaking a row-oriented database into columns

boon—data are easy to search, and time-series analysis necessary in so many financial applications is a snap!

Several database providers deliver column-based offerings; among them are KDB, created by KX Systems, and MCObject. Still, some institutions store data in simple text files, one column per file, with names of the files indicating the date and the type of data stored. For example, the column containing best bids on NYSE:SPY for August 29, 2016, may be stored in a text file as simple as bid_SPY_20160829.txt. Such a file would contain all the best bids recorded sequentially for SPY on August 29, 2016. A separate companion file with timestamps of all data points (typically recorded as a number of micro- or milliseconds from midnight) could be called timestamps_SPY_20160829.txt. When working with asynchronous data streams and recording bids, asks, and trades that arrive independently and at random times, the system would generate entries in all the columns simultaneously for each given timestamp. The columns without new information would receive a 0 or the previous value of the data.

Of course, this kind of data takes up a huge amount of storage space. Just think about this: A day's worth of orders for just one exchange takes about 10 GB of disk space, and 100 GB for one day of equity options. The latest Apple MacBook Air comes with a 256 GB hard drive. That amount is the total storage space, some of which is claimed by various apps. In other words, only two days of market data may fit in your laptop.

To save space, people have turned to some ingenious tricks. For instance, to save price as a decimal number requires at least four bytes (a byte is a computer storage unit, the 'B' in the GB of the hard drive space). Saving a whole number, an integer, on the other hand, often requires only 2 bytes, depending on one's computer system. So, one can cut computer storage by half by just multiplying out the equity prices by 100, and recording them as a whole number instead of a decimal. Other nifty examples abound.

Instead of dealing with data locally, some people choose to outsource the storage entirely to *clouds*—machines and storage managed by someone else, and accessible through the Internet. Clouds like Microsoft's Azure or Amazon's are indeed inexpensive and a straightforward way to store data. Google's cloud is free altogether. Of course, when someone else manages your data, there is a remote risk that a third party will monitor what you do with the data, potentially leaking your expensive data and your priceless intellectual property.

TECHNOLOGY

What single factor has most affected finance in the last 20 years? Some say derivatives, some say portfolio management, some say data. Without a doubt, our understanding of the mathematics of derivatives, and of how to use them and how to quantify the embedded risk, has significantly improved the way financial institutions operate. Similarly, advances in portfolio management and related risk theories have enhanced the operations of many pension funds, mutual funds, hedge funds, and individual portfolios. Finally, data have enabled us to fine-tune our strategies and become even more sophisticated investors through historical replay of our strategies, profitability analyses, and econometric brilliance.

Although the aforementioned accomplishments in the field of finance are undeniable, they simply would not be possible without a single most important factor. That factor is technology. Yes, plain old technology.

Some 20 to 30 years ago, technology usually comprised extra large and super-expensive machines that required not only a special staff that knew how to communicate with those machines, but also often required their dedicated refrigerated offices—the machines emitted so much heat that it was necessary to cool them off to avoid literal meltdown. A typical Alpha DEC, a popular model of the late 1980s and early 1990s, was a giant cube that measured about 6 feet in height, 6 feet in length, and 6 feet in depth, could only be accessed by a tiny black-and-white text-only terminal, and cost about $20 million (yes, we are talking about US dollars here, and in today's money, those $20 million translate to $35 million).

Fast-forward to today, and a computer of the same power, the same processing capacity, and the same memory size takes up about the size of a tablet or a laptop, requires no special maintenance cost, let alone air-conditioning, and costs (drumroll, please...) some $200 at a local Best Buy. That's it.

How is this possible, you may ask? The significant drop in the price of computing is likely due to the mass-production of computer components overseas. Taiwanese, Korean, and Chinese computer chips can be found in pretty much every computer, no matter how big or how small. Figure 2.2 shows the geographic distribution of computer chip manufacturing by region around the world. Taiwan still leads the pack, yet China's share is growing rapidly.

While overseas production of technology components has drastically reduced costs, it was not the single factor behind the dramatic plunge in prices of computer equipment. The second biggest reason is probably the

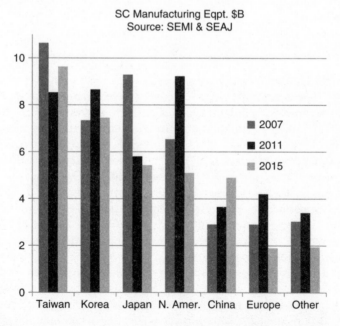

FIGURE 2.2   Volume of computer manufacturing in US billions by geography

amazing expansion of the market for computer technology in the individual space. Who does not own a device today? In the United States in particular, it seems that every six-year-old is now entitled to his or her own iPhone, correspondingly in blue or pink. Considering that many of the iPhone components are closely related or are even the same as those in other devices, such as laptops, tablets, security alarms, car computers, and many more average household items, the demand for these components and their volume is so large that it is indeed profitable for manufacturers to sell the parts at extremely low costs.

The shrinking costs of technology have eliminated entry barriers for thousands of startups wanting a piece of the pie. Fintech was born and has been booming. Still, the plunging costs alone do not tell the whole story about technology's influence on finance. Another component of the fintech revolution was the exponential upgrade in computing power per every square inch (or millimeter, depending on your background) of computing surface—core computer components can be infinitesimally thin.

The Alpha DEC, the monstrous computing engine that sent tremors of awe to prospective clients, employees, and investors, could run a complex forecasting procedure known as Monte Carlo simulation on just one financial security over a course of a day or two. Today's $200 laptops are capable of replicating the same operation on a universe of 10,000 financial instruments overnight. The million-time increase in computing power was once again brought on by the demands of computing retail public, and video gamers in particular—the ever-complex games and their real-life simulation required finer and more computing-intensive rendering within the same consumer budget. Because of the proliferation of video games across the globe, computer manufacturers have been able to leverage the masses to deliver super-low-cost products and still turn significant profits. Figure 2.3 summarizes evolution of technology costs and computing power over time.

Technology was the enabler of such market innovations as exchange-traded funds (ETFs), alternative trading systems (ATS) or venues, and, of course, high-frequency trading (HFT). ETFs require daily rebalancing and their valuations need to be reconciled with their underlying instruments—something that would be too hard for individuals to do without having their eyes glazing over from monitoring such vast amounts of relevant data and the inevitable errors that follow.

ATS are a class of execution venues, like new exchanges and dark pools, which, in most cases, have completely automated execution and settlements of orders. The precision, speed, and sheer power required to match countless orders in real time make some of these players nothing short of technological wonders.

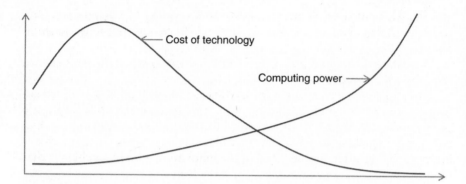

FIGURE 2.3 Evolution of technology and computing power over the past century

Finally, high-frequency trading is simply not possible to perform at human speed (hence, the high-frequency component). Computers are required by default.

In a nutshell, what is the impact of all the technological advances that we've experienced over the past 50 or so years and feel so keenly today? First, automation is definitely cheaper, and the costs still keep falling. That, in turn, implies that many functions traditionally performed by people can now be automated, resulting in faster, cleaner, less error-prone, and much cheaper business processes. Take loan evaluation, for instance. Aside from mitigating factors that can still only be assessed by relationship managers, frameworks based on past borrowing behavior, revenues, expenses, and other loans are predictive, fast to compute, and do not require human intervention, saving businesses billions in lending-related costs every year.

BLOCKCHAIN

Faster production is another consequence driven by technology. The settlement process, for example, used to take as long as three days to complete. Numerous agents and clerks compared tickets and other records to reconcile stock trades and trades in other financial instruments. Now, with technology, those clerks are largely replaced by electronic systems, reducing settlement times to at most one day. The new generation of settlement envisions technologies such as blockchain enabling real-time or near-real-time settlement. Speedy settlement, in turn, will make sure that traders and other market participants do not exceed their account limits and have money in a bank for the securities they trade, enhancing market stability and fairness in the process.

Part of the way that we manage risk is the agreements that we enter into when we transact. Whether it's a bond or a baseball, the act of buying and selling always includes contracts and record keeping. Blockchain is a new technology that changes the way we make an exchange and how we think about risk.

Imagine if you could buy a stock with instantaneous settlement. That's the future with blockchain.

Developed for the crypto currency Bitcoin, blockchain is the infrastructure of how to buy and sell, and can be used to securely trade and settle pretty much everything, from insurance to prescription drugs. Rather than two people agreeing to make a trade, blockchain is a ledger that records every trade, one after another. Part of the innovation with blockchain is that the contracts and agreements are part of the ledger.

Blockchain enables a transaction to happen instantly because all of the elements of a trade are satisfied in the structure of the distributed ledger. Terms are standardized so that there does not need to be any negotiation. Any pretrade activity is either avoided through anonymity or prearranged through processes such as know-your-customer (KYC) and any further suitability or accreditation processes. Blockchains can operate either for anonymous trades or permissioned where some level of pretrade clearance is required. The transaction also needs to be funded. Cash accounting is part of the ledger and when a trade occurs, changes in cash balances are recorded immediately.

The distributed ledger is an innovation of the blockchain. Everyone transacting in this manner has a ledger that records individual trades. Additionally, there are centralized ledgers that record all trades. Since these trades are funded, peer-to-peer, instantaneous, and centrally recorded, the methodology is a unique way to manage settlement and reconciliation.

All trades are recorded in the order that they are entered, and all trades are fulfilled at the time they are executed.

WHAT ELEMENTS ARE COMMON TO ALL BLOCKCHAINS?

A blockchain is distributed across many computers in almost real time. It is decentralized, and a copy of the entire record is available to all users. This feature reduces the need for intermediaries such as banks and brokerages to play the role of record-keeper.

It has a system for generating consensus among participants in the network. Everyone in the network needs to authenticate and verify any new information. This ensures that the same transaction does not occur more than once. New blocks need to pass the test by a majority to be added to the chain.

Rather than use actual signatures, a blockchain uses cryptography and digital signatures to prove identity. These may seem to be anonymous but can be tied back to the actual person. Blockchains can be either permissioned or public. Public chains are truly anonymous, where permissioned chains require some kind of accreditation.

It is difficult to change archived data. Once data enters, it generally remains permanently. Additionally, all records are timestamped, which helps with verifications and record keeping.

A blockchain can contain instructions embedded within blocks, such as "if" this "then" or "else" do that.

Why is this important? The appeal of instant transactions with stream-lined recording and reconciliation is obvious. It's a revolution compared with the manual and intensive processes that happen today. The risk is that many of the important pretrade processes, such as KYC, or posttrade processes such as funding will be difficult to complete or will create new risks to the businesses using blockchain.

What Is Different about Blockchain from Previous Technologies?

Traditional databases were essentially tables with information stored neatly in rows and columns. To avoid duplication, the tables stored as diverse data sets as possible, but were linked with an index, also known as a *key*. Sorting through traditional databases was a nontrivial task, but the most critical component of the system was how entries can be modified: For one person to change the database, that person would most often need to "check out" or "lock" the table he was working on to avoid the table being simultaneously modified by someone else, and thus losing changes in the process.

Consider how hard it is to use the conventional database in trading. When you send your order to the exchange, the exchange needs to record it, but many simultaneous orders may also be taking place at the same time. Locking the database to record each trade is impractical, as it would slow trading down to a screeching halt, raise issues about market timeliness and access priorities, and many other problems. As a result, conventionally, exchanges used to do *settlements*—transaction aggregation and recon-ciliation first over several days after the transactions occurred and, most prevalently now, the next day after the transactions.

Still, in our age of real time, next-day settlement is probably too slow. Here comes blockchain—the technology that gained popularity and acceptance with Bitcoin, the latter being a digital currency of unclear polit-ical affiliation. Regardless of Bitcoin's future, it accomplished something momentous—a proof of concept of blockchain technology.

The revolutionary change that brought us blockchain is the scientists' way to allow simultaneous database updates at once. While the computer scientists have worked on problems of database updates forever, and multiple solutions have been proposed over the years, the blockchain approach proved solid, easy, and sensible.

Here is how it works. Every transaction is recorded twice: once in the virtual ledger of the buyer and once in the ledger of the seller. These transactions are linked to the central blockchain node that reconciles them and records them in perpetuity in real time. Transactions that are submitted where the buyer spends less than the seller receives are automatically rejected. However, whenever there are transactions showing the buyer spending more than the seller receives (whether in error, or intentionally) the surplus may be captured by the blockchain operator for the operator's benefit, making errors particularly costly!

All of the money flowing in a blockchain system has to come from some initial transfers into the blockchain and then the funds float into other transactions, ensuring a fixed money supply within the blockchain ecosystem.

Which Fintech Sectors Are Adopting Blockchain?

Banking   Traditionally, buying or selling a security takes three days to transfer ownership. With blockchain, a lot of investment is directed at a concept called $T + 0$. This would result in same-day settlement. Why such a change? Buying and selling has involved working through brokerages, custodians, and exchanges. It takes time for these institutions to execute a trade through an exchange, transfer funds, and execute the contracts that transfer ownership. All of these activities can be part of a blockchain transaction, and this would be instant settlement.

One challenge that is being considered is how to incorporate margin trading, trades that involve customized or a fair amount of administration. Innovation is pointing in the direction of blockchains that are programmed with instructions that may make it possible to instantly trade on margin, but not yet!

Payments and Money Transfers   Sending money through international money transfers is one of the industries that align with blockchain's development. Transfers into a foreign currency often need to exchange first to US dollars and then to the local currency, and the transfer comes with cumbersome paperwork.

Using blockchain for international transfers makes sense because it enables parties to agree directly on the exchange and for the terms of the exchange to be captured within the transaction itself.

One example of this innovation is a company named Circle. Founded in 2013, it is developing money transfers with China. The vision is to speed up the time it takes to make a transfer by incorporating the process that is currently quite cumbersome into blockchain and integrating it into social applications. Investors are rallying to this cause with $140 million raised so far from players such as IDG Capital Partners, Baidu Inc., China International Capital Corp., Everbright Securities Co., and others.

Cybersecurity Blockchain can also safeguard data and systems from cyber-attacks. In an extreme example, darkness spread across several Ukrainian cities in December 2015 as hackers accessed the central electrical system. By controlling the electrical grid centrally, the hacker was able to cause widespread "darkness" once inside the system.

One of the advantages of the approach for blockchain is its distributed nature. Records can be maintained on many computers and servers around the world. With command and control distributed rather than centralized, it will take more than one hacker in one command center to turn off the lights.

Additionally, blockchain networks often seek consensus with each other before allowing changes to be made to the blockchain. If a hacker needed to gain control over many of the distributed nodes in order to gain consensus to do something, then it would be a much more difficult system to break.

Insurance The process of collecting information on customers could be streamlined if the manner of collecting such information were standardized. Insurance companies are growing in markets with less stringent government identification systems. This increases the potential for fraud. If a blockchain could improve verification of identity, this would accelerate the pace at which insurance companies could offer their services.

Imagine if a blockchain could keep track of every item in a warehouse. If that warehouse were to burn to the ground, the insurance company could accurately gauge the loss, and the records would be verified and reside at the insurance company and the client. Currently, this detailed tracking is not possible, so insurance companies need to insure the maximum possible loss.

Algos

Most computer automation is accomplished with algorithms or *algos,* for short. The idea of algos in finance is periodically discussed in the media. Some market participants love algos and cannot imagine life without them. Some claim algos can be scary and inflict damage on the markets, and for a good reason: a bad algo deployed at Knight Capital Group cost the company US$440 million in the span of 45 minutes on August 1, 2012. Still, some have a very limited understanding of algo operations, and fear the uncertainty algos can create.

An algo is a set of rules designed in a way that is easy to explain to a computer. An algo is not a computer program or an app, but is instead logic set out in step-by-step procedures.[1]

Once translated into a computer language, an algo becomes a computer program or an app. Apps are computer programs themselves, but in a computer science understanding, apps are designed for human interaction, while computer programs are of a much more general nature.

Wild or "run-away" algos indeed present a problem and occur relatively often. A great social benefit from data science is that even the wildest runaway trading algos can be detected and stopped. For example, Able-Markets.com detects runaway algos within one minute of incidence so that companies are aware of issues in the markets and can take appropriate protective measures.

The Internet

Most of the changes in today's financial markets originated from the Internet. Indeed, the Internet can be blamed for every single market problem, questionable regulatory action, and, of course, multiple successes of recent years, such as lower transaction fees, increased market transparency, and the like.

Before the Internet, trading took hours, if not days. A trader would record a customer order over the phone. Next, he would wait for orders from other customers to fill up a "lot"—typically, a round number of shares. Then, the trader would forward this round lot order to another trader up the food chain, the latter trader aggregating a larger, bulkier order from several round-lot orders. The iteration would pass several layers of traders, until it would finally reach a guy in a bright jacket milling about on the exchange floor. That floor trader would negotiate the purchase or sale with another floor trader, setting off a reverse reaction.

By the time the order confirmation reached the client, markets may have moved, wars could have erupted, and the portfolio assumptions made by the client could be invalidated. The important saving grace of clients, however, was that most traded at the same super-slow speed. As a result, news took a long time to trickle into the markets, and some gains were to be had by all. In late 1990s, financial technologists began to realize that the Internet could be harnessed to securely transfer trading information. Financial standards, like the Financial Information Exchange (FIX), began to develop. FIX

---

[1]In a linguistic twist, "algo" has a separate meaning in Spanish: "something." The "something" translation has no relation to algos as abbreviation of "algorithms" in the computer science sense!

soon became the dominant method of carrying trading information, replacing multiple levels of brokers communicating via phones and special voice deal-negotiation networks.

With the reduction of headcount and associated operating costs on trading desks, competitive offerings of ultra-low transaction costs promptly emerged. These drove the momentum for faster, lower-cost, and more effective trading communication systems and led to a "nuclear arms race" in financial services. From proprietary data communication protocols, like NASDAQ's ITCH and OUCH, to cross-Atlantic cables for faster data delivery to telecom and microwave communication towers built and operated by trading firms, the trading speed landscape has never looked the same.

Various data transfer and packaging technologies are deployed today to gain a competitive speed advantage and offer a faster, better, and cheaper service. Regardless of these high-level innovations, the technology underlying all communication has changed little since the Internet of the early 1990s. All message traffic floats through two underlying communication protocols: TCP/IP (Transmission Control Protocol / Internet Protocol) or UDP (User Datagram Protocol). TCP/IP protocol, that most of today's population uses as a channel for email, counts the number of message packets sent and resends the message stream if the entire package did not reach its destination. TCP/IP guarantees delivery of a message, making it a must in areas like order communication and confirmations. However, the reliability of TCP/IP makes it sacrifice its speed, as every resend takes up time.

TCP/IP itself runs on a protocol known as UDP. UDP is one of the most basic communication tools in the Internet domain. UDP broadcasts messages, and if some are lost, it does not retransmit them. By its function, UDP is most suitable to applications such as quote dissemination—lost market quotes are immediately rendered stale by new quotes, so losing a packet of data occasionally does not deprive the receiving party of observing the current market dynamics.

Technical details aside, the Internet has really changed the way financial services are delivered. Want to trade in the middle of a park on a nice sunny day? There is an app for that on your phone. Interested in finding the best stock to invest in? Again, the Internet is at your fingertips to do the research.

As the Internet made access to data and research increasingly easy, the complexity of analysis to identify successful investments has risen exponentially. As more and more people are competing and using identical resources to pick rising stocks, the gains from basic analyses evaporated. Today's financial market researchers are pushed to even greater depths to uncover investing ideas and leading market indicators untapped by others. Even though the trading costs have declined due to the Internet, allowing greater profitability across all trades, the profits on investing ideas have narrowed simply because the Internet has democratized generation of investing ideas.

Of course, the democratization of communication brought on by the Internet has also produced new challenges and risks. Believe it or not, most of the financial communication in today's world happens on unencrypted Internet lines. Yes, you read it correctly: billion-dollar accounts exchange orders without any encryption. It is true that some of the communication is conducted in binary, which makes it difficult for people to read, but easy as pie for machines. Still, most trading communication is conducted in clear text. Orders to buy and sell thousands, millions, and sometimes billions of dollars, along with account numbers and other sensitive information you would not find in the street is streamed down the Internet channels.

Why are billion-dollar entities so careless about their information? The answer consists of several parts. First, any sort of encryption kills data-processing speed. To successfully transmit an encrypted message, the sender first needs to spend time actually encrypting the message, then the often fattened-up message needs to be sent over, and, finally, the message needs to be decrypted by the message receiver. The encryption and decryption, however fast, puts the message transmitter at a relative disadvantage in today's world of high-paced orders. Thus, most institutions choose to forgo encryption altogether.

Another argument some make against encryption is the construction of the public Internet pipeline. Figure 2.4 illustrates a typical scenario of how data travels from its origin to its destination through public networks. After a message is broken down into small packets on the sender's machine, the packets join the exhaust pipe of the Internet provider that sorts the messages by their destination and ultimately delivers them. The anti-encryption camp argues that once the small packets of messages enter the carrier's exhaust pipes, they are so small and indistinguishable from other packets that reconstructing the entire message is pretty much impossible. However, just like your individual post mailbox is the weakest link in your snail mail communication (even though it is illegal to steal one's mail, doing so at your house is probably the easiest place for those criminally inclined), the Internet lines coming in and out of your office or building are vulnerable to illegal surveillance. Consider this doomsday scenario: A few foreign-speaking guys in hard hats are digging the pavement outside your office building for a couple of weeks under a guise of road repair. In reality, they are tapping into your fiber-optic Internet communication at its source—your office. Screening through all the outbound message packets, the perpetrators have a reasonably easy job of reconstructing all your messages—after all, they do not have to sort them out from random strangers' flow. How do you feel about your Internet security now?

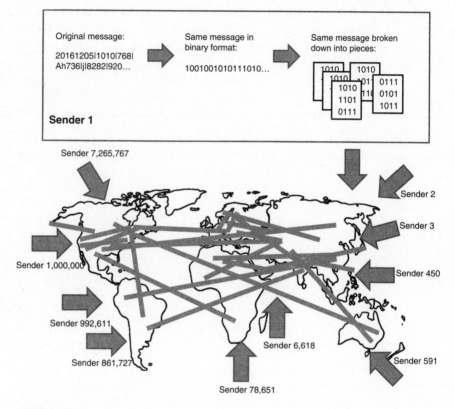

FIGURE 2.4 Simultaneous input of broken down information packers into the world's network systems

There does exist one near-bullet-proof solution to the speed/security trade-off. If you seal off the sender and the receiver of information in the same secure bunker, then the risk of someone tapping into the real-time information source narrows down to the rogue employees of the facility. In today's world of big-brother surveillance, rogue employees with critical impact can be monitored in real time, further reducing the risks of data leakage. Wouldn't it be nice to avail yourself of this peace of mind?

The great news is, the setup exists. Ironically, this solution has attracted the wrath of many market participants, some of whom are potentially the most vulnerable targets of electronic perpetrators. The solution is called colocation, or *colo*. The monthly cost per colocated server with, say, NASDAQ, ranges from $3,000 to $5,000—an affordable amount to most institutions.

Furthermore, colocation centers ensure the fairness of their facilities to every 1 mm of cable length: the servers that sit physically closer to the exchange server have their connecting cables measured and coiled next to the server to ensure identical lengths of cables.

CONCLUSIONS

Where is technology taking us from here? The trends clearly point to ever-increasing automation and introduction of robotics. Computers are not going away; they are becoming better, cheaper, and ever more powerful.

With the adoption of new technology come risks, many previously unknown. Security remains a number-one risk in the financial markets—the threat of a sophisticated yet malicious party breaking into the modern financial system and obliterating its components is ever so real. Brand-new technologies like blockchain are promising to secure transactional data, but may still be vulnerable to attacks with fake identities and the like. Physical security of data transmission results in overall security of data and is delivered by a much-discussed colocation.

Data analysis itself is also full of pitfalls and may deliver faulty algorithms. However, most problems with the latter can be contained through extensive testing and run-time safety checks, presenting little risk to the markets.

END OF CHAPTER QUESTIONS

1. What is the most significant driver in the development of modern finance today?
2. What is unstructured data?
3. What is an algorithm?
4. What are the biggest data and technology-related risks in today's markets?
5. How can blockchain help mitigate some of the market risks?

CHAPTER 3

Dark Pools, Exchanges, and Market Structure

—Who is the compliance manager chasing on the trading floor?

—A runaway algo.

In addition to enabling record-breaking data processing and storage capacity, technology is also responsible for a fair share of previously unthinkable risks. When billions of dollars are moved around the globe at breathtaking speed, the dynamics can be outright dangerous. Ensuring the legitimacy of accounts and identifying and blocking malicious behavior are very difficult tasks to execute in real time.

The financial markets used to comprise just one exchange for each class of financial instrument. If you traded equities, you did so at the New York Stock Exchange (later, NASDAQ was created with the explicit purpose of trading new technology stocks). If you traded commodities or futures, you would do so at the Chicago Mercantile Exchange. Another exchange existed solely for options. Foreign currency pairs and most of bonds never formally traded on an exchange, having been intermediated privately by banks and specialized dealers. The bottom line is that you had clarity and consistency in where you would go to trade a specific financial instrument.

This is no longer the case. Today, there are 21 "national securities exchanges" registered with the US Securities and Exchange Commission, the top regulatory body for just equities, ETFs, and equity options. The names of exchanges registered to trade equities at the time this book was written are shown in Table 3.1. The last entry in Table 3.1 is the notorious IEX exchange, which made copious news aided by a timely book by Michael Lewis, *The Flash Boys*.

While there are still only two exchanges trading commodity futures, Inter-Continental Exchange (ICE) and Chicago Mercantile Exchange (CME), there are six exchanges registered to trade equity futures, including futures on ETFs and commodity ETFs, documented in Table 3.2.

For US equities, along with the 21 exchanges, we now have 36 alternative trading systems (ATS), also known as alternative trading venues or,

TABLE 3.1 List of National Securities Exchanges (Stock Exchanges) Registered with the U.S. Securities and Exchange Commission under Section 6 of the Securities Exchange Act of 1934, as of August 4, 2016

NYSE MKT LLC (formerly NYSE AMEX and the American Stock Exchange)
Bats BZX Exchange, Inc. (formerly BATS Exchange, Inc.)
Bats BYX Exchange, Inc. (formerly BATS Y-Exchange, Inc.)
BOX Options Exchange LLC
NASDAQ BX, Inc. (formerly NASDAQ OMX BX, Inc.; Boston Stock Exchange)
C2 Options Exchange, Incorporated
Chicago Board Options Exchange, Incorporated
Chicago Stock Exchange, Inc.
Bats EDGA Exchange, Inc. (formerly EDGA Exchange, Inc.)
Bats EDGX Exchange, Inc. (formerly EDGX Exchange, Inc.)
International Securities Exchange, LLC
The Investors Exchange LLC
ISE Gemini
ISE Mercury
Miami International Securities Exchange
The Nasdaq Stock Market LLC
National Stock Exchange, Inc.
New York Stock Exchange LLC
NYSE Arca, Inc.
NASDAQ PHLX LLC (formerly NASDAQ OMX PHLX, LLC; Philadelphia Stock
   Exchange)
IEX

Source: SEC, https://www.sec.gov/divisions/marketreg/mrexchanges.shtml

TABLE 3.2 Exchanges Registered by the SEC to Trade Equity Futures, as of August 4, 2016

Board of Trade of the City of Chicago, Inc.
CBOE Futures Exchange, LLC
Chicago Mercantile Exchange
One Chicago, LLC
The Island Futures Exchange, LLC (formerly registered)
NQLX LLC (formerly registered)

Source: SEC, https://www.sec.gov/divisions/marketreg/mrexchanges.shtml

simply, dark pools. Table 3.3 shows the distribution of trading volume of "Tier 1 NMS stocks" (the big guys) for the first quarter of 2016. Notice that IEX is present and is #3 out of all exchanges by the number of shares and by the dollar amount traded—not bad for a little startup! Dark pools trade anonymously and without displaying order information before trades are

TABLE 3.3 Dark Pools Trading Equities in the United States, Tier 1, 1st Quarter, 2016, Tier 1 Stocks, Ordered by Total Share Volume

ATS Name	MPID	Total Trades	Total Shares	Average Trade Size
UBS ATS	UBSA	49,047,755	8,089,201,874	165
CROSSFINDER	CROS	33,339,407	6,343,434,705	190
IEX	IEXG	28,244,595	6,131,146,711	217
SUPERX	DBAX	22,272,463	4,519,968,650	203
MS POOL (ATS-4)	MSPL	13,362,208	3,590,847,590	269
JPM-X	JPMX	10,107,387	2,588,077,060	256
INSTINCT X	MLIX	11,259,098	2,452,877,139	218
BARCLAYS ATS ("LX")	LATS	12,360,051	2,246,958,412	182
LEVEL ATS	EBXL	12,725,055	2,213,199,100	174
SIGMA X	SGMA	11,165,962	2,171,686,977	194
INSTINET CONTINUOUS BLOCK CROSSING SYSTEM (CBX)	ICBX	7,961,839	1,838,821,958	231
BIDS TRADING	BIDS	2,971,107	1,817,897,065	612
KCG MATCHIT	KCGM	10,658,342	1,765,576,712	166
POSIT	ITGP	4,201,987	1,225,928,000	292
CROSSSTREAM	XSTM	2,214,926	974,427,132	440
MS TRAJECTORY CROSS (ATS-1)	MSTX	3,818,025	781,362,300	205
DEALERWEB	DLTA	1,500	689,843,781	459,896
MILLENNIUM	NYFX	1,929,992	656,649,514	340
LIQUIDNET ATS	LQNT	11,200	533,875,600	47,667
PDQ ATS	PDQX	2,532,572	524,673,185	207
CITI CROSS	CXCX	1,973,084	476,121,106	241
IBKR ATS	IATS	1,508,554	464,127,980	308
BLOCKCROSS	BLKX	32,430	416,573,635	12,845
LIGHT POOL	LTPL	1,782,994	336,065,331	188
LIQUIDNET H2O	LQNA	18,161	225,951,700	12,442
INSTINET CROSSING	XIST	38,147	185,616,240	4,866
TRADEBOOK	BTBK	731,093	180,375,389	247
MS RETAIL POOL (ATS-6)	MSRP	253,251	71,630,440	283
LIQUIFI	LQFI	3,135	60,340,170	19,247
LUMINEX TRADING & ANALYTICS LLC	LMNX	1,574	49,184,737	31,248
AQUA	AQUA	1,992	25,469,615	12,786
MERRILL LYNCH (ATS-1)	MLVX	59,256	20,137,700	340
XE	WDNX	8,051	12,057,427	1,498
RIVERCROSS	RCSL	53,941	11,714,860	217

(*continued*)

TABLE 3.3 *(Continued)*

ATS Name	MPID	Total Trades	Total Shares	Average Trade Size
USTOCKTRADE SECURITIES, INC.	USTK	4,355	999,953	230
BARCLAYS DIRECTEX	BCDX	44	978,397	22,236
PRO SECURITIES ATS	PROS	26	90,800	3,492
Grand Total		246,655,559	53,693,888,945	218

Source: FINRA, http://www.finra.org/industry/otc/ats-transparency-data-quarterly-statistics

executed. The lack of displayed information is the key difference between dark pools and registered "lit" exchanges. Exchanges show the entire limit order book, down to how many shares are in each limit order, while dark pools hide all limit-order book information. Institutional investors that trade large blocks and lack appropriate algorithmic expertise (more on this in later chapters) may go to dark pools and "hide" their large orders from other traders. The same orders would be displayed in the limit order books of exchanges, potentially scaring away other traders by the sheer size of their bets. Note that neither lit exchanges nor dark pools display the identity of traders: Both lit exchanges and dark pools are anonymous!

The explosion of exchanges and alternative trading venues is driven by a singular factor. Way back when, in the 1950s and '60s and early '70s, trading was limited to a single exchange per type of a financial instrument, and that exchange was a not-for-profit organization. The not-for-profit construct was not a mere convenience, it was a necessity—order matching, settlement, and auxiliary record-keeping was so labor-intensive that exchanges simply could not turn a profit. Technology enabled the exchanges not only to move away from a nonprofit model, but also to create a cottage industry of extremely profitable businesses, all backed by very powerful technological infrastructure.

Let's pause for a moment to consider the enormity of changes due to fintech in the exchange arena alone. We are not yet talking about blockchain—the next fintech train steaming over the exchanges in the next decade (yes, it is already in the exchanges' collective backyards). The changes that end customers are feeling right now are related to data. If you are of a certain age (ahem), you may remember those days when to find a quote for the stock you owned, you had to look in the newspaper. Not just any random freshly printed newspaper, but a thick newspaper that contained a section of *yesterday's* quotes for stocks, bonds, and everything else under the sun. Furthermore, for each stock there were only five data points from the previous trading day available: open, high, low, close, and daily volume. That's it.

Could you tell if there was a flash crash? Hardly. You had no idea what was going on beside the news articles written by people who traded rumors or relied on the same limited data set.

What about Bloombergs and TVs? Yes, the Bloomberg terminal did change things around a bit. Few people may remember, but Bloomberg started as a terminal-renting company, leasing out personal computers at the time when they were prohibitively expensive for most banks to buy. As a convenient segue, Bloomberg gradually built its own operating systems for the terminals the firm offered. Its operating system allowed users to query a computer's databases of data instead of relying on the newspapers. Still, even with all the search power, the data was limited to open, high, low, close, and daily volume, as trade-by-trade data was just too expensive to store. Additionally, no one really cared what happened intraday—when the transaction costs per trade were as high as 0.5 percent of the amount traded, an intraday drop of 0.5 percent was a mere drop in a bucket, not a cause for concern. To top it off, few Wall Streeters could care about anything after lunch—the times were good, the markets kept rising at an average of 8 percent per year, and those liquid three-martini lunches were all the rage.

What happened next? As the technological power continued to increase, and overseas manufacturers managed to reduce the costs of computer components to unprecedented lows, it became feasible to deliver data and transact with an unprecedented speed, frequency, and cost that was unthinkable at the time. Regulators took notice and adapted governance, allowing competition in the space via regulation alternative trading systems (Reg ATS) in 1999, enacted on April 1, 2000.

Reg ATS was limited to equities and equity derivatives. Not surprisingly, it affected many institutional investors working with equities. Equity trade sizes have fallen from thousands of shares per order to uniform 100-share orders, sliced with precision by complex algorithms. *Traders Magazine* (2015) reported that two-thirds of US and European long-only investors missed bygone natural blocks, which are the pools of liquidity where hedge funds, asset managers, and wealth managers can execute large orders without retaining personnel or specialty firms to manage their order execution, like in the long-gone days when only one exchange existed.

Despite the proliferation of trading venues, the landscape of the market is not necessarily a "wild west," as many similarities among trading venues exist. Most trading venues deploy the centralized limit order book to record and match the orders. It is also known as the double-sided continuous auction, or more commonly, the *limit order book*.

An order book is a way exchanges keep track of all buy and sell orders, order cancellations, and other communication with brokers and traders. In some sense, an order book is like a shelf in a grocery store that contains tomato soup offered by different companies at different prices. Some choose to sell their tomato soup at $2 a can, while others sell tomato soup for $5 a can. These offers of essentially the same product at different prices are what the exchange order book is about, at least on the ask side of the market. Each unit of tomato soup may be thought of as a unit of volume offered, its price a corresponding ask or offer. When customers interested in purchasing tomato soup arrive, they may choose one of the following actions:

1. Buy the best-priced tomato soup available on the shelf at the moment, a method known as buying via a market order.
2. Create a bid on tomato soup, by leaving a ticket with the store clerk asking him to call you if the price on any tomato soup drops to $1.99—your desired price level. This method of purchasing via a bid is known as a limit order: you as a trader specify the limit on the price you are willing to pay.

The above example is, of course, an oversimplification of how the exchange's order books work, yet it illustrates a point: trade instructions at exchanges are straightforward and make sense. The actual exchange limit

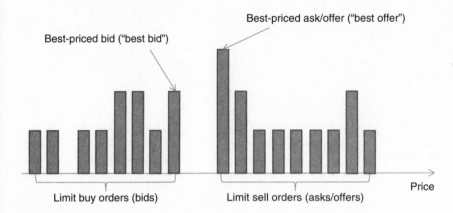

FIGURE 3.1 Sample limit order book

order books are two-sided, meaning that not only the sellers can display their wares on a shelf but the buyers can do so, too, by submitting their bid tickets, formally known as limit buy orders. The exchanges stock all the buy and sell tickets along one shelf in the direction of increasing price, ultimately coming up with a limit order "book" like the one shown in Figure 3.1.

In a limit order book, the best-priced bid and ask define a bid–ask spread, the difference between the best ask and the best bid. The minimum spread is always equal to one tick, one division on the limit order book number line defined by regulators and, possibly, trading venues. At the time this book was written, in equities one tick was $0.01, or 1 cent. In foreign exchange, one tick could be as little as $0.00001, or 1/100,000 of a dollar. During times of uncertainty, for instance, ahead of major news announcements, the spread typically widens as limit-order traders avoid risk by removing orders too close to the market price to avoid being "run over" or "picked over" by traders with superior news services or analysis. Limit orders can be removed by cancellations—separate requests placed with exchanges. All limit orders collectively create "liquidity," defined in academia as the immediacy with which a trader may execute a market order. The more limit orders are present, the deeper the liquidity, the faster a market order of an arbitrary size can be executed.

All market orders, orders to immediately buy or sell, are matched with the best available bid and ask limit orders "resting" in the limit order book at the time of the market order arrivals. A limit buy order priced higher than that of the best offer is treated as a market buy order and is immediately matched with the best offer. Similarly, a limit sell order or ask priced below the best bid is deemed "marketable" and is treated as a market sell order.

In addition to buy and sell limit and market orders, many exchanges provide hybrid orders that may restrict the display of size of the order (e.g., iceberg orders), and other custom types of orders. All custom orders tend to be more expensive than the plain-vanilla limit and market buy and sell orders.

How do investors choose between placing market, limit, and other types of orders? To answer this question, consider an average investor, Joe, who wants to do something mundane: buy or sell a stock or another financial instrument at the market open prices. To do so, Joe has two basic methods at his disposal (other order types are typically variations of limit and market orders):

1. Joe can place a market order that tells his broker or an exchange to fill his order as soon as possible at the best price available.
2. Joe can place a limit order specifying a particular price, but no time limit for his trade.

If Joe chooses the market order route, he is guaranteed to have bought his desired security, but possibly at a much worse price than the opening bid or even ask price. During the few minutes immediately following the market open, prices strive to incorporate all of the information pent up from overnight, when the markets are closed. This information is transmitted into the markets through orders, and the disparity of views causes the prices to bounce violently up and down. This continues until traders reach a consensus on prices. Due to the volatility, Joe's market order may be filled at the worst possible price, possibly erasing Joe's projected gain from the trade.

As an alternative, Joe may choose to place a limit order and specify the price at which he is willing to buy it. Here, Joe is facing another decision, the price itself. If Joe chooses a price that is too low, his order may never execute. If the price is too high, he does nothing to outperform his market-order scenario. How can Joe determine a price that is just right, that is both favorable and results in a timely execution?

A simple, yet effective strategy could be to place a limit order at a *mid-price*—a price that is the average of the bid and ask at the market open. To do so, however, one needs a timely source of market data, from which to calculate the mid-price. (Most brokers provide their clients with free access to data that are 15-minutes delayed—too slow for Joe to successfully identify and execute upon his strategy.)

All orders, order executions, and order cancellations are received and processed by the majority of the exchanges in the first-come, first-served fashion. However, exchanges may offer variations to distinguish themselves from their competitors.

In equities, trading is further complicated by the national best bid/offer (NBBO) requirements.

The requirement, a product of regulation national market systems (Reg NMS, 2005), stipulates that all trading venues have to continuously submit to the government the best limit buy and sell prices (best bid and best offer/ask) available on their respective venues. This is done simultaneously for all securities traded. The best bid and best offer quotes then enter the security information processor (SIP) run by the US Securities and Exchange Commission. From there, the quotes are aggregated in real time, the very best bid and the very best offer are picked out from all submitted data. These NBBO numbers are then distributed back to trading venues with the identification of the exchanges that have the best quotes.

And here comes the fun part: An exchange that has a local best bid and best offer that is inferior to the NBBO in a given security cannot execute the incoming market orders for this particular security. Instead, the exchange with the inferior NBBO is required to route the market orders to the exchange that has the best NBBO quotes for market orders at that particular time. If at any time, the exchange receives limit orders that are better than the prevailing NBBO, that exchange will now own the NBBO, and all the market orders will be routed there. The order routing may or may not be free of charge, depending on the venue.

As an example, suppose that the current NBBO for IBM stock is $155.14 for bids and $155.15 for offers (a spread of the minimum tick, $0.01, is usually present in all markets, otherwise arbitrage opportunities exist; the spread is also often the only compensation that the market-makers obtain—more on this later). Suppose further that BATS BYX exchange has the following best quotes for IBM: $155.13 bid (200 shares) and $155.15 offer (100 shares). As always, the best quotes are determined by the best buy and sell limit orders present in the limit order book: the price associated with the best buy order becomes the best bid, and the price associated with the best sell limit order forms the best offer. If a market order to buy 100 shares of IBM arrives at BATSY, the market order is executed at $155.15, since this is the prevailing NBBO. If a plain market order to buy 200 shares of IBM arrives at BATSY, only 100 shares will be executed, and the other 100 may be routed to an exchange where NBBO is present, unless that exchange is still BATSY at a different price level. If a 100-share sell market order arrives at BATSY, it will be forwarded to an exchange where the prevailing national best bid of $155.14 exists.

Figure 3.2 illustrates the idea.

Although the idea of NBBO works well in general, imperfections exist. First, the technology still has a finite speed as far as the collection, processing, and redistribution of quotes is concerned. As such, it is possible for investor

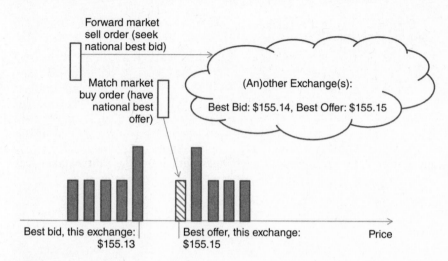

FIGURE 3.2 How NBBO execution works

orders to "fall through the cracks" and to be matched on exchanges where NBBO no longer exists. To the SEC's credit, the SEC mandates regular revisions to the NBBO submission and redistribution frequencies, making the data collection faster and execution fairer. As of August 2015, the government guaranteed the round-trip aggregation and redistribution time of best quotes of at most 500 milliseconds (one half of one second). Since, proposals have been made to reduce the quote redistribution speed to as little as 5 milliseconds.

Although all exchanges are obligated to observe the SEC Regulation National Market Systems (Reg NMS) that mandates all market orders are executed at NBBO or better, due to the competitive nature of the modern trading landscape, exchanges differentiate themselves by deploying different pricing and matching combinations. Some equity exchanges offer traders monetary incentives to provide liquidity in an attempt to attract limit orders, and thus deepen available liquidity. Exchanges doing so are known as *normal* and offer "rebates" for providing liquidity (posting limit orders), while charging fees for taking liquidity (placing market orders). Other exchanges, known as *inverted,* do the opposite. They charge for limit orders and pay for market orders. The NYSE is an example of a normal exchange, while the Boston OMX is an inverted exchange. A few exchange firms have offerings in each category. BATS, for example, has separate normal and inverted exchanges.

Some liquidity is considered to be "toxic," or detrimental to investors. Typically, toxic liquidity comprises orders that are canceled rather promptly, raising other market participants' questions about the intent of the providers of that said liquidity. Fees and other properties of exchanges affect the toxicity of their liquidity. Some researchers find that, on average, the fees across all the exchanges are in equilibrium, balancing the explicit fees with implicit costs, such as observed spreads. The lower the fee imposed on "liquidity makers" providing limit orders, the higher is the observed spread on a given exchange, potentially implying higher toxicity levels. Order cancellation rates are lower on exchanges with lower liquidity maker fees (higher liquidity taker fees), also indicating lower toxicity levels.

Still, gaps persist. Besides periodic data outages on exchanges, an illegal activity called spoofing can really distort the NBBO, as described in Chapter 4.

THE NEW MARKET HOURS

In addition to new trading venues and data standards, many other changes have occurred in the financial markets over the last 20 years. The markets are undergoing continuous innovation with the ever-expanding presence of computers on the trading floors. Some products of automation, such as high-frequency trading (HFT), have generated unprecedented attention, while other changes, significant to investors, have largely gone unnoticed. This section focuses on just one such change, extended market hours, and discusses the implications for investors, large and small.

Many years ago, when markets were dominated by human traders, financial markets worked standard hours: 9:30 AM to 4:00 PM. The timing allowed sufficient leeway for market professionals to prepare for the market opening, including gathering the latest news and other requisite information, and organize daily trade "tickets" at the end of the day prior to departing the exchange. The market "open" and "close" prices, often reported in the next day's newspaper, corresponded to trade prices recorded at 9:30 AM and 4:00 PM, respectively.

The trading hours were designed to suit a business schedule normal for most market practitioners. News that arrived outside of market hours, however, often caused much volatility and could not be traded in a timely manner. In response, an innovation ensued: About 10 years ago, many exchanges began offering extended trading hours beginning at 4:00 AM ET and closing at 8:00 PM ET. The extended morning opening hour coincides with the market open in London, and the extended closing time suits professionals in Asia, also allowing the US-based market practitioners to trade closer to a 24-hour format, capturing latest news in the markets.

While extended hours provide a longer window to execute trades, they also set a stage for several issues unanticipated by large and small market participants:

1. *Changes in open prices.* Quantitative financial analysis has traditionally been developed and taught on daily open and closing prices. With the introduction of extended market hours, the open prices are now often recorded at 4:00 AM, not at 9:30 AM as before. As a result, financial analysts trying to develop portfolio rebalancing or trading models based on market open may need to recalibrate their approaches.
2. *Significant market movement outside of regular market hours.* A considerable portion of market movement now occurs from the "new" market open to 9:30 AM. Traders and investors expecting to wake up and enter the markets past 9:30 AM may be subject to the "you snooze—you lose" formula, whereby most of the relevant news has already been incorporated by the markets prior to the regular-market open prices at 9:30 AM.
3. *Corporate earnings announcements again often fall during trading hours.* In the 1990s, there was a lot of concern related to corporate earnings announcements during normal market hours, and the resulting volatility and potential market manipulation around the earning announcements. To circumvent the issues, more and more public companies began reporting earnings outside of the "regular" 9–4 trading hours, often at 8:00 AM and 6:00 PM. The new extended trading hours, however, put the issues surrounding earnings announcements back on the table.

These issues are not dealbreakers for trading, or an argument to revert the market structure back to its 9:30 AM to 4:00 PM format. However, investors large and small need to be aware of the changes in order to understand and optimize risk factors in their portfolios.

WHERE DO MY ORDERS GO?

The order maze befuddles many investors. So, you press that "Submit" button, and your order is executed, right? Wrong. Plain wrong. And what happens in reality depends on a multitude of factors.

First, was the order you sent in a market or a limit? Limit orders specify the execution price. If the market price is far away from the specified limit price, the limit order may execute with a considerable delay and may never execute at all.

Market orders are orders to buy and sell here and now, at the best available price. Still, even market orders have to wait their turn. Most investors' orders first end up on their brokers' systems when submitted. Brokers are entities such as Charles Schwab, JP Morgan, Pragma Trading, and Quantitative Brokers. They carry a special designation to do the best possible job on behalf of their clients. The designation is administered by the SEC and Financial Industry Regulatory Authority (FINRA) for equities, ETFs, and equity options, and CFTC and National Futures Association (NFA) for commodities and futures. Foreign exchange brokers tend to be unregulated.

At the point when the order reaches the broker, the order contains all identifying information: who the order is from (institution or individual), your account number, and so on. Next, the broker may choose one of the five ways to handle your order:

1. Send the order to the exchange for execution.
2. Send the order to a market maker.
3. Send the order to an Electronic Communication Network (ECN).
4. Send the order to a dark pool.
5. Match the order internally with other orders sent to the same broker.

For most publicly traded equities, brokers can send the orders to an exchange, such as NYSE. Some exchanges will compensate brokers for the flow with rebates. As discussed earlier in this chapter, some exchanges pay rebates for the market orders and some do so for the limit orders. Depending on whether your order is a market or a limit order, your broker may forward the order to a different exchange to maximize the fees the broker receives from exchanges. You, the end client, may or may not see some or all of the fees your broker receives on your behalf. The exact distribution of fees is typically stipulated in the fine print of your broker services agreement.

As an alternative to sending your order to an exchange, the broker may choose to send your order to a designated market maker. A market maker is a broker-dealer who keeps inventory on hand and is available to match orders out of their cache. A prominent example of a market maker is Knight Capital Group (KCG). Market makers may also pay your broker for bringing in your orders, and you may or may not see any of those payments.

Still further, the broker may send your order to an electronic matching service known as an electronic communication network (ECN). An ECN is an alternative trading system (ATS) that matches orders outside of exchanges. ECNs match orders electronically. Unlike dark pools, ECNs display their quotes in the consolidated quote feed (SIP tape) that redistributes NBBO. An example of an ECN is NYSE Arca. The very first ECN was Instinet, founded as an inter-broker dealer back in 1969. ECNs may also pay your broker for bringing in flow.

A broker may also choose to route your order to a dark pool. For example, Interactive Brokers (IB) clearly states on its website:

> *IB maintains connections to "dark pool" ATS's (including the IB ATS) that execute a portion of IB customer stock orders. IB customers benefit from IB's access to dark pools. Dark pools provide a source of substantial additional liquidity. Dark pools charge no execution fees or lower execution fees than exchanges. Dark pools also provide fast executions and the possibility of executions at prices more favorable than the prevailing NBBO.*
> *Source:* https://gdcdyn.interactivebrokers.com/Universal/servlet/
> Registration_v2.formSampleView?ad=order_routing_
> disclosure.html

Finally, your broker may not choose to send your order anywhere at all, and instead match it internally with an opposite order on its internal books. For example, if you submit a limit buy for 100 shares of IBM at $155.14 and it comprises NBBO, and your broker receives a market sell order for IBM, the broker will match your order with an incoming market sell order without forwarding your order on. The process of intra-broker execution is called *internalization*. Brokers are required to internalize all commodity and commodity futures orders by law. The law was created to avoid money laundering that was apparently happening when the "dirty" money was traded on the exchange into a "clean" account by the brokers who housed both accounts. The broker may still charge you the same commission as it would have if the broker forwarded your order on.

As long as your order stays on the broker's premises, your account information is visible and attached to the order. When the order leaves the broker, it automatically loses all its individual account identity and becomes associated only with broker ID. That's right—by the time your order reaches an exchange, it effectively becomes anonymous, lost in hundreds if not thousands or millions of orders your broker processes on a daily basis. No market participant outside of your broker knows who you are and what you trade, unless, of course, you dominate your broker-dealer flow.

EXECUTING LARGE ORDERS

Brokers' orders may be more numerous than one would expect. Part of most brokers' business is best execution: The ability to slice large orders and massage the parts into the exchange order flow without causing panics, crashes, or market exuberance. In other words, many brokers are commissioned to process a large order while leaving as little impact as possible in the markets. How do brokers do that? Why, with the algorithms, of course!

Execution algos are computer programs that are designed to break down orders into small chunks and then optimize order timing and routing so that the order obtains the best execution. Suppose you want to sell $1 billion of British pound, GBP/USD. If your order hits the markets in one piece, two things happen: First, it will immediately wipe out all available limit orders, possibly causing a crash; second, the price of your execution will be horrendously low as you will "sweep the book," picking up all terribly priced orders to satisfy your appetite. If, on the other hand, you break down your order into small chunks and spread those mini-orders over time, you will give a chance to limit orders to rebuild naturally, and may obtain execution close to what the market price would be if your order did not exist at all!

Two common execution algos are used across all markets. The simpler one breaks down a large order into an equal number of pieces, where the number of resulting mini-orders is specified by the client or is a function of the broker's secret sauce. With this algo, known as time-weighted average price (TWAP), the number of the orders corresponds to the desired frequency of execution times the length of execution. The main advantage of TWAP is its simplicity.

The main disadvantage of TWAP is that it is very mechanical and completely ignores regularly occurring trading patterns. For instance, it is normally the case in equities to have high trading volume at the 9:30 AM market open, a slower late morning, and even slower lunch hour, and then somewhat of a resurgence ahead of the market close. In other words, the trading volume in the equity markets follows something of a U-shaped pattern. The higher the volume, the easier it is to massage in larger orders without moving the markets with those particular orders. Furthermore, across individual stocks, the volume patterns are similar from one day to the next, allowing for a fair degree of intraday volume predictability based on its historical patterns. Enter the volume-weighted average price (VWAP) algo—essentially, a TWAP, with TWAP timing of orders, where the size of the individual orders is modified according to the historical volume curve: higher in the morning, lower through the midday, and higher again at the market close.

VWAP has been such a hit in equities that it has become a de-facto standard in execution, against which all other execution methodologies are measured. Of course, it is not 100 percent perfect. For one, you can outperform it with an *overlay*: a strategy that requires a slight modification of VWAP and potentially delivers a substantial gain. Companies like Able-Markets deliver overlay services, among other data. Second, while the small packets of orders are mixed up in the anonymous markets, the patterns may still be clearly visible.

TRANSACTION COSTS AND TRANSPARENCY

Regulators, aware of data capabilities and the risks hidden in today's markets, have proposed higher transparency requirements on the whole industry. For example, the new pan-European market regulations from MiFID II have a direct impact on the structure of brokerages in Europe. Specifically, MiFID II dictates that all brokerages are required to demonstrate best execution and provide full disclosure and transparency on the following items: price, transaction costs, speed of execution, likelihood of execution, trading venue selection, and so on. While these metrics seem to be obvious priorities for investor disclosure that should be adopted by the US regulators as well, these long have been the "secret sauce" of many execution brokers.

So where is the brokerage industry going under the new regulations? Technology is certainly not only enabling the requirements of transparency, it is also leveling the field as far as investors are concerned, making broker-shopping easier. How are brokers to retain their clients?

The answer, once again, lies with technology. Smart order-routing solutions should enable brokers to compete for clients beyond taking them to beer outings and popular concerts. A solid example of someone who has been doing this well for the past decade in US equities is Pragma Securities: leveraging PhD-level research and the technology to deliver benchmark-beating routing to their clients. However, even Pragma cannot fully disclose its secret sauce—doing so would make it vulnerable to the competition and likely affect its business considerably.

Research on how to enhance order routing is not straightforward and does not come cheap—retaining the brains from defecting to competition and spilling their knowledge there is not just a matter of bullet-proof contracting. And the competition does not come just from other brokers—many successful hedge funds and prop trading shops are now setting up their own execution divisions to avoid brokerage costs and leaking information about their trades to a third party. Companies like AbleMarkets provide off-the-shelf solutions to beat the competition in execution, by tracking aggressive HFT activity, for example, making the job of executing brokers easier and more profitable. The long-term future of many brokers, therefore, depends on sound investing and partnerships with the right research providers—competing on price and intangible perks like beer outings alone is a treacherous path for survival.

CONCLUSIONS

The changes sweeping the financial markets can be mind-boggling. Most are driven by advances in technology at an ever lower cost, be it in data processing or storage. Computers take market paradigms to previously unthinkable constructs. These are changing trading and execution as a business, creating a slew of previously unknown risks, and magnifying the impact of formerly marginal risks. Investors should be aware of the developments in the market microstructure space and use the latest technology advances to protect their portfolios.

END OF CHAPTER QUESTIONS

1. What are alternative trading systems (ATS)? What categories do they comprise?
2. How does a limit order book work?
3. What is NBBO? How is it produced?
4. How do brokerages execute client orders?
5. What new regulations are proposed in the order execution space?

CHAPTER 4

Who Is Front-Running You?

—What do quants eat for dinner?

—Depends on their risk appetite.

Many investors feel that someone can see their orders and place orders immediately ahead of them to draw liquidity and capture a small profit at the investor's expense. Often, investors sense that they can observe such market behavior in real time through a brokerage app screen. Take a quiet market; see a specific bid; place a sell order, and the bid evaporates just before the order happens to execute. How can this happen? This chapter discusses the peculiarities of front-running in the electronic trading world we live in, as well as broader implications of liquidity, order book depth, spoofing, and more.

First, the basics—front-running is illegal. Front-running is defined as an activity whereby an ill-intentioned market participant observes an incoming market order. Knowing that the order is likely to move the price just due to its basic liquidity-taking property, the observer places a similar order directly ahead of the original investor's order. As such, the observer runs to place an order ahead or in front of the investor with the expectation of taking a better price. Next, the investor's order is executed, possibly at a worse price due to reduced liquidity, courtesy of the front-runner. Following, the price likely moves further since the investor's order also takes out liquidity from the market. The front-runner can now liquidate his temporary position and realize a small profit.

Thus, suppose you are an investor and want to sell 1,000 shares of IBM at the best price available, with a market order. You look at the market and see that the best bid available across all markets at the time you are placing your order is $162.96. You diligently enter your 1,000 share order into your order entry/management system (OMS), and click "Submit." As discussed in the previous chapter, your order travels on a public network that is most-likely unencrypted to your broker, who then decides what to do with it. Your broker may choose to match your order with opposing orders your broker has accumulated up to that point, in what's called *internalization*. If your order is internalized, your order never actually hits the markets; instead, you receive a confirmation of order execution without touching any of the big boards. Even when your broker chooses to internalize your order, your order may still be moving the needle on the price display in which means that you did not receive the best price you observed when you placed the order. More on this later.

Alternatively, your broker may choose to route your order to an external trading venue, such as an exchange, an ECN, a dark pool, another broker, or a third-party market maker. And here is an important detail: When your broker sends your order on to the next execution venue, your order loses your identifier. Instead of your order being identified with your account number, your name, or your corporate identity, once your order leaves your broker's realm, your order takes on your broker's identification. The span between your computer and the order-receiving brokerage is the only environment where you are represented and identified as yourself, be it individual investor, a large hedge fund, or another legal entity. In other words, when your order hits the financial markets at large, it does so anonymously, save for your broker's identification. Your broker uses the same order identification on all the orders it sends on to other market participants for execution. Tracing your particular order from an exchange board to your account, therefore, becomes virtually impossible, unless your broker is primarily dealing with your orders and your orders alone. Figure 4.1 illustrates the point.

Front-running your specific orders may occur in two ways: (1) when the alleged front-runner knows who you are, and (2) when the alleged

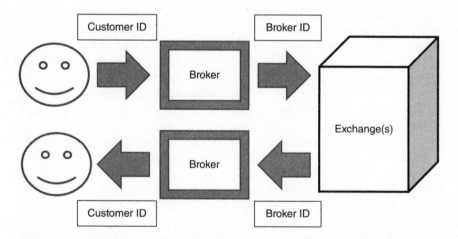

FIGURE 4.1 Stages of order identification

front-runner does not know who you are. The first case, when the alleged front-runner is well aware of your identity, can only occur within your broker's realm, since your broker is the only party who legally has access to your identity in the financial markets (we are ruling out guys spying on your identity illegally via computer hacks here).

How can your broker front-run you? Technically, your broker is bound by the code of *best execution*—that is, your broker is morally obligated (and regulated) to deliver the best possible work for the client like you and the others like you who choose to use your broker's services. Of course, the broker also needs to stay in business, and the execution business can be a tough endeavor in the age of electronic trading. Some brokers, therefore, resort to prehedging, which loosely works as follows: The broker sees your order, realizes that she may be exposed if she holds inventory and you have better information than she does (in a situation known as *"adverse selection"*), determines that you are likely to move the market, and jumps ahead and executes a similar order ahead of yours in the markets to ensure that she ends up on the winning side, should the markets move considerably. The broker's trade erases some of the previously available liquidity, your order gets a much worse fill than you expected, and, worst of all, the market returns back to its prior level after your order is filled, since the broker disburses the purchase for their own account following your trade. *Prehedging* is also known as *anticipatory hedging*, as in preempting and hedging the risks of impending execution.

While prehedging is currently forbidden on the CME, foreign exchange is still a wild west and equities regulators allow the use of derivatives to prehedge. Thus, once your 1,000-share order to sell IBM hits the broker, your broker may turn to IBM options and buy 500 put options on IBM before executing your order, with the explicit purpose of protecting itself against your information asymmetry—suppose for whatever reason you know that IBM is about to crater, and your broker does not. If your broker is holding any IBM inventory, it will be at a disadvantage as the IBM price is about to sink. The seemingly innocuous options purchase by the broker has wild ramifications in today's interconnected markets. Aggressive high-frequency traders (HFTs), discussed in the next chapter, continuously scan markets for arbitrage opportunities, and will see the temporal discrepancy between the options activity and the still-lethargic IBM stock (your order still has not hit the markets). The HFTs will take off the price you saw when you placed the order just before your order had a chance to execute. Figure 4.2 illustrates the idea.

Are any changes for the better on the horizon? To an extent, yes. For example, in June 2016, the Bank of International Settlements, the body loosely coordinating the standards in foreign exchange transacting,

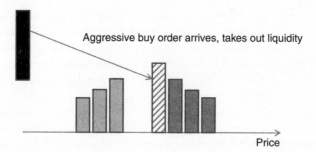

FIGURE 4.2 Aggressive HFT's orders impact bid-ask spreads
This figure illustrates that an arriving aggressive order wipes
out the best limit order(s) on the opposing side of the limit
order book, widening spreads and increasing volatility
through larger bid-ask bounce.

proposed to eliminate prehedging from foreign exchange practices. The
proposals are nonbinding at this point, and require substantial industry
buy-in to take effect, yet, this is likely a step in the right direction.

Several initiatives have tried to circumvent this situation altogether. For
example, a Legal Entity Identifier (LEI) program, currently administered by
the Office of Financial Research (OFR), is promoting requirements for things
like mandatory trade identification, with each end-user being a part of the
record. The idea behind LEI, at least in part, is to track who is front-running
whom and help regulators make better rules about what market participants
may and may not do. This initiative, conceived in the wake of Lehman Brothers' collapse in late 2009 and the mess of financial records that followed, has
been adopted in markets such as swaps and insurance distribution. However,
real-time adoption of such identifiers may be far away, as the industry is still
struggling to shorten its settlement cycle, often from as many as three days.
In fact, as this book was written, NASDAQ announced the formation of an
industry group to discuss moving settlement from the three day to a two-day
cycle ($T + 3$ to $T + 2$). As blockchain technology proliferates, however, and
enables true real-time settlement, legal entity identifiers may gain traction for
trade-by-trade reconciliation. Still, why would a trader want to be publicly
recognized on every exchange? Wouldn't that make the front-running situation even worse? Imagine the world with all the market participants, not
just brokers, knowing which trader has a high betting average?

Another possible reason for front-running: stale quotes. In other words,
the best prices you are seeing on your computer screen are simply out
of date. The breakdowns of exchange feeds are still too common when
sending quotes to the SEC's security information processor (SIP) tape

that redistributes the best quotes back to everyone. Companies like the New York Stock Exchange (NYSE), traditional bastions of human trading, have had a hard time adjusting to new-age technological requirements, 24/7 operational mandates for their systems, and so on. Still, even the brand-new exchange entrants like IEX may wittingly or unwittingly be distributing stale quotes, and here's how.

IEX's innovation is to delay all orders by 350 microseconds. In all fairness, this innovation is not really IEX's: foreign exchange electronic broker EBS, a subsidiary of ICAP, introduced the 250-microsecond-delay loop years ago. The official reason for the delay, as explained by IEX, is that the delay stops aggressive HFTs from arbitraging price discrepancies between dark pools, giving dark-pool prices a chance to adjust to market levels prior to execution. And that works great for ICAP in dark-pool-like distributed foreign exchange execution and worked fine for IEX when IEX was a dark pool. Fast-forward to the present, IEX is a lit SEC-registered exchange subject to national best bid/offer (NBBO), and the same delay essentially produces stale quotes and explicitly allows for front-running.

How does that work? Suppose IEX has a limit order for IBM. IEX delays all incoming market orders by 350 microseconds (μs) "to deter high-frequency traders"—a nonstarter measure due to the NBBO dynamics, as discussed in the next chapter. Suppose another market order has already arrived to IEX ready to claim that available liquidity that you are seeing on screen. Since the market orders are delayed, you are seeing phantom liquidity, as those orders are already spoken for by the orders that have arrived before you even looked on screen—IEX simply provides artificial or "stale" quotes by forcing delays in execution. Not only that, IEX distorts the dynamics of the entire market.

Consider this scenario: There is some unexpected news and the market is moving super-fast. IEX has a backlog of quotes, all of which have already been spoken for by incoming market orders, sitting in their respective 350-microsecond-delay pens. IEX quotes are thus the best in the markets, as all of the other exchanges have moved way beyond these levels. IEX is going into the SIP (NBBO collector) as the best available quote of the moment, forcing a ton of new orders to be routed their way due to the NBBO requirement. The end result? IEX obtains a huge share of the orders by law, most of which are executed at the subpar prices, IEX captures untold commissions, and investors feel ripped-off more than ever.

IEX introduces other opportunities for front-running as well. All of the quotes in the SIP are already at least 1 ms delayed due to the back and forth of quote transmission and another 0.5 ms or so in SIP own quote aggregation. IEX introduces another 1 ms or so delay into the SIP quotes when accounting for data transmission speeds in excess of IEX's own delay loop.

So now you have the following hierarchy: real best quotes, quotes delayed by 1 ms by IEX, and quotes delayed by 2 ms by SIP. Most of the time, markets are reasonably quiet and 1 ms delay will not matter much. However, when the markets move rapidly—for example, in response to news—the following high-frequency arbitrage opportunity presents itself. Suppose the true best bid/offer for IBM is $150.09/$150.25, and IEX is still quoting $150.45/$150.87 into the SIP. Since the SIP-based national best bid is at $150.45, exchanges with true market values cannot execute market orders, and instead are obligated to forward them to IEX, where the NBBO currently resides. IEX, as a result, is accumulating a backlog of market sell orders with limited liquidity to support them all. Feeding $150.00 and lower-priced bids into the IEX system, therefore, while placing limit orders to sell at $150.09 prevailing in other markets results in virtually risk-free short-term arbitrage opportunity, stemming simply from IEX design.

SPOOFING, FLAKY LIQUIDITY, AND HFT

Not all that appears to be front-running is technically that. Some perceived front-running is flaky or vaporized limit orders—the market depth that somehow is ephemeral, easily disappearing in times of even minute stress. Not surprisingly, many investors have been blaming high-frequency traders, and specifically, high-frequency trading market makers, for providing this phantom liquidity and pulling it at their convenience, leaving the rest of the market in disarray.

First, the basics. *High-frequency trading* (HFT) refers to a category of computer programs designed to process vast arrays of market information and trade the markets, typically in an intraday framework and only occasionally holding positions overnight. Broadly speaking, all HFT can be split into two large groups: aggressive HFT and passive HFT. The key difference between the two categories is their built-in impatience. Aggressive HFTs tend to trade on time-sensitive information and typically prefer to use market orders that deliver immediate execution at the best available price. Aggressive HFTs are discussed in detail in the next chapter. Passive HFTs engage in market making and other, less time-sensitive strategies. As a result, passive HFTs mostly use limit orders. Most successful aggressive HFTs require ultra-fast connectivity and speed of execution to reach the markets ahead of their competition.

Passive HFTs tend to reduce volatility by propping up the limit order book and reducing spreads and the bid-ask bounce of prices. Of course, traders deploying passive HFTs can cancel their limit orders, as can everyone else placing limit orders. However, they cannot run away once their orders have been selected for matching by the exchange. In other words, just by placing a limit order, a passive HFT is committing to honor that order in the period of time before the order may be canceled. No matter how soon the order cancellation may be sent, if the limit order is the best-priced order on the market, and if a market order arrives in the time span between the placement of the limit order and its cancellation, the limit order will be executed. Stated differently, any limit order always has a positive probability of execution. Figure 4.3 summarizes actions of passive HFTs' provision of liquidity.

Limit orders form liquidity. Liquidity is a measure of how big of an order one can place in a market, where the "market" is usually considered to be the order book for one given financial instrument. The higher the liquidity in a particular market, the less price disturbance a large order will incur there. In a perfect market with infinite liquidity, an investor may process an infinitely sized market order and not move the price 1 tick. Of course, such perfectly liquid markets tend to exist only in the imagination of academics.

In reality, in order for a buy or sell market order to be fulfilled, the market order needs to be matched with one or more limit orders of the opposite direction, buy market orders being matched with sell limit orders, and vice

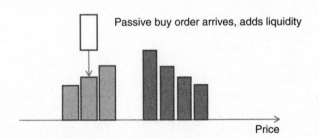

FIGURE 4.3 Illustration of a passive HFT order placement

This figure shows that an arriving passive limit order enhances liquidity, adding depth to the limit order book.

versa. The larger the market order, the more limit orders it will consume. Conversely, as more limit orders are available for matching the arriving market order, the larger the market order can be. Thus, in technical terms, *liquidity* is the set of all available limit orders that can be used for immediate execution. Figure 4.4 illustrates a snapshot of a limit order book, containing "displayed" liquidity: resting buy orders ("bids") and sell orders ("offers"), aggregated by price from lowest to the highest. Besides displayed liquidity, most exchanges offer the opportunity to send in "hidden" limit orders that, similarly to traditional dark pools, are not revealed until they are executed.

According to folklore, modern liquidity has two subsets: "natural" liquidity and "toxic" liquidity. *Natural liquidity* is thought to consist of dependable limit orders ready to be matched with incoming market orders or to put it another way, liquidity placed by traders who generally plan to hold the position for longer than one day. *Toxic liquidity*, also referred to as *opportunistic liquidity*, comprises the limit orders that are not dependable or stable. Just as the toxic market order flow leaves market makers at a disadvantage in a process referred to as adverse selection, toxic liquidity can be disadvantageous to non–market-making participants such as institutional portfolio managers. Toxic limit orders are often canceled, only to be replenished by another set of identical limit orders after a brief pause. The goal of such on-off flickering is to be intentionally harmful to the markets along the following dimensions:

- Some market participants believe that flickering quote behavior is present to deceive market participants about the depth of the order book.
- Others believe that flickering quotes are used to prompt large traders into revealing their true position execution sizes. Such information-mining on behalf of entities deploying flickering orders is known as *phishing* or *pinging*.

FIGURE 4.4   Buy-side available liquidity exceeds sell-side liquidity

The figure illustrates that an incoming market buy order faces a sparser limit order book, and hence a less certain execution, than an incoming market sell order.

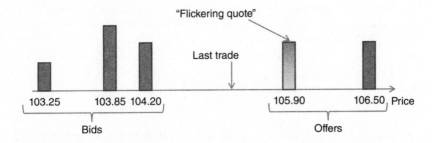

FIGURE 4.5 Example of impact of flickering quotes

This figure shows that a trader using a market buy order observes the best quote at price 105.90, but is filled at 106.50 since the 105.90 quote is canceled before the market buy order reaches the exchange, resulting in worse execution.

- Overall, flickering or disappearing liquidity can be toxic because it can accentuate the market impact of incoming orders. Figure 4.5 shows an example of market toxicity.

Due to the often-intense speed of flickering observed in toxic limit orders, some consider toxic liquidity to be generated by machines more so than by humans. People are constrained; we need to physically observe and click the orders. Indeed, human market makers and institutional market participants are often described as generating the most natural liquidity. As a direct consequence, the presence of toxic liquidity has prompted debates on the usefulness of high-frequency trading in market making. The next section discusses strategies deployed by passive high-frequency traders and their activities in the markets.

A particular concern surrounding passive HFT has been a perceived rise in fast order cancellations and the resulting toxicity of liquidity. Some recent research went as far as to suggest that in today's markets, as many as 95 percent of all limit orders are canceled, creating wasteful clogging of networks. The same research proposed that such clogging is a result of potentially malicious activity by high-frequency traders. New research suggests that the number of canceled orders has been significantly overstated, and, therefore, the risks associated with HFTs were blown out of proportion.

The miscalculation of the proportion of limit order cancellations happened for simple and innocuous reasons. In the exchange databases, most orders are recorded with one of the following four monikers:

A for limit order addition

X for limit order cancellation

E for order execution

P for hidden order execution

Notice that there is no code for limit order revision. Instead, when a trader sends in a request to update the price of his limit order from $33.56 to $33.58, the update is recorded as two separate transactions: a cancellation of the limit order at $33.56 and an addition of the new limit order at $33.58. When one counts X orders vis-à-vis the number of all orders in the database, the proportion of cancellations indeed appears to exceed 90 percent. A more detailed review, of course, presents a different picture. The vast majority of X orders are not just simple order cancellations, but are immediately replaced by another A order with a more favorable price. In other words, the majority of limit orders are not simply canceled, but are instead revised. Indeed, only 12 percent of limit orders are canceled outright without immediate replacement.

Can we be sure that a given order is canceled and then replaced? How do we know that the observed A order is not a completely separate limit order arriving and then being canceled? All orders have unique order identifiers. In the case of BATS Y-exchange, for instance, the order identifier is a unique 12-digit alphanumeric sequence. When an order is revised, instead of being simply canceled, the 12-digit ID on the order cancellation (message type X) and the following re-addition of the order (message type A) share the common identifier. Studies citing unusually large order cancellation ratios make no mention of order identification counting, likely misreading the order classification statistics.

What happens with the other 88 percent of limit orders that are not simply canceled? On BATS Y-exchange, just 0.1 percent, or one in every thousand, of all limit orders are matched with limit orders in the limit order book—a tiny number that is a function of BATS pricing, customers, and the resulting appearance of quotes matching the NBBO in the BATS limit orders. Another 1 percent of limit orders are executed immediately upon arrival, since they hit the so-called hidden limit orders, the limit orders of the opposite side (buy vs. sell), placed at the same or better price as the newly arriving limit orders, yet not shown in the limit order book until their execution. An increasing number of exchanges offer hidden limit orders that are a feature in the spirit of dark pools, where all the limit orders are hidden. The remaining 86 percent of all limit orders are revised, not canceled outright, until the end of the trading day.

Hidden orders are not a feature of BATS alone. Many of the exchanges have been moving in the direction of dark-pool-like functionality, allowing *iceberg orders.*

Hidden or dark orders have certainly taken their fair share of criticism over the last few years, in both dark pools and lit exchanges. Dark pool operators have been sued and accused of amoral and unscrupulous behavior and generally singled out as shady characters. People trading in the dark pools were likewise thought to be tarnished and were scrutinized for phishing, pinging, and an array of other, previously unheard of, market activities.

Specifically, phishing and pinging are two techniques traders may use to induce a behavioral response from hidden market participants in a dark pool as well as in a lit exchange utilizing hidden orders. Phishing and pinging are related concepts and work as follows. Assume there is a large dark or hidden order in the order book of the dark pool or a lit exchange. To find out where the order is and to approximate its size, a phishing trader may send out a sequence of very small orders at different price levels within the limit order book, as shown in Figure 4.6. At a certain point, the phishing orders will be picked up or executed, indicating the approximate location of the dark orders. The speed of the dark order's response to phishing orders also matters: The faster the response, the closer are the phishing orders to the dark orders—a phishing order hitting upon a price point with dark liquidity present is executed instantaneously. Think of this as slow creatures moving along a dark ocean floor—whoever drops the bait directly in front of the creatures is rewarded instantaneously with a catch!

Several dark pool and exchange operators have been screening their traders for phishing behavior. Automated Trading Desk (ATD), long since acquired by Citi, was famous for creating negative financial incentives for phishing participants in its markets. The fees ATD imposed were in proportion to the benefit the phisher received, and the fees thus worked to discourage phishing behavior. Other trading venues may terminate phishing participants altogether, but each exchange has leeway to treat their phishers differently.

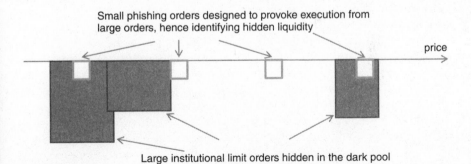

FIGURE 4.6 Limit order book in the dark pools and phishing

What should investors do? It's worth remembering that the original purpose of dark pools and dark orders on lit exchanges was to hide large order blocks. Michael Lewis suggested that all markets are doomed and investors really have no choice but to turn to the one dark pool, IEX, that he was promoting. Aside from marketing messages, sophisticated algos help investors break down their large positions into single-digit share or dollar trades, and process those trades in lit and well-regulated exchanges. With an algo in hand, investors simply do not need dark pools—lit regulated exchanges work just fine. The reality is that algos are a necessity for managing many execution venue-related risks, and should be considered a must-have in every large investor's toolkit.

Today's most sophisticated execution algos do not just break large positions into small orders according to the VWAP or TWAP. The best execution algos take into account fees paid or received from exchanges and trading venues, and various available order types. A typical exchange may offer dozens of order types to traders of all categories, including institutions and HFTs. As of September 2015, NYSE had 25 active order types, including six types of "immediate or cancel" (IOC) orders comprising variations of a market order, five types of displayed limit orders, and four types of nondisplayed or hidden limit orders (Intercontinental Exchange 2015). Out of all the order types, NYSE IOC market-order types comprised 32.61 percent of all orders in aggregate, displayed limit orders of all stripes accounted for 41.51 percent of all orders, and nondisplayed limit orders totaled just 2.46 percent of all orders. By comparison, the following is the distribution of orders on BATS exchanges in September 2015: BATS IOC, including vanilla market orders, occurred 13.84 percent of the time, with displayed limit order variations submitted 48.91 percent of the time, and nondisplayed orders accounting for 37.26 percent of the total order count (BATS Global Markets, 2015). The differences in order prevalence by type may be a function of market structure divergences among exchanges. However, most exchange order types have at least one commonality: the structure of order transmission to and from the exchanges.

The commonalities in order transmission are not to be confused with the language of transmission, formally known as *transmission protocol.* Many exchanges use FIX communication protocol to transmit messages, while some exchanges, such as NASDAQ, have proprietary data transmission models that allow information exchange to be faster and more reliable than FIX. However, most protocols deploy a message structure that includes message additions, message cancellations, and message executions, with individual messages often linked by unique order identifiers to track order arrivals and existing order modifications.

TABLE 4.1 A Sample from the Level III Data (Processed and Formatted) for GOOG on October 8, 2015

This table presents a snippet of detailed order flow for GOOG recorded on October 8, 2015, by BATS. A messages represent limit order additions and X messages are limit order cancellations.

Unique Order ID	Message Time (ET)	Symbol	Original Order Placement Time	Order Size	Limit Price	Order Type
C91KT9003TDS	9:39:01.688	GOOG	9:39:01.688	100	637.33	A
C91KT9003TDS	9:39:02.790	GOOG	9:39:01.688	100	637.33	X
C91KT9003UU4	9:39:09.213	GOOG	9:39:09.213	100	629.23	A
C91KT9003UU4	9:39:10.212	GOOG	9:39:09.213	100	629.23	X
C91KT9003W7J	9:39:16.794	GOOG	9:39:15.799	100	648.45	X
C91KT9003OBR	9:39:19.967	GOOG	9:39:00.270	100	641.00	X

For instance, Table 4.1 shows a stylized excerpt from a message log recorded for GOOG on October 8, 2015, by BATS BYX exchange. The fields included in Table 4.1 are Unique Limit Order ID, used to identify all limit order additions and subsequent executions and revisions; the time the message was sent out by the exchange; the time when the original limit order was added; the size of the original limit order or revision; and the price of the original limit order. Table 4.1 shows two order types: A for a new limit order addition and X for limit order cancellation. Additional order message types may include partial or full executions of limit orders, market orders, and hidden order executions.

In the snippet of messages shown in Table 4.1, the first two messages pertained to order ID C91KT9003TDS. The first C91KT9003TDS message was an addition of the limit order with a price of 637.33 recorded at 9:39:01.688 AM ET. The timestamp originally was reported in milliseconds since midnight, but was converted into regular time for reader convenience. The second message pertaining to the same order ID, a cancellation, arrived just over one second later. A similar pattern occurred with the next order ID, C91KT9003UU4. The message to add the 100-share order, this time with a price of 629.23, occurred at 9:39:09.213, while the message to cancel the same order was recorded by the exchange at 9:39:10.212, just 999 milliseconds later. The last two messages displayed in Table 4.1 are cancellations of orders placed earlier in the day and not shown in the table. On October 8, 2015, GOOG had 50,274 messages that were of one of the following types: (1) limit order additions, (2) full or partial limit order cancellations, (3) regular limit order executions, and (4) hidden order executions.

TABLE 4.2 Distribution of Order Sizes in Shares Recorded for GOOG on October 8, 2015

This table illustrates distribution of order sizes for orders of different types. Order types are: A—add limit order; E—resting limit order executed; P—hidden limit order executed; and X—limit order cancellation.

	A	E	P	X
Average	94.26877	87.36691	68.49554	94.21459
Standard deviation	21.39916	40.30215	102.4454	21.38267
Maximum	400	300	2283	400
99%	100	207.56	138.79	100
95%	100	100.6	100	100
90%	100	100	100	100
75%	100	100	100	100
50%	100	100	86.5	100
25%	100	74	20	100
10%	80	37.3	5	80
5%	47	5.5	2	47
1%	2	3	1	2
Minimum	1	2	1	1
# Messages	24,824	139	561	24,750
Total Size	2,340,128	12,144	38,426	2,331,811

Out of those messages, 24,824 (49.3 percent) were limit order additions, 24,750 (49.2 percent) were limit order cancellations, 139 (0.3 percent) were limit order executions, and 561 (1.1 percent) were records of hidden order executions. Table 4.2 summarizes size properties of each category of orders. Out of all the added limit orders, only 49 were greater than 100 shares, and the maximum order size was 400 shares. The posted limit orders exclude hidden or dark orders that are now available in most public exchanges ("lit" markets).

After a limit order is added (message type A), it can be canceled or executed in part or in full, or it can remain resting in the order book until its expiry, typically at the end of the trading day or "until cancel." The trader who placed the order completely determines the cancellation. The execution is a combination of factors: a resting limit order is executed when it becomes the best available order and a matching market order arrives, given that the order is not canceled before the market order arrival. A limit order may be canceled all at once or in several cancellation messages, each message chipping away at the limit order's initial size. Similarly, a limit order may be executed in full if the matching market order size is greater or equal to that

TABLE 4.3 Distribution of Difference, in Milliseconds, between Sequential Order Updates for All Order Records for GOOG on October 8, 2015

This table shows the duration of time since the last order update for each given order ID for various order types. Order types are: A—add limit order; E—resting limit order executed; P—hidden limit order executed; and X—limit order cancellation. A and P type orders are first recorded when added and executed, respectively.

	A	E	P	X
Average	0	17932.87	0	8299.751
Standard deviation	0	82984.99	0	211621.9
Maximum	0	687989	0	18326189
99%	0	496794.7	0	29535.6
95%	0	33518	0	11545.15
90%	0	25900	0	6599.4
75%	0	10049	0	2237
50%	0	3010.5	0	567
25%	0	626	0	68
10%	0	29.9	0	4
5%	0	0	0	1
1%	0	0	0	0
Minimum	0	0	0	0

of the limit order. If the limit order is larger than the matching market orders, it will be partially executed.

Table 4.3 summarizes the distributional properties of time since the last record of each order appeared. For additions of limit orders as well as for executions of hidden orders, the times are identically zero. Limit order cancellations average 8.3 seconds since the last action on the order ID: at the order placement or previous partial cancellation. The time distribution is highly skewed, with the median time between the last order action and following order cancellation of just a half a second. Executions (order types E) on average occur 18 seconds since the last order action, with the executions following limit order additions just 3 seconds at the median value.

Out of 24,824 limit orders added to GOOG on October 8, 2015, 21,698 (87 percent) were canceled in full, with just one order cancellation. On average, single cancellations arrived just five seconds after the limit order was added to the limit order book. The median shelf life of a limit order with a single cancellation was even shorter: just over half a second. Table 4.4 illustrates that most of the orders were 100 shares or smaller, but greater than 1 share. As Table 4.4 shows, most of the orders were in 100-share lots.

TABLE 4.4 Size and Shelf Life of Orders Canceled in Full with a Single Cancellation for GOOG on October 8, 2015

This table shows the summary statistics for limit orders canceled in full, as opposed to partial order cancellations.

	Size	Time Until Cancel
Average	93.50871	5210.672
Standard deviation	22.55583	154922.7
Maximum	400	18326189
99%	100	27946.44
90%	100	6543
75%	100	2284
50%	100	630
25%	100	97
10%	80	30
5%	47	1
1%	2	0
Minimum	1	0

The limit orders not canceled in full with a single order cancellation can be subsequently executed or canceled at a later time. Figure 4.7 displays a histogram of the number of order messages for each added limit order when the order messages exceed two (typically, addition and cancellation, or addition and execution). As Figure 4.7 shows, some limit orders end up with as many as 50 limit order cancellations.

The most interesting part of the limit order dynamics could be in the intraday evolution of orders. Until 9:28 AM ET, limit orders arrive and are promptly canceled, without any limit orders visibly resting in the limit order book for longer than five minutes. Displayed limit orders alternate between buys and sells, and various price levels. Then, at 9:28:30.231 AM ET, two orders arrive, a buy at 596.57, order ID C91KT9000RU8, and a sell at 684.27, order ID C91KT9000RU9. The buy order is left untouched until 11:52:25.912 AM, at which point the buy order is modified through a simultaneous cancellation message and another added with the same order ID and size, at 590.16. At 14:59:30.895, the same order ID is in play again, this time receiving a simultaneous cancellation message and an A message with price of 596.64. At 16:00:00, the limit order is finally canceled. The sell order C91KT9000RU9 is updated with a simultaneous cancellation and an order addition at 9:49:44.619, when the price is reset to 677.88, and then 11:56:21.674, when the price is reset to 671.49, and then 14:39:58.082, when the price is changed to 677.95. This order too is finally

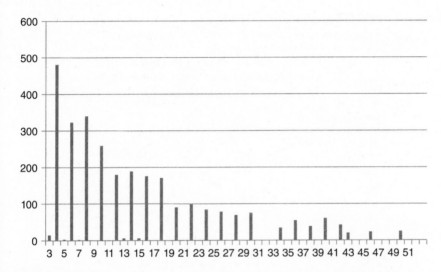

FIGURE 4.7 Histogram of number of order messages per each added limit order

This figure shows the number of order messages for each added limit order excluding order additions followed by single order cancellations. Addition of the limit order (A message) is included in the total order count, displayed on x-axis. The y-axis shows the number of order IDs corresponding to each message count.

canceled at 16:00:00.000 by the exchange, probably because it was a day limit order.

When a limit order is adjusted, it is recorded not as a separate message, but as a sequence of two messages with the same order ID: an order cancellation followed by an immediate order addition with revised characteristics. In GOOG data for October 8, 2015, 4,794 messages existed pertaining to limit order adjustments, comprising 9.5 percent of the total message traffic. An average revision occurred 30 seconds after the last order update, indicating likely human direction. Out of all the revisions, 99.0 percent occurred within 40 seconds from the original order addition or last revision. Table 4.5 summarizes the distribution of inter-revision times for limit orders on GOOG on October 8, 2015.

Out of all order revision traffic messages, only 488 (10.2 percent) referred to singular order updates; the remaining (89.8 percent) of revised orders incurred several sequential revisions in a row. For example, the limit sell order C91KT9003EDZ was revised five times within six seconds from 9:38:05.139 to 9:38:11.424, with the limit sell price dropping with each consecutive order from 641.26 to 641.25 to 641.14 to 641.07 to 641.05. For the 3,244 messages pertaining to the sell order revisions, the price on

TABLE 4.5 Distribution of Times (in milliseconds) between Subsequent Order Revisions for GOOG on October 8, 2015

	Shelf Life of Limit Orders between Subsequent Revisions (in milliseconds)
Average	31119.4
Standard deviation	469658.7
Maximum	11224983
99%	40072.72
95%	10763.8
90%	5458
75%	1201
50%	45
25%	1
10%	0
5%	0
1%	0
Minimum	0
Message count	4794
% of all messages	0.095357

This table shows distribution of time between subsequent order revisions.

95.0 percent of the orders was revised downward (i.e., improved with each revision). Similarly, for the 1,550 buy order revision messages, the price was raised to be closer to the market in 96 percent of cases. In other words, the vast majority of the 9.5 percent of all limit order traffic comprising limit order revisions was beneficial: the limit order updates tightened spreads.

Unlike order revisions, 6,168 messages, or 12.3 percent of the 50,274 total order messages for GOOG recorded on October 8, 2015, were short-lived flashes of liquidity that can be considered "flickering liquidity." For example, a 100-share buy limit order C91KT9000W09 is placed at 9:30:02.763 for 632.55 only to be canceled 678 milliseconds (ms) later without a simultaneous replacement. At 9:30:09.376, another buy limit order C91KT9000XZ0 arrives for a higher price of 638.01, and is held for precisely 1,000 ms, at which point it is also canceled without an immediate replacement. Two more buy orders turn on and off sequentially, first for 636.55 at 9:30:11.403 for 1,001 ms, and then for 629.09 at 9:30:14.422 for 5,352 ms, before a hidden order execution trade print arrives: 23 shares at 642.27 executed at 9:30:47.035. A similar dance of short-lived quotes followed by hidden order executions continues throughout much of the trading day. Of the flickering orders, 1,622 message pairs (each flickering order

TABLE 4.6 Distribution of Duration (in milliseconds) of Limit Orders Canceled with an Order Message Immediately following the Order Placement Message

	Shelf Life of Flickering Limit Orders (in milliseconds)
Average	1293.185
Standard deviation	7682.144
Maximum	268397
99%	11430.36
95%	4960.8
90%	2633.7
75%	1001
50%	196
25%	4
10%	0
5%	0
1%	0
Minimum	0
Message count	6168
% of all messages	12.2688%

This table shows the distribution of visibility of flickering limit orders.

comprises an order addition and an order cancellation) pertained to sell limit orders, and 1,462 pairs were on the buy side of the limit order book. Table 4.6 summarizes distribution of the shelf life of orders that are canceled without immediate replacement, and can, therefore, be considered flickering.

While the flickering orders identified in Table 4.6 are likely candidates for pings or phishes, the results present a drastically different picture from that of some previous studies on the dynamics of limit orders, who find that 95.0 percent of limit orders are pings canceled within one minute of their addition.

Of the remaining 78.2 percent of the entire message traffic not accounted for in order revisions and pings, only 700 orders (1.3 percent of the total daily message traffic) were order executions. Out of those, only 139 orders (0.3 percent) were executions of limit orders displayed in the limit order book—message types E. The remaining 561 executions (1.11 percent of total message traffic) were type P messages—matches of market orders with hidden limit orders, special order types that do not appear in the centralized limit order book.

The finding that most order executions are accomplished with hidden limit orders is not entirely surprising. Some studies find that hidden orders accounted for 20.4 percent of all executions. This percentage is probably increasing as lit exchanges are moving toward structures akin to dark pools.

ORDER-BASED NEGOTIATIONS

According to some recent research, market participants may use lit limit orders to signal their willingness to buy and sell at specific prices. Most of the execution, however, happens in the interaction with hidden or dark liquidity that cannot be directly observed in the limit order book. A swift negotiation may follow an indication of interest, resulting in a hidden order execution. A hypothesis can be put forth that the institutions and other market order and hidden order traders are influenced by flickering, suboptimal, liquidity provided by high-frequency traders. Next, we present simple tests of the order interactions in today's markets.

To test the interaction of various order types, each order message within the data set is separated and labeled into one of the following categories: a message revision, a ping, a regular limit order addition, and a regular limit order cancellation. The message revision orders are picked out by matching limit order IDs of sequential orders where the order addition follows order cancellation with slightly different parameters. Pings are identified as order cancellations following order additions with the same order ID without subsequent order additions.

We tested two frequencies of order interactions: high, sampling orders every 10 exchange messages, and low, with considering the impact of orders every 300 messages.

The observed impact of various order types appears to change considerably from high-frequency to lower frequency. On average throughout the day, 10 exchange messages were timestamped every five seconds, with a median time of two seconds, and the lowest decile of 67 milliseconds. Conversely, 300 messages were processed every 2.5 minutes, on average, with a median processing time falling to 1.8 minutes, and 10 percent of all 300-message blocks crowding into 1 minute. Although a human trader can theoretically follow every 10 trading messages in just 2 seconds, a more likely scenario is that speed is processed by a machine, whereas human traders would more likely observe data at a minute scale (i.e., 300-message horizon).

At higher (10-message) frequencies, both regular market order executions and hidden order executions exhibit dependence on the dynamics of other order types of the following nature:

1. Flickering orders bear little impact on the execution of hidden orders—at higher frequencies, the rate of execution of hidden orders

remains unchanged whether flickering orders are present or not. However, flickering orders appear to deter market order traders from sending in the market orders.

2. Limit order revisions do not change the dynamics of incoming market orders, but increase the rate of hidden order execution. Potentially, limit order revisions serve to identify hidden orders and approach hidden orders faster, resulting in matching.

3. Regular limit order placement and cancellation has the greatest impact on the execution of both market orders and hidden orders. Surprisingly, in the cases of market orders and hidden orders, the impact of new limit order arrivals and cancellations is negative: the more regular (nonrevision, no-flicker) limit orders arrive or are canceled in the limit order book, the fewer market orders and hidden orders are executed. Potentially, new limit orders are simply alternatives to market orders, with traders choosing limit orders whenever the impending market movement is not perceived as urgent. Similarly, additions and cancellations of regular limit orders may delay hidden order discovery, reducing the hidden order cancellation rates.

At the 10-message frequency, both hidden and lit order execution is determined by factors unrelated to the order messages immediately preceding execution. At a lower 300-message frequency, a much stronger dependency exists between the preceding pings and order revisions. Specifically, at lower frequencies, flickering orders have a stronger impact on market and hidden order execution. An increase in pings leads to an increase of market orders and hidden order executions with 99.9 percent confidence. This finding starkly contrasts with findings about the flickering order impacts at higher frequencies where the execution of market orders declines with increases in flickering quotations.

It is as if, at lower frequencies, traders are drawn to flickering orders, while at higher frequencies, traders are repelled by pings. If higher frequency orders are machine-generated, and lower-frequency ones are placed by humans, then human traders are disproportionally hooked on pings, while machines find ways to ignore or even run away from them.

Similarly, at lower frequencies, limit order revisions present a much stronger influence on increased market order and hidden order execution than at higher frequencies. Finally, at lower frequencies, while the impact of regular order addition on market and hidden order executions is present, it is less statistically significant than that observed at higher frequencies—human traders do not care about the depth of the order book as much as machines do, potentially exposing the human limits to absorbing limit order book information.

The divide in how market participants perceive and interpret flickering quotes is informative on many levels. First, it could reveal a weakness in the SIP tape, administered by the SEC. The routine operation of SIP involves gathering quotes from various trading venues, finding the best bid and the best offer among the quotes, and then redistributing the best quotes back to market participants. Trading venues might use SIP to determine to which exchange to forward a market order in the absence of best quotes on a given exchange. The presence of flickering quotes on a particular exchange could cause SIP to post the flickering order as the best nationwide quote, and cause a spike in market order routings to that exchange. As a result, the routed market orders may or may not be filled up at best prices. Alternatively, people watching market data on screens could perceive the flickering quotes as the true available liquidity and attempt to execute against the quotes using either market or hidden orders.

Finally, flickering orders could be pure pings seeking to identify pools of hidden liquidity within the spread in a given limit order book. In this case, a small match of a flickering order with a hidden order establishes the location of a potential liquidity pool in the limit order book.

In the context of signaling, both hypotheses postulated at the beginning of this section appear to hold true: (1) machine traders identify and filter behavior of other machines, disregarding issues such as flickering quotes or pings, and (2) lower-frequency traders appear to interact with flickering liquidity. While the results presented in this chapter are a case study of an individual stock, GOOG, on just one trading day, October 8, 2015, the results are easily extended to a larger stock universe where similar conclusions hold.

CONCLUSIONS

Front-running is an often misconstrued problem. Due to the anonymity of exchanges, most perceived front-running is due to the practice of pre-hedging often used by brokers to diversify the risk of information asymmetry. Diversifying brokers helps investors protect their trading decisions from front-running by avoiding information leakage via the single broker.

Contemporary equity markets are evolving to best meet institutional investors' needs in other areas of market execution. Some issues, however, particularly those pertaining to the collaboration of human and machine traders, remain unresolved. Most regulated (lit) exchanges are accommodating the demand for block trading by converging to a model that supports large hidden block orders, producing substantial liquidity readily available to execute institutional investors' mandates. In BATS data, for instance, the vast majority of order executions are conducted with hidden limit orders, and just a small fraction is carried on with market orders.

HFT market making, often considered the worst due to the flickering liquidity it delivers, is only a small fraction of available liquidity. While not as copious as previously thought, flickering liquidity appears to have a dual impact at distinct frequencies. At high frequencies, the flickering liquidity is mostly detrimental to itself, as it is readily observed and avoided by other high-frequency market participants. At lower frequencies, however, flickering liquidity appears to attract execution of both market and hidden orders, potentially causing order routing toward flickering order books by the SEC's consolidated tape via SIP and disadvantaging human traders.

Finally, regular limit order additions and, separately, cancellations appear to deter the execution of market and hidden orders. The observed negative impact of order additions and order cancellations is more statistically significant at higher frequencies. Traders observing the markets may want to be aware of the market's responses to individual orders and reconsider their processing of market data as well as placement of their orders with the market signaling context in mind.

END OF CHAPTER QUESTIONS

1. What is liquidity?
2. What is passive HFT?
3. What is prehedging?
4. What is pinging?
5. What order types are out there?

CHAPTER 5

High-Frequency Trading
in Your Backyard

—What do experienced bond traders and typists have in common?

—Computers ate their lunch.

High-frequency trading (HFT) is another fintech innovation capitalizing on plunging costs of technology. When programmed correctly, HFT software has built-in advantages over manual trading. Computers seldom become ill, are hardly emotional, and make, in short, superior cool-headed traders who stick to the script and don't panic.

Of course, some recent research purports that some people, especially those attuned to their intuitive or biological responses, can outperform machines. Well, good for those few! By and large, however, human traders tend to be a superstitious, irrational lot prone to, well, human behavior, and no match for their steely automated trading brethren.

Perhaps one of the largest advantages of machines, however, is not that they can contain their nonexistent feelings, but in their information processing power. Humans have a finite ability to process data. We may, possibly, be able to stare at some 16 screens all at once, but our eyes can still only process 24 distinct visual frames per second. Should the information update faster than that, we simply miss it. Computers, on the other hand, can process unlimited volumes of data at the speed of light.

Even more importantly, following just a few news sources and several price charts in today's interconnected continuously arbitraged markets is simply not enough. News leaks out into the markets in chaotic and often unforeseeable ways. Processing the entire realm of information, including quotes for some 6,000+ stocks, hundreds of thousands of options, interest rates, futures, and social media is what separates today's successful traders from the not-so-successful ones. And machines simply do it better. No extreme human physiology allows us to simultaneously read in-depth news and analyses on even 100 financial instruments.

The HFT, on the other hand, are generally well-equipped to process reams of information on the fly. Still, as discussed in Chapter 4, all HFTs do not fit in the same mold. Some are market makers, using predominantly limit orders, passively waiting for the market-order-armed liquidity takers to arrive. Others are aggressively pursuing the best price available at a given point in time. Both categories, passive HFT and aggressive HFT, have their parallels in the world of human traders: passive HFTs are automated versions of their human market-maker predecessors, and aggressive HFTs are modeled on former prop traders and day traders.

Passive HFTs, described in Chapter 4, are a set of HFT strategies mostly placing limit orders. As such, passive HFTs end up buffering market liquidity, and making markets. Prominent passive HFT firms include Virtu and Knight Capital Group. The market makers, whether human or robotic, follow the same basic principles. Market-making strategies consist of often-simultaneous placement of limit orders on both the buy and the sell side of the limit order book, shown in Figure 5.1. The simple two-sided quotation works great when markets are quiet or range-bound. However, when the markets move rapidly in one direction or another, market makers risk severe losses.

The market makers' risks are largely a result of their potential information asymmetry. For example, suppose that the latest trade price of IBM stock is $155.76, and a market maker is quoting $155.74/$155.77, as shown in Figure 5.2. Suppose further that another trader with better information strongly believes that the IBM market is about to fall, say, to $155.00 in

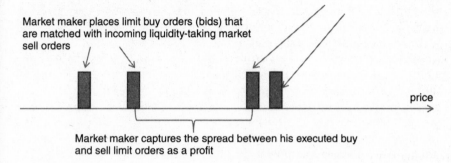

FIGURE 5.1 Stylized representation of market making in a limit order book of a given financial instrument

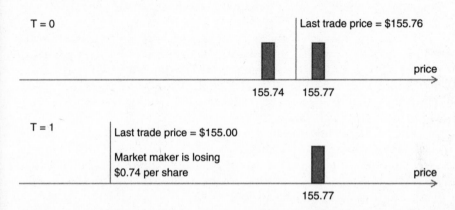

FIGURE 5.2 The consequences of adverse selection for market makers

the next 20 minutes. To capitalize on his fleeting informational advantage, the second trader places the market order to sell IBM stock. The trading venue matches the market sell order with the market maker's limit buy order at $155.74, leaving the market maker holding a long position in IBM in a rapidly falling market. Fast-forward 20 minutes, and the market maker is in the hole at $0.74 for every share he bought. The phenomenon is known as *adverse selection* whereby the uninformed market makers and other traders are "picked off" by better-informed market participants.

Is being better-informed illegal? Of course not. Some superior information costs a pretty penny, and substantially reduces the informed traders' gains from trading, when netted out at the end of the day. What is a market maker to do? The market maker needs to (1) hedge his exposure, and (2) become better informed. Hedging exposure is always costly. For instance, the market maker may decide to purchase options or other derivatives to hedge his exposure to the underlying. A put option will do the trick, but at an upfront premium.

Another route is to obtain better information. One way of gearing up on the information frontier is segmenting traders into better-informed and worse-informed, and essentially front-running better-informed traders using prehedging or anticipatory hedging, as discussed in Chapter 4. The strategy works mostly at a broker-dealer's market maker, since order flow on exchanges and other venues outside of a broker-dealer are largely anonymous. Another, more ethical route comprises investing into premium data that is indicative of the market's near-term direction, shrinking the information barrier and preempting sharp moves. Once again, computerized market makers win the bots-versus-humans debate as information is king, and the ability to process vast amounts of information simultaneously is cash.

Bots using market orders that trade using intricate strategies of professional traders are collectively known as aggressive HFT, as opposed to passive market makers. Unlike passive HFTs, aggressive HFTs tend to use market orders to capitalize on fleeting information at their fingertips. In the industry, the return advantage from fleeting information is often referred to as *rapidly decaying alpha*.

What kinds of inferences do aggressive HFTs deploy? To put it simply, all kinds. The most successful aggressive HFTs, like QuantLab and others, use a multitude of information sources to create an informational haystack, from which big data-driven inferences are extracted about the prospective market movements.[1]

Not everyone agrees with the premise that the usually-private HFTs are a success. Recently, some articles have declared HFT dead. One author even suggested that "poor" HFTs should be "pitied" as their strategies have been wiped out by volatility and dog-eat-dog competition for faster, better, ever-more expensive technology undermining all profits. According to the research of AbleMarkets.com, discussed here, however, nothing could be farther from the truth: aggressive HFTs quietly, but significantly, prosper, and more so in the currently volatile market conditions.

Just how profitable are aggressive HFTs? It's impossible to know the full range of profitability of all the HFT firms. However, just a set of aggressive HFTs that hold positions for one minute on average can achieve a Sharpe ratio of 39 (that's right, thirty-nine) trading all 500 stocks in the S&P 500. Aggressive HFT in all of the 500 stocks produces nearly

---

[1]Many of the HFT strategies are discussed in detail in Irene Aldridge, *High-Frequency Trading: A Practical Guide to Algorithmic Strategies and Trading Systems* (Hoboken, NJ: John Wiley & Sons, 2009, 2013, translated into Chinese).

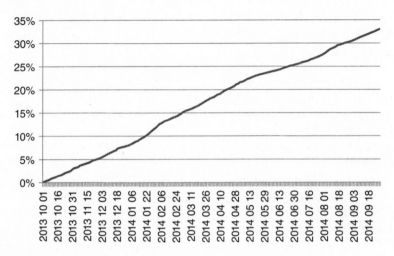

FIGURE 5.3 One-minute performance of aggressive HFTs identified by AbleMarkets.com Aggressive HFT Index

35 percent return per year without any additional leverage, generating almost no volatility in the performance, regardless of market conditions.

Figure 5.3 illustrates the performance of selected aggressive HFT algorithms detected by the AbleMarkets.com Aggressive HFT Index. The index estimates the participation of aggressive HFT by volume in real time. The profitability of aggressive HFTs is computed as follows: Whenever the proportion of volume estimated to be initiated by aggressive HFT sellers exceeds the proportion of volume the index attributes to aggressive HFT buyers by at least 10 percent, a hypothetical sell order is generated and the position is "held" for the following 1 minute, at which point the position is considered to be closed at the prevailing market price and the gain or loss of the trade is recorded. Similarly, whenever the AbleMarkets Aggressive HFT Index reports the proportion of aggressive HFT buyers exceeding that of aggressive HFT sellers by 10 percent or more, a paper buy order is generated, followed by an offsetting sell order 1 minute later.

The resulting trading strategy illustrates just how good aggressive HFTs are at their game. While highly sensitive to transaction costs, a Sharpe ratio as high as 39 makes a compelling case for investors to invest in super-fast processing power in order to maximize the net gain. The strategy may also be used to optimize the execution of other strategies with large positions in individual securities: deciding when and how to send in slices of large orders to exchanges, as discussed in the following section. Briefly, when the percentage of aggressive HFT buyers is higher than that of aggressive HFT sellers, aggressive HFTs wipe out liquidity in offers, but create a surplus of bids—it is a good time to withhold buy orders and place sell orders instead.

Should we be surprised by such performance results of HFTs? Not really—the performance is perfectly in line with HFT giants such as Virtu Financial, who have not experienced a single losing week in a few years. In other words, reports of premature death of HFT appear to be, well, premature.

Latest research shows that stocks with higher participation of aggressive HFT experience higher intraday volatility. Comparing intraday volatility, as measured by the difference between the daily high and low and normalized by the daily closing price, with aggressive HFT participation captured by AbleMarkets Aggressive HFT Index shows that every 1 percent increase in aggressive HFT participation by volume drives up same-day volatility by 2 percent on average! As discussed earlier in this chapter, aggressive HFTs comprise a set of trading strategies that predominantly use market orders (as opposed to limit orders) to execute their trading decisions. As such, aggressive HFT strategies are usually characterized by short profitability windows and strive to capture gains as soon as possible with the most immediate order execution. How much does aggressive HFT participation change from one day to the next? According to AbleMarkets research, the answer is 80 percent of the time (across all the S&P 500 stocks), aggressive HFT increases or decreases by at most 3 percent from one day to the next. However, outliers exist, and aggressive HFT may spring up in some previously untapped names. For example, on February 26, 2015, aggressive HFT participation in Graham Holdings Company (NYSE: GHC) spiked up to 66 percent by volume from just 34 percent observed on the previous business day only to drop back down to 34 percent on the following trading day, February 27, 2015.

On days when the participation of aggressive HFTs across all of the S&P 500 stocks sparked up by 3 percent or more, observed intraday volatility on average was 2.4 percent with a standard deviation of 2.0 percent during the first six months of 2015. On the other hand, on days when the participation of aggressive HFTs across all the S&P 500 stocks declined by 3 percent or more from the previous trading day, observed intraday volatility on average was 1.5 percent with a standard deviation of 0.8 percent. For a baseline comparison across all days and across the S&P 500, observed intraday volatility was 1.7 percent on average with a standard deviation of 1.1 percent.

The aggressive HFT is "sticky." Stocks with high aggressive HFT retain high aggressive HFT participation as HFT developers ramp up and down their algorithms slowly over time. In fact, the previous day's aggressive HFT participation is a great predictor of the next trading day's aggressive HFT. The analysis of the S&P 500 shows that a daily value of AbleMarkets Aggressive HFT Index explains 86 percent of variation in the aggressive HFT participation (measured by AbleMarkets Aggressive HFT Index) on the following trading day, as measured by a statistical metric known as Adjusted R-squared.

How do these findings translate into the prediction of volatility? Both day-to-day changes and absolute values of the AbleMarkets Aggressive HFT Index are predictive of the next day's volatility. AbleMarkets Aggressive HFT Index helps to make the detection of aggressive HFT and the resulting volatility prediction easier and more manageable.

IMPLICATIONS OF AGGRESSIVE HFT

As a natural consequence of aggressive HFT market-taking activity, aggressive high-frequency traders tend to wipe out limit orders in the direction that they trade, increasing bid-ask spreads and resulting in higher realized volatility from the bid-ask bounce. Figure 5.4 shows the basic mechanics of

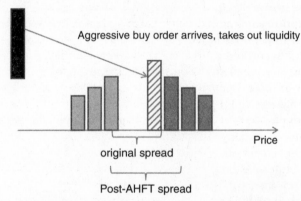

Panel a) An arriving aggressive order wipes out the best limit order(s) on the opposing side of the limit order book, widening spreads and increasing volatility through larger bid-ask bounce.

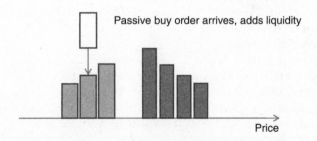

Panel b) An arriving passive limit order adds liquidity.

FIGURE 5.4   Stylized liquidity taking (panel a) and making (panel b)

how aggressive HFT increases bid-ask spreads. The average proportion of aggressive high-frequency traders in stocks varies from stock to stock, but changes little over time.

Like many recurring events in the financial markets, trades initiated by aggressive HFTs leave a specific signature in the markets, according to research from AbleMarkets.com. As a result, aggressive HFT activity can be measured and recorded in even perfectly anonymous markets, and the impact of the activity can be readily and objectively examined. Table 5.1 shows the daily average aggressive HFT participation in selected financial instruments on August 31, 2015.

While the mechanics shown in Figure 5.4 may follow all market-taking orders, two key issues pertaining to aggressive HFT behavior may particularly exacerbate available liquidity. Aggressive high-frequency traders tend to execute bursts of market orders at once, potentially deeply affecting the liquidity on one side of the limit order book. This situation may occur at any time. Another liquidity-draining tactic occurs when aggressive HFTs act in response to major market announcements. At those times, aggressive HFTs use their fast infrastructure to reach the markets just ahead of competing institutional traders, substantially worsening execution for the latter. Avoiding trading in the same direction as the bursts of aggressive HFT for about 20 minutes allows liquidity to replenish itself. A wait-and-hold strategy following bursts of aggressive HFT activity can significantly help performance of execution traders.

TABLE 5.1   Average Aggressive HFT
Participation in Selected Commodities and
Equities on August 31, 2015

Crude Oil	20.0%
Silver	10.0%
Gold	17.9%
Natural Gas	10.4%
US Treasuries	12.4%
Less than Silver, out of the S&P500:	
ZNGA	7.4%
VVUS	8.3%
RAD	9.8%
Highest aggressive HFT, out of the S&P 500:	
GOOGL	39.6%
AMZN	38.1%
GOOG	37.6%

Following aggressive HFT can also significantly improve the performance of portfolio managers. Several studies confirm the aggressive HFT impact on market volatility. Some find that aggressive HFTs are more active during the periods of high market volatility, potentially causing said volatility. AbleMarkets.com estimates that stocks with higher aggressive HFT display consistently higher volatility.

Volatility is risk. With higher volatility come higher returns, as the holders of riskier assets demand compensation for the risk in their portfolio. Risk generated by aggressive HFTs is also linked with returns, remarkably consistent across various financial instruments and asset classes. Specifically, financial instruments with higher aggressive HFT participation have higher risk and higher returns. In addition, the risk generated by aggressive HFT falls into the "instrument-specific" or "idiosyncratic" category, and not only is it uncorrelated with that of other financial instruments, but it can also be diversified in a portfolio. Thus, if one prefers to increase returns while increasing diversifiable idiosyncratic risks, one should pick financial instruments with higher aggressive HFT participation. If, on the other hand, one is more concerned about minimizing risk, investing into instruments with lower aggressive HFT participation allows the portfolio manager to increase the Sharpe ratio of the portfolio. With reduction of aggressive HFT across financial instruments, volatility declines faster than do returns, allowing for a Sharpe ratio decrease.

The insights gleaned from understanding aggressive HFT activity in various financial instruments do not last just microseconds or milliseconds. HFT is sticky across time, as well-performing algos do not get turned off suddenly, but may be phased out incrementally as their performance begins to wane. Due to the HFT stickiness, the volatility driven by the aggressive HFT participation detected today can persist for hours, weeks, months, and even years. In fact, even portfolio managers that choose to reallocate their investments only once a year would do much better if they included aggressive HFT participation as one of the factors in their allocation decision framework.

Incorporating aggressive HFT in a short- or long-term portfolio management framework can be as easy as multiplying or dividing existing portfolio weights by a simple factor: (1 + AHFT), where AHFT is the average aggressive HFT participation in a given financial instrument over the past day, week, month, quarter, or year. The horizon of aggressive HFT averages should match your projected holding period. For example, managers reallocating their portfolios once a month would use the last month's average of aggressive HFT activity in tweaking their portfolios. Those with quarterly or annual investment horizons would incorporate the average aggressive HFT activity for the preceding quarter or year, respectively. For portfolio managers seeking extra returns at the expense of portfolio risk, the existing portfolio weights should be multiplied by (1 + AHFT) to increase allocations to stocks with proportionally more active AHFT. For portfolio managers seeking a higher Sharpe ratio, the same weights should be divided by (1 + AHFT) to scale down investments with higher AHFT exposure.

Most interesting to other traders and investors, however, is the fact that this type of insight has the power to move the markets not in microseconds, but in minutes and, sometimes, for as long as half-hour spans. As a result, observing and following aggressive HFT strategies can lead to highly profitable results for short-term investors and execution traders alike.

Using the insights from aggressive HFT to understand the half hour before a news event is a particularly novel finding. The following is an example. On Friday, October 2, 2015, traders worldwide watched for the news release for nonfarm payrolls by the US government at 8:30 AM. The news was worse than expected and the markets plunged over 1 percent nearly instantaneously. What role did aggressive HFTs play in the collapse of the market in response to the news announcement? Were aggressive high-frequency traders to blame for the market's response?

According to Bloomberg, the consensus forecast for the month-to-month nonfarm payrolls figures was an increase of 203,000 (see Table 5.2), while

TABLE 5.2 Employment Figures as Reported by Bloomberg

Released On 10/2/2015 8:30:00 AM for Sep, 2015					
	Prior	Prior Revised	Consensus	Consensus Range	Actual
Nonfarm Payrolls—M/M change	173,000	136,000	203,000	180,000 to 235,000	142,000
Unemployment Rate—Level	5.1 %		5.1 %	5.0 % to 5.2 %	5.1 %
Private Payrolls—M/M change	140,000	100,000	195,000	175,000 to 246,000	118,000
Participation Rate—Level	62.6 %				62.4 %
Average Hourly Earnings—M/M change	0.3 %	0.4 %	0.2 %	0.1 % to 0.3 %	0.0 %
Average Workweek—All Employees	34.6 hrs		34.6 hrs	34.5 hrs to 34.6 hrs	34.5 hrs

the actual figures clocked in much below at 142,000, prompting Bloomberg to report the following:

> *Forget about an October rate hike and maybe forget about a December one too. The September employment report came in weaker than expected on all scores with nonfarm payroll at 142,000, well under the low estimate for 180,000. To seal the matter, downward revisions to the two prior months total 59,000. Average hourly earnings also came in below the low end estimate, at an unchanged reading and a year-on-year rate of 2.2 percent which is also unchanged. And the labor market is shrinking! The labor participation fell 2 tenths to a nearly 40 year low of 62.4 percent.*

The disappointing numbers sent the US equities markets straight down. For example, the S&P 500 ETF (NYSE:SPY) dropped nearly instantaneously from $193.50 to $191.00 in a matter of seconds. However, the impact was rather temporary—as the news was absorbed throughout the day, the market improved and SPY rose to $195.30 by the end of trading on Friday, as Figure 5.5 shows.

According to AbleMarkets research, prior to the news announcement, the pattern of aggressive HFT activity oscillated from selling to buying and back to selling, as shown in Figure 5.6 for the S&P 500 ETF (NYSE:SPY).

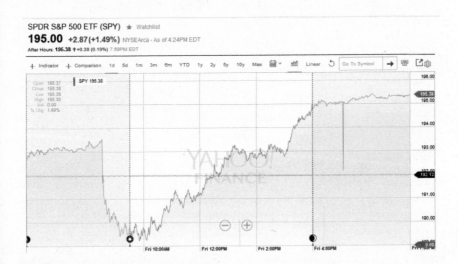

FIGURE 5.5 S&P 500 ETF (NYSE: SPY) on October 2, 2015. A sudden drop in price circa 8:30 AM coincided with smaller-than-expected job gain figures. *Chart source:* http://finance.yahoo.com

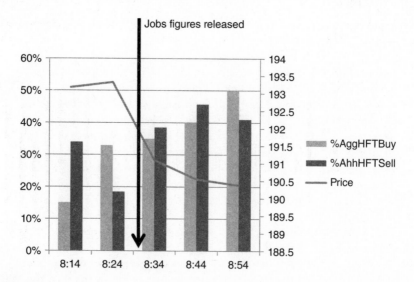

FIGURE 5.6 Proportion of aggressive HFT buyers and sellers in the S&P500 ETF (NYSE: SPY) on October 2, 2015. Shown: 10-minute moving averages of aggressive HFT buyer and seller participation

As Figure 5.6 shows, aggressive HFT sellers outnumbered aggressive HFT buyers from 8:04 to 8:14, and again from 8:24 to 8:34, although to a much smaller extent the second time around. The heightened aggressive HFT seller activity from 8:04 to 8:14 in SPY cannot rule out an insider trading activity on the then-embargoed soon-to-be-released jobs data; however, further analysis is needed to ascertain or dispute such activity.

Aside from equities, it is noteworthy to mention the euro foreign exchange rate following the jobs announcement on October 2, 2015. While most currencies and commodities had aggressive HFT buyers and sellers at comparable levels until 9:00 AM on October 2, 2015, the EUR/USD exchange rate had a distinct spike in aggressive HFT buyers from 8:31 to 8:41 AM (41 percent for aggressive HFT buyers by volume among all buy trades in EUR/USD vs. 11 percent for aggressive HFT sellers). This sudden spike in the HFT buying activity illustrates that, in response to announcements, aggressive HFTs participate in short-term arbitrage.

Throughout the rest of the day, aggressive HFTs helped prop the market back up. Figure 5.7 shows average participation of aggressive HFTs for all the market and marketable buy orders and sell orders by volume across the Dow Jones Industrial stocks. As Figure 5.7 shows, from 9:30 AM to 4:00 PM ET, aggressive HFT buyers exceeded aggressive HFT sellers on average in every one of the stocks shown. Throughout the

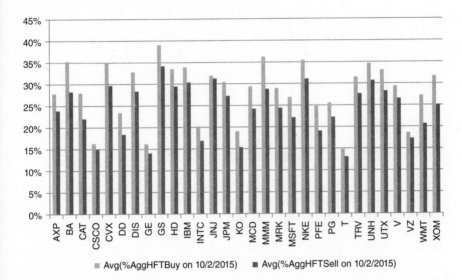

FIGURE 5.7 Average participation of aggressive HFT buyers and sellers, as percentage by volume traded, among all the Dow Jones Industrial stocks on October 2, 2015

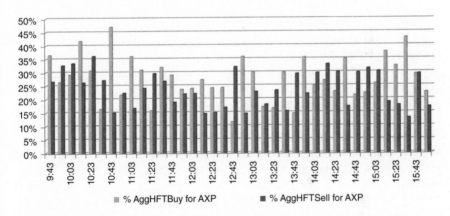

FIGURE 5.8 Aggressive HFT buyers and sellers in American Express (NYSE:AXP) on October 2, 2015

day, however, aggressive HFT participation varied, as shown in Figure 5.8 for a case of American Express stock.

Are aggressive HFTs to blame for the sharp sell-off following the news? The data indicate that most likely not, since aggressive HFT activity was quite balanced after the news announcement period, with the proportion of aggressive HFT sellers exceeding that of aggressive HFT buyers by a mere 3.5 percent (38.5 percent and 35 percent, respectively). However, aggressive HFT trading on fully embargoed information at the top of the hour prior to the news announcement when the aggressive HFT sellers exceeded aggressive HFT buyers by 19 percent (34 percent versus 15 percent) cannot be completely ruled out.

AGGRESSIVE HIGH-FREQUENCY TRADING IN EQUITIES

Aggressive high-frequency trading (HFT) is a classification of electronic trading strategies that rely on ultra-fast infrastructure and market orders to take advantage of news, predictive analytics, or short-lived information asymmetries. Unlike passive HFTs that tend to provide market-making services, aggressive HFT models attempt to reach the markets prior to others to capitalize on short-term market inefficiencies. AbleMarkets.com Aggressive HFT Index tracks aggressive HFT activity in real time and has developed statistical insights into aggressive HFT behavior, some of which are summarized here.

Among the S&P 500 stocks, for instance, aggressive HFTs are more prevalent in equities with

- Higher prices
- Lower dividend yield
- Higher volatility, measured as a standard deviation of daily returns

On average, a $100 difference in stock prices attracted 3 percent more aggressive HFTs by volume. Not surprisingly, Google (NASDAQ:GOOGL) is the stock with the highest average participation of aggressive HFTs registering close to 38 percent average daily aggressive HFT participation in 2014. With a stock price well over $500 per share at the time this chapter was written, Google is one of the most expensive issues in the S&P 500. An explanation for the phenomenon may lie in the value of fixed costs, such as a bid-ask spread, of trading using market orders relative to prices of stocks: for high-priced stocks, the spread and other fixed costs account for a smaller percentage of the price, allowing the traders to keep a larger share of the gains.

Stocks with lower dividend yields also attract aggressive HFTs. On average, a 1 percent decrease in dividends accounts for a 1.1 percent increase in aggressive HFT participation and explains 8.5 percent of variation in aggressive HFT participation among the S&P 500 stocks. Companies paying high dividends tend to be mature businesses and may detract aggressive

HFTs seeking a volatile environment. This suggests that firms may be able to manage aggressive HFT participation in their stocks by adjusting their dividend policy, in conjunction with other factors.

Stocks with higher volatility also have a higher proportion of aggressive HFTs. A 1 percent increase in volatility measured as an annualized standard deviation of daily returns based on closing prices translates into a 0.23 percent increase in aggressive HFT participation.

It is not immediately clear, however, whether aggressive HFTs seek out high volatility, whether aggressive HFT participation induces higher volatility in stocks, or both. However, a 1 percent increase in aggressive HFT participation translates into 0.17 percent in additional annualized volatility across all the stocks in the S&P 500 index. Overall, differences in aggressive HFT participation account for 2 percent of variation in volatility among all of the S&P 500 stocks. Aggressive HFT participation is, therefore, a highly predictive metric of volatility: in comparison, the celebrated and often-used GARCH model only accounts for 5 percent of variation in volatility among the same group of stocks. With higher volatility comes higher average returns, so, indirectly, aggressive HFT contributes to better performance of stocks. Specifically, a 1 percent increase in aggressive HFT participation drives up average annualized returns by 0.23 percent among all of the S&P 500 stocks. Even long-only portfolio managers may want to take aggressive HFT participation into account in order to fine-tune the risk allocations in their portfolios.

As the latest research shows, both the participation of aggressive HFTs and the propensity of a stock to have a flash crash can be influenced by carefully chosen corporate actions. Before any preventative measures can take effect, however, investors can perform due diligence to ascertain their chosen stock's vulnerability and portfolio risk.

The aggressive HFT is here to stay, and understanding its presence is more necessary than ever before. Today, participation of aggressive HFTs can be readily included in portfolio and trading decisions, as well as risk management and, specifically, collateral valuation. As big data analytics and computer technology continue to proliferate in finance, the applications surrounding aggressive HFTs will only expand further.

In the last few years, a number of exchanges and dark pools emerged claiming that their businesses will exclude high-frequency traders (HFTs) detrimental to institutional investors. Almost invariably, the HFTs in question happened to be the so-called aggressive HFTs: HFTs that execute mostly using market orders and have been shown to erode liquidity, causing short-term volatility in the process. Although the idea of excluding aggressive HFTs may be appealing to investors, the realities of modern microstructure preclude this from happening. Given the NBBO require-ments, in the US equity markets all orders are routed to an exchange with the best available quotes. As such, all orders, whether HFT or not, are herded to the same spot at the same moment—precluding any one venue from shunning aggressive HFT. As a result, most of today's exchanges in the United States have a similar proportion of aggressive HFTs by volume of executed trades.

AGGRESSIVE HFT IN US TREASURIES

US regulators have recently questioned the role that high-frequency trading plays in the bond market. The latest research shows that aggressive HFTs initiate, on average, 20 percent of trades in the US Treasuries market. Aggres-sive HFTs also often trade US Treasuries when no one else does. It accounted for nearly all of the trades on the post-Thanksgiving Monday in 2014 and the post-Memorial Day Tuesday in 2015. Third, the participation of aggres-sive HFTs in the US Treasury market has declined slightly in 2015 from 30 percent in much of December 2014 and January 2015 to 13 percent at the end of July 2015.

Figure 5.9 shows aggressive HFT participation as a percentage of vol-ume traded for US Treasuries for the period of October 2014 to July 2015.

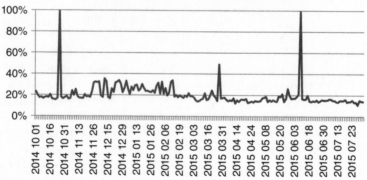

FIGURE 5.9 Evolution of aggressive HFT participation in the US Treasuries as a percentage of volume traded, measured by the AbleMarkets Aggressive HFT Index (HFTIndex.com)

While aggressive HFT in US Treasuries made up 20 percent by volume, it varied over time. There were clear periods of volatile aggressive HFT behavior (e.g., December 2014 to January 2015), where aggressive HFT ranged from 15 percent one day to 35 percent the next day, and stable aggressive HFT behavior (e.g., June to July 2015), where aggressive HFT participation changed by less than 1 percentage point from day to day.

The observed patterns of behavior can be due to several factors, such as news, microstructure issues, and the volatility in the participation of other non-HFT traders. The lower is the number of non-HFT in the US Treasury markets, the higher is the relative participation of aggressive HFTs, as documented in Figure 5.9.

Overall, aggressive HFTs do not appear to be a driving force of the US Treasury markets or to be significant enough to warrant a concern, at least not yet. By comparison, the participation of aggressive HFTs in equities markets routinely tops 30 percent in many S&P 500 equities.

Notwithstanding the current aggressive HFT levels, the participation needs to be proactively monitored to capture any further developments and to develop timely responses and regulations to aggressive HFT in US Treasury markets, the markets of strategic importance to the US economy.

AGGRESSIVE HFT IN COMMODITIES

In general, aggressive HFT participation in commodities has been growing but is still far behind equities. As shown in Table 5.1, on August 31, 2015, a typical trading day, average aggressive HFT participation in selected commodities ranged from 10 to 20 percent by volume, while average aggressive HFT in equities went as high as 40 percent.

Lower aggressive HFT by volume in commodities likely reflects the fact that commodities are still dominated by human traders as opposed to algorithmic systems that comprise a fair portion of the volume in equities.

Most commodities share another important property with equities as it relates to aggressive HFT: One day's average aggressive HFT participation accurately predicts the next day's volatility in most commodities. Thus, a rise in aggressive HFT tends to be followed by a hike in the next trading day's one-month implied volatility. Similarly, a drop in aggressive HFT activity observed on a particular day is often followed by lower implied volatility on the next trading day. Figure 5.11 shows a rescaled version of Figure 5.10, where the relationship between aggressive HFT in crude oil and one-month implied volatility on crude oil is a lot more obvious.

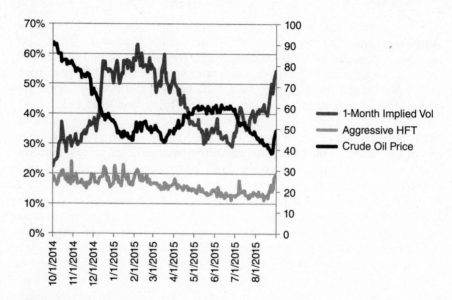

FIGURE 5.10 Daily average aggressive HFT on crude oil and corresponding price and implied vol on crude oil

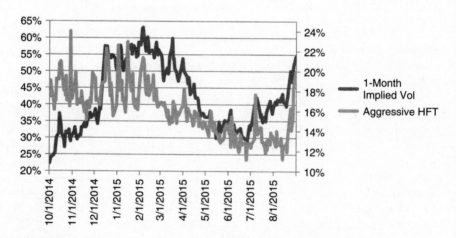

FIGURE 5.11 Daily average aggressive HFT on crude oil and implied vol on crude oil

The dependency between aggressive HFT participation and implied volatility can be further verified mathematically. The relationship of implied volatility and aggressive HFT is highly persistent from one day to the next. For instance, the correlation of *today's* average aggressive HFT level with *tomorrow's* implied volatility is 38.21 percent, a number similar to the correlation of *tomorrow's* average aggressive HFT level with *tomorrow's* implied volatility. Furthermore, day-to-day changes in average aggressive HFT are even more predictive of the next day's implied volatility than day-to-day changes in the implied volatility itself. In other words, both the levels and the changes in aggressive HFT behavior can help predict future implied volatility in crude oil, and, more generally, in commodities.

In general, daily values for implied volatility closely follow the prior day's averages of aggressive HFT participation. Not shown in the study is an even higher dependency that exists between implied volatility and aggressive HFT in the intraday setting. Investors can harness levels of aggressive HFT data to predict future volatility in optimizing execution and pricing options.

AGGRESSIVE HFT IN FOREIGN EXCHANGE

The behavior of aggressive HFTs in foreign exchange is comparable to that in other instruments in the fixed income space, and in Treasuries in particular. In foreign exchange, the relative proportion of aggressive HFTs has been holding steady at 10 to 15 percent in most major currencies, such as Japanese yen, Swiss franc, British pound sterling, Australian dollar, and Canadian dollar, as Figure 5.12 shows.

Foreign exchange is the notorious wild west of an asset class. Unregulated and traditionally clubby, it is also the most liquid and voluminous market, accounting for some $1.5 trillion in trading volume per day. In the face of automation, even foreign exchange trading and portfolio management has seen a push to HFT. While aggressive HFT is still nascent in most currency pairs, it is growing. Figure 5.12 shows the evolution of aggressive HFT as a percentage of daily trading volume in major foreign exchange pairs. As the figure shows, proportion of aggressive HFT in currencies may vary significantly from one day to the next, potentially impacted by institutional flow, such as quarterly cross-border rebalancing. In fact, the nature of foreign exchange participants may drive a fair bit of observed variation of aggressive HFT participation: a single large cross-border flow resulting from a foreign acquisition, for example, may dominate the markets for just one day resulting in a lower relative proportion of aggressive HFT by volume. Just as in equities, commodities, and Treasuries, however, aggressive HFT in foreign exchange is "sticky" as the algorithms are tweaked infrequently and the capital allocated to the aggressive HFT tends to change slowly.

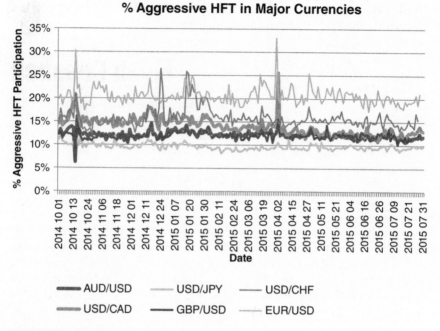

FIGURE 5.12 Aggressive HFT participation as a percentage of volume traded in foreign exchange (daily averages)

CONCLUSIONS

Aggressive HFT is an important market participant that most other participants want to track and have a set of rules to use to harness aggressive HFT behavior. Aggressive HFT is also becoming an established player, and its impact is becoming clearer and easier to quantify and analyze. All types of financial market professionals are affected by aggressive HFT, as it raises risk across all time frames and all electronically traded asset classes. Understanding aggressive HFT behavior helps market participants mitigate the impact of HFT.

END OF CHAPTER QUESTIONS

1. What is aggressive HFT?
2. How does aggressive HFT impact the markets?
3. What can investors do to harness their aggressive HFT exposure?
4. Are some exchanges more conducive to aggressive HFT than others?
5. What are the differences in aggressive HFT across different asset classes?

CHAPTER 6

Flash Crashes

— Who do you call when the markets are in a panic?

—Your system administrator.

Nothing shouts real-time risk like seeing a stock's price plummet for no apparent reason. How is it possible that on a day when there isn't much news to speak of, a stock's value can crater? Sometimes the entire market collapses, but often the crashes are contained to individual stocks. At times, the price recovers during the day, prompting investors to ask about the causes of this phenomenon. This chapter describes the spanner in the works.

A flash crash is a significantly negative intraday return coupled with high intraday volatility, collectively known as severe downward volatility. A flash crash does not necessarily span multiple financial instruments; it may affect only one stock, bond, or futures contract.

To complicate matters further, high volatility alone does not guarantee a crash. For a highly volatile day to become a crash day, the price of the asset under consideration has to significantly drop. Few investors can be heard complaining about flash rallies, when the price is driven significantly higher intraday.

Likewise, a steep intraday loss alone may just be considered a "crash" and may or may not constitute a "flash" crash. Most market events commonly considered to be flash crashes are characterized by a sharp reversal or correction of prices. For example, during the infamous flash crash of May 6, 2010, the markets mostly recovered from the intraday losses by the end of the day. A steep drop in prices alone may be reminiscent of a more traditional crash like the one of October 1987 and not a flash crash of the modern day.

WHAT HAPPENS DURING FLASH CRASHES?

Flash crashes are a frequent occurrence. In the Dow Jones Industrial Average (DJIA) index alone, aggregate intraday prices dropped by at least 2 percent on 431 separate trading days since 1985. In individual financial instruments, flash crashes can be even more prevalent. The common shares of IBM, for instance, registered an intraday drop of at least 2 percent 966 times since 1985, nearly double the number of marketwide crashes. Let's consider the question of why and how price crashes in individual securities sometimes lead and sometimes do not lead to marketwide crashes with a specific example of the flash crash of October 15, 2014.

First, we shall review some flash crash statistics. The number of marketwide flash crashes per year has varied from year to year, as shown in Figure 6.1. The periods with the fewest flash crashes included 1992–1995, 2004–2006, and 2012 to present, roughly corresponding to periods of economic expansion in the US markets. The incidence of flash crashes per year in individual securities, for example IBM stock, is highly correlated with the number of annual flash crash occurrences in the markets overall, reaching 59 percent for IBM (in relation to the market) over the 1985–2015 period. Still, flash crashes in individual stocks remain far more numerous, as Figure 6.2 shows, yet not all individual instrument crashes translate into the marketwide pandemics. The silver lining for both marketwide and individual-security-level flash crash is that both have been declining since 2008.

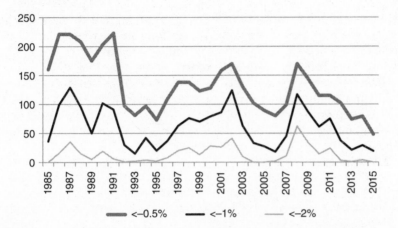

FIGURE 6.1 The number of flash crashes in the Dow Jones Industrial Average index per year. Flash crashes are defined as the intraday percentage loss in the DJIA index from market open to the daily low that exceeds −0.5 percent, −1 percent, and −2 percent, respectively.

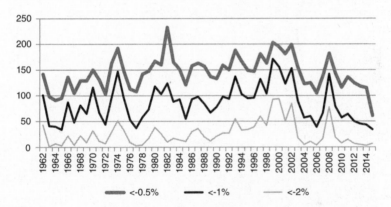

FIGURE 6.2 The number of flash crashes in IBM per year, defined as a percentage loss in the IBM stock from market open to the daily low

Flash crashes may be caused by human "fat fingers," sending in exaggerated orders. Flash crashes may also be due to poorly written and subsequently runaway algorithms. Most flash crashes, however, are contained within one financial instrument and do not necessarily cause a market-wide pandemic.

How do market-wide flash crashes occur? Some researchers believe that ETFs are at least partially responsible for major market flash crashes. These financial products are considered a passive investment and are merely mandated to track established indexes; however, ETFs can also play a role in wild intraday fluctuations.

ETFs became popular as passive investments whose owners enjoy diversification at a much lower cost than that of a traditional mutual fund or even a hedge fund. Issued by an investment manager that collects small fees for fund management, today's ETFs come in all shapes, sizes, and flavors and seem to span most portfolios imaginable. Investors can even access alternatives though mutual funds. The classic ETFs include those tracking the S&P500 (NYSE:SPY) and other common indexes.

Some ETFs are thematic: if you don't like tobacco, there is an ETF for you. For example, the iShares MSCI socially responsible ETF (NYSE: DSI) "excludes companies with significant business activities involving alcohol, tobacco, firearms, gambling, nuclear power or military weapons."[1] Like solar power? There is an ETF for you! PowerShares WilderHill Clean Energy Portfolio (NYSE: PBW) covers "predominantly clean energy companies (wind, solar, fuel cells, and biofuels)."[2] There are ETFs even for leverage-loving credit-constrained consumers: Want to lever up 3x on the S&P 500? There is an ETF for that (NYSE:SPXL)! And if you want to short the S&P 500 and experience the effect of a 3x downside, there is an ETF for you as well (NYSE:SPXS is designed for that!). In short, there is pretty much an ETF for every taste.

The Investment Company Institute estimates that as of December 2014, there were 1,411 ETFs traded on the US markets provided by 52 "sponsors"—as ETF issuers are known. Those 1,411 ETFs attracted $1.974 trillion and accounted for 13 percent of net assets managed by long-term mutual funds, other ETFs, closed-end funds, and unit investment trusts—the most powerful asset managers grouping in the United States (Figure 6.3). The demand for ETFs has been increasing, fueled by the ease of investment (just tell your broker what you want), and the low costs of participation in an ETF. Most ETFs include large-cap stocks and fixed income, including treasuries, other bonds and potentially foreign exchange, as Figure 6.4 shows.

ETF trading volume has been growing off the charts as well. Figure 6.5 shows the average monthly volume of ETF trading on Deutsche Borse's Xetra exchange over the past 15 years.

---

[1]MSCI, "November 2014 Index Methodology MSCI Global Socially Responsible Indexes Methodology," November 2016, p. 13, available at: https://www.msci.com/eqb/methodology/meth_docs/MSCI_Global_SRI_Methodology_November_2014.pdf.

[2]PowerShares Exchange-Traded Fund Trust Supplement Dated December 18, 2012, to the Prospectus Dated August 31, 2012, available at: https://www.kgibank.com/cosmos/T06/docs/ETF/PBW.pdf.

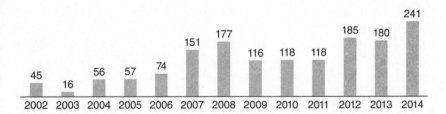

FIGURE 6.3 Net Share Issuance of ETFs, billions of dollars, 2002–2014
Note: Data for ETFs that invest primarily in other ETFs are excluded from the totals.
Source: Investment Company Institute (https://www.ici.org/etf_resources/background/faqs_etfs_market)

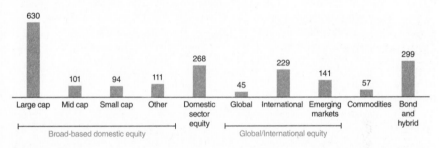

FIGURE 6.4 Total net assets of ETFs concentrated in large-cap domestic stocks, billions of dollars, December 2014

Although the proliferation of ETFs has certainly reduced costs and improved the investment lives of many, it has also delivered some unintended consequences. Remarkably, the product that is considered a passive investment, merely tracking established indexes can also play a role in wild intraday fluctuations. According to some researchers, the proliferation of ETFs facilitates *stock return synchronicity*—a condition whereby portfolio diversification is tossed out the window as the prices of all stocks move south at the same time. Some researchers deduce that ETFs propagate shocks and cause instabilities in the markets, framing the discussion in the direction of the information spillover theory. Others propose alternative theories of ETF behavior, pinning responsibility for the ETF and flash crash effect on the market makers. Still other researchers link the so-called smart beta models and the ETFs among the causes of flash crashes.

How do ETFs cause flash crashes? For one, many ETFs are created using derivatives on underlying assets, such as futures and options, not the

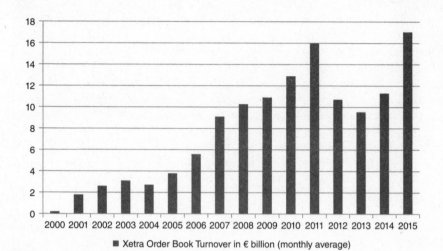

FIGURE 6.5 Average monthly ETF turnover on Deutsche Borse Xetra
Source: Deutsche Borse, 15 years of ETF trading in Europe & on Xetra, Facts and
Figures (http://deutsche-boerse.com/INTERNET/MR/mr_presse.nsf/0/
3F0529D170C9E1BFC1257E2100298622/$File/Fact%20Sheet%2015%20years
%20ETF_e.pdf?OpenElement)

instruments that the ETFs are designed to track. As such, they are potential
booby-traps with unchecked risk exposure ticking away in the markets.
Prospectuses for ETFs typically mention the composition of an ETF in
general terms, the details are often murky and kept rather confidential for
competitive purposes. Instead, most ETF prospectuses contain the following
"buyers beware" passage:

> *The U.S. Securities and Exchange Commission has not approved
> or disapproved these securities or passed upon the accuracy or ade-
> quacy of this prospectus. Any representation to the contrary is a
> criminal offense. Securities of the Trust ("Units") are not guaran-
> teed or insured by the Federal Deposit Insurance Corporation or any
> other agency of the U.S. Government, nor are such Units deposits or
> obligations of any bank. Such Units of the Trust involve investment
> risks, including the loss of principal.*[3]

---

[3] "Principal U.S. Listing Exchange for SPDR® S&P 500®, ETF Trust: NYSE Arca,
Inc., under the symbol 'SPY,'" Prospectus Dated January 20, 2016. https://www
.spdrs.com/library-content/public/SPDR_500%20TRUST_PROSPECTUS.pdf.

While such derivative exposure makes ETF manufacturing cheap and easy, it is not at all straightforward to assess the true risks of such opaque instruments. One 2014 research paper examined nearly 7,000 ETFs and found that only 11 percent of the ETFs are within 1 percent of the actual mean return and volatility that they are designed to reproduce! In other words, only 89 percent of all ETFs are doing their job of replicating their target baskets of financial instruments! The exact risk profile of ETFs is usually not accessible to investors.

The flash crashes, however, are not influenced by a potential implosion of a single ETF. In the age of electronic trading, ETFs are a target of statistical arbitrage (stat-arb), a technique employed by high- and low-frequency traders alike. In a nutshell, a stat-arb strategy seeks to arbitrage the "law of one price"—one of the pillars of finance. The law of one price says that in perfectly efficient markets, a basket of securities, say the S&P500, should have the same price as the ETF tracking the S&P 500 in real time. Most modern markets, although rapidly approaching efficiency, allow for temporary inefficiencies—that is, situations where prices deviate from their equation-based model linking the price of the basket of securities and the corresponding ETFs. Such abnormalities are perfect for traders possessing ultra-fast technology: Whoever identifies the mispricing first and trades it away making the most money.

For example, suppose the basket of securities representing the S&P 500 is in aggregate priced relatively lower than the ETF tracking the S&P500 (NYSE:SPY). Since the basket and the ETF should follow the law of one price, sooner or later, the prices will equilibrate. In the meantime, a fast trader can pounce and buy up shares of individual S&P 500 equities, buoying their price, while simultaneously short-selling the SPY ETF, lowering its price, and effectively making the equilibrium between the basket and the ETF happen sooner than it would otherwise. Once the equilibrium is reached, the fast trader would liquidate his position, realizing a tidy profit in the matter of milliseconds or seconds or, possibly, minutes in the process.

While, most of the time, statistical arbitrage facilitates market efficiency by bringing the baskets and the corresponding ETFs into price equilibria, in many cases the market-ETF dependency may cause a flash crash. Consider the following scenario: One of the financial instruments in a basket tracked by an ETF experiences a sharp fall. Stat-arb traders trade the ETF to reflect the law of one price. Once the ETF's price falls, however, a new force comes to influence the markets, potentially causing widespread contagion among other financial instruments in the markets. This new force is macro arbitrage. The macro arbitrage traders and systems often rely on a macro factor model to evaluate the prices of major securities. According to the macro model, the price of a major security is tied (within a range) to the price of a major index, nowadays most often approximated by an ETF, such as the one tracking the S&P 500. Once the price of the ETF drops, most of the securities in the underlying basket are revalued by the macro traders and algorithms, dragging down the prices of most individual securities in the basket. The basket is now once again priced below the corresponding ETF!

Next, the vicious cycle repeats itself: the ETF tracking the basket is repriced downward, causing the macro-repricing of the underlying securities. In what the US Securities and Exchange Commission dubbed a "hot potato effect" in one of its reports on the flash crash of May 6, 2010, the prices of all instruments across the market fall in a death spiral, creating a flash crash.

Once the flash crash begins in a particular market, it can rapidly spread to other instruments, affecting markets across all asset classes and continents. The recovery can be just as swift: All it takes is for one market participant or system to realize the artificial absurdity in the present crash and the low valuations of the securities to begin to repurchase the underpriced instruments. The impact of a flash crash on volatility is much-longer lived: the heightened volatility and "jitteriness" in the markets may persist for days and months following a substantive crash.

Is the proliferation of ETFs actually increasing flash crash frequency? Figure 6.6 plots the peaks and troughs in the number of flash crashes in the S&P 500 per year against the annual trading volume in the S&P500 ETF (NYSE:SPY). As Figure 6.6 shows, the volume of SPY exactly tracks the number of flash crashes in a given year since 2007. While the chart alone does not establish causality of trading volume, the relationship speaks for itself. At the same time, the overall growth in trading in the S&P 500 does not appear to have a hand in flash crashes. As Figure 6.7 shows, the annual volume in the traded shares of the S&P 500 index appears to lag the number of flash crashes per year.

Are traders and their machines choosing to use ETFs during flash crashes, and, if so, why? A branch of research speculates that ETFs are an easier option to trade when it is urgently required to liquidate positions. Some researchers emphasized the liquidity advantages of ETFs as compared with other forms of investing. Indeed, ETFs are often used in the following solution: Sell anything closely correlated and highly liquid with one's target portfolio first and then slowly rebalance the position to neutralize the portfolio as a whole. The desired effect can be achieved with derivatives and, of course, plain ETFs. Anecdotally, the technique has proved effective and gained popularity with pension funds, hedge funds, and other large institutions charged with capital protection.

Over time, the traded volume of the S&P 500 ETF (NYSE:SPY) has been increasingly correlated with the intraday downward volatility of the ETF. Figure 6.8 shows the 250-day rolling correlation of intraday downward

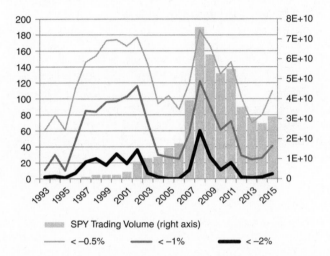

FIGURE 6.6 Number of flash crashes per year in the S&P 500 ETF (NYSE:SPY) and the annual trading volume in the S&P 500 ETF. The number of flash crashes appears to be exactly tracking the volume in the S&P 500 ETF.

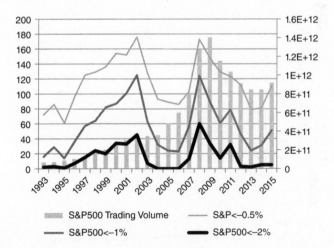

FIGURE 6.7 Number of flash crashes in the S&P 500 index (not ETF) and the respective annual share volume in the stocks comprising the S&P 500. The S&P 500 trading volume appears to lag the number of flash crashes—increase following an increase in flash crashes.

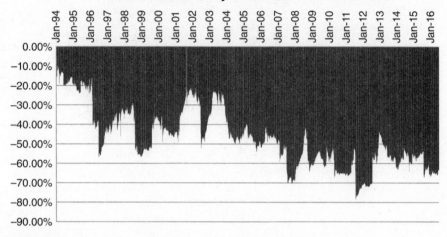

FIGURE 6.8   250-day rolling correlation of the intraday downward volatility (low/open −1) and daily volume of the S&P 500 ETF (NYSE:SPY)

volatility (daily low versus daily open, expressed as a percentage) versus the daily volume for the same day. As Figure 6.8 shows, in SPY, the correlation has been sloping down to −70 percent, implying an increased dependency between the relative intraday lows and the traded volume. As Figure 6.8 also illustrates, the effect is not as palpable in the S&P 500 itself, implying that SPY is indeed used as a quick liquidation tool in falling markets. Correlations become less pronounced when volume lags downward volatility by one day, implying that trading is really concentrated on the day of the sell-off. The correlations almost disappear altogether when the downward volatility lags trading volume—it is the trading volume that drives down prices, not volatility.

Is the existence and behavior of ETFs limited to the US equity markets? Far from it. The prices of the constituents in the index were often tracking the ETF. For instance, major constituents of GREK, an ETF following the Greek economy, are closely tracking the index.

Is banning ETFs a solution? Probably not. ETFs deliver a convenient and quite transparent way to trade portfolios of securities. Managing ETF risks, however, is a barely charted territory. In light of this, some researchers, like Professor Maureen O'Hara of Cornell University, suggest that ETFs should be restricted to baskets of widely traded instruments.[4] As the analysis

---

[4]A. Bhattacharya and M. O'Hara, "Can ETFs Increase Market Fragility? Effect of Information Linkages in ETF Markets" (working paper, Cornell University, 2016).

presented in this chapter shows, however, it is precisely the ETFs on the baskets of widely traded securities, often used as proxies for the broader market, that are most often used as factors in the macro models and are therefore most likely to cause marketwide crashes.

And what if ETFs like SPY were banned? At present, SPY provides a convenient function: It tracks the composition of the S&P 500 index and enables short-term stat-arb and macro traders to immediately reference the index in their quest for a quick profit. Banning SPY, however, would not eliminate stat-arb and macro traders—instead of using a readily available SPY to benchmark intraday price movements, the traders and their algorithms would instead track the composition of the S&P 500 themselves. The implementation of pseudo-SPY would probably entail some 100 lines of code, and would allow the traders to continue deploying their present strategies for a foreseeable future. In fact, banning any sort of ETFs would probably give rise to a new cottage industry of synthetic ETF proxies potentially traded over the counter—that is, outside of exchanges, without the transparency afforded to them at present. Thus, banning ETFs, as O'Hara suggests, may not have the desired effect.

Another recommendation by O'Hara is to improve information quality; abstract the noise of temporary would-be flash crashes with a sound understanding of where the fundamentals and other traders stand and whether the markets are ripe for a flash crash. This is where the uncommon data and the Internet of things come in, discussed in Chapter 8.

How do flash crashes in individual instruments spread to other securities and result in marketwide crashes in practice? In this chapter, we will dig into an example from October 15, 2014. The flash crash of October 15, 2014, rattled fixed-income traders. The day was dominated by the institutional activity that is illustrated on Figure 6.9. The day started with institutions selling off two particular names: MRK and MSFT. Following the sell-off, institutional activity switched to *buying* natural gas, gold, and euro, possibly in anticipation of a broad market crash across most asset classes. The resulting sell-off eventually prompted the sell-off in gold and natural gas as well, in a presumptive reversal of the previous accumulation. This was also accompanied by a sell-off in U.S. Treasuries. A subsequent reversal across most equities, commodities, and rates buoyed market expectations.

As with all sudden market crashes and reversals, one always wonders whether the crash was intentionally driven by an unscrupulous market participant in search of a quick yet illicit gain. In the case of the October 15, 2014, crash, the AbleMarkets' analysis cannot rule out such a possibility. The analysis indicated significant institutional purchases of natural gas, gold, and EUR/USD preceding the US equities market crash by as much as one hour. Following the downturn, however, gold and natural gas positions were

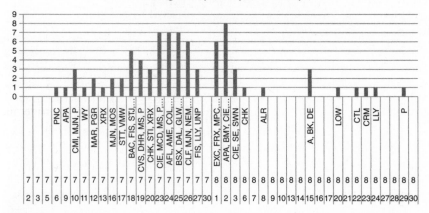

FIGURE 6.9 Timeline of cross-asset institutional activity on the day of the flash crash of October 15, 2014, as estimated by AbleMarkets
Source: AbleMarkets, 2015, "The Flash Crash of October 15, 2014—What Happened?"

reversed in tandem with a turnaround in equities. It is, therefore, conceivable that the accumulation of euros and commodities served as a hedge for a flash-crash market strategy in the US stocks.

Was the crash caused by institutions, and how might you know? One of the questions about the events of October 15, 2014, is about institutional participation on that day and its influence on the markets. We can look to the AbleMarkets Institutional Activity Index to glean some answers for the Dow Jones 30 companies as well as selected commodities and currencies. The AbleMarkets Institutional Activity Index is an index based on a proprietary methodology that tracks the participation of institutional traders by classifying each trade initiated by a market or a marketable order as institutional or noninstitutional with a high degree of accuracy.

According to the AbleMarkets Institutional Trading Index, the first 30 minutes of the trading day witnessed a considerable institutional sell-off in Merck & Co. (NYSE: MRK) and Microsoft (NYSE:MSFT). The proportion of institutions originating market(able) sell orders exceeded those in buy orders by 92 percent in MRK and 85 percent in MSFT from 9:30 AM to 10:00 AM. Interestingly, institutional sell-offs in MRK and MSFT were accompanied by institutions purchasing Johnson & Johnson stock (NYSE:JNJ), gold, and Japanese yen. Specifically, from 9:30 to 10 AM, the proportion of institutional buyers of JNJ, gold, and Japanese yen exceeded the proportion of institutional sellers by 94 percent, 59 percent, and 69 percent, respectively.

In the following 30 minutes, from 10:00 AM to 10:30 AM, the institutional activity briefly stabilized among the Dow Jones 30 stocks. However, institutions retained their focus on buying commodities, such as the natural gas, where the proportion of institutional buyers exceeded that of sellers by 77 percent. The institutional buying of commodities, however, was reversed from 10:30 AM to 11:00 AM, with institutional sellers outnumbering institutional buyers by 91 percent in natural gas and by 76 percent in crude oil. During the same time period, 16 out of Dow Jones 30 stocks experienced a mild sell-off, where the proportion of institutions among all entities placing market and marketable sell orders exceeded the proportion of institutions in buy orders.

From 11:00 to 11:30, the relative percentage of institutions placing sell orders further increased, with 22 out of Dow Jones 30 stocks being dominated by institutional sellers. The trend continued from 11:30 to 12 PM, where 23 stocks of the Dow Jones 30 were affected. Simultaneously, institutional buyers outnumbered institutional sellers in gold and the euro. However, institutional sellers dominated in the Canadian dollar, Australian dollar, Swiss franc, and emerging currencies such as Mexican peso and Turkish lira.

From 12:00 PM to 12:30 PM, the trend continued to exacerbate, with 26 out of 30 DJIA stocks being under heavy institutional selling pressure. Institutional sell-off in US stocks spread to crude oil and most currencies, including UK pound sterling, Canadian dollar, Australian dollar, Swiss franc, Mexican peso, Turkish lira, Chinese yuan, and Brazilian real. At the same time, however, institutional buyers outpaced institutional sellers in commodities, such as gold, silver, and natural gas, and also in currencies, such as Japanese yen, Russian ruble, and, in particular, euro, where the proportion of institutional buyers among all market(able) buy orders exceeded the proportion of institutional sellers among all seller-initiated trades by 82 percent.

By 1:00 PM, institutional sellers overtook institutional buyers in most equities, commodities, and currencies, with notable exceptions of natural gas and euro, where institutional buyers exceeded institutional sellers by 94 percent and 82 percent, respectively. The stock of McDonald's Corporation (NYSE:MCD) and the Turkish Lira were particularly disbursed by institutions. By 13:30, institutions were dominating the sell-off across the board in stocks, commodities, currencies and even U.S. Treasuries, with exceptions (institutional buyers-favored) including American Express (NYSE:AXP), Goldman Sachs Inc. (NYSE:GS), Japanese yen, Brazilian real, and Russian ruble. Euro, crude oil, natural gas, gold, and silver were all registering heavy institutional selling pressure.

By 2:00 PM, there was a sharp reversal in institutional activity among equities and currencies. Twenty-two out of 30 constituents of the DJIA registered significantly higher institutional participation among market buy orders and marketable limit buy orders than sell orders. Heavy institutional buying activity was also observed in Japanese yen, Australian dollar, Canadian dollar, Swiss franc, British pound sterling, Chinese yuan, Brazilian real, Mexican peso, Korean won, and Russian ruble. Institutional activity in the euro reversed direction, resulting in a sell-off. Institutional sell-off persisted in silver, gold, and US Treasuries. At the same time, institutional activity in crude oil and natural gas was already mostly dominated by buyers.

This pattern largely persisted until the end of the North American trading session with a couple of notable changes. Around 3:00 PM, crude oil underwent a sharp institutional sell-off, only to stabilize by the end of the trading day. Institutional activity in silver and gold reversed (became buyer-dominated) by 3:30 PM, while the sell-off in the US Treasuries persisted until the end of the day.

DETECTING FLASH-CRASH PRONE MARKET CONDITIONS

Can flash crashes occur independently of ETFs? Absolutely, yes. As Figure 6.10 shows, flash crashes in individual securities are incredibly common. Market-wide flash crashes, however, are much less frequent, in part because a dropping stock does not necessarily precipitate contagion in other securities. Accordingly, the number of market-wide flash crashes has been steadily decreasing over a number of years, as depicted in Figure 6.1. In particular, 1974, 2002, and 2008 were "high-flash-crash years," where the number of market-wide flash crashes with over 2 percent intraday plunges reached and surpassed 45 trading days out of 251 available for a typical trading year, resulting in one flash crash every six trading days on average!

What is the solution to the problem of flash crashes? According to research, the onset of flash crashes can be detected in much the same way as the human propensity to have heart attacks and other diseases. AbleMarkets has identified certain markers that, like tests on human blood, point to whether the markets are susceptible to price agitation, potentially leading to flash crashes. Specifically, flash crashes can be spotted in deformities of the limit order book as many as two days ahead of the flash crash. Erratic micro-movements of prices that can only be detected in the limit order book are also reliable predictors of subsequent market-wide crashes.

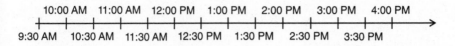

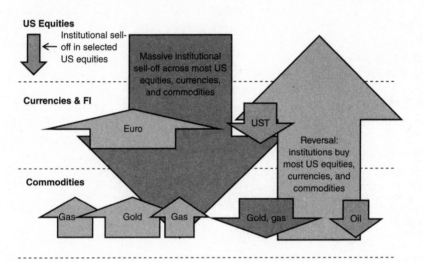

FIGURE 6.10 Number of single-stock crashes (when daily low fell below the daily open over 0.5 percent) among the 30 constituents of the Dow Jones Industrial Average
Source: AbleMarkets Analysis.

This phenomenon is not that different from conventional physics. Consider this experiment: Take a sealed bottle of water ("the market") and start warming it up slowly. What happens next? The water molecules ("prices of individual financial instruments") inside the bottle begin moving at an increasingly high pace. Heat the bottle more, and the molecules will ultimately erupt out of the bottle, not unlike a flash crash in the markets. Cool the water bottle, however, and the molecules stabilize and return to their business as usual, giving us hope that swift detection of abnormal flash-crash-leading market conditions may actually help spare the markets from flash crashes. A limit order book filling exercise may be the answer to rescue the market but much more research is needed to determine exactly what kind of remedy works best for this purpose.

The sharp movements of prices preceding flash crashes can be modeled as high-frequency runs. When there is too much one-sided trading activity, it erodes liquidity on the opposite side of the market, resulting in drastic price precipitations. In the time before flash crashes, trading data also ceases following regular patterns.

Under normal market conditions, trades often form "sequences" or "runs." Under flash-crash prone conditions, the runs exacerbate—like the molecules in the heated water bottle, the one-dimensional runs of prices become longer and more pronounced. A run is a one-directional price movement. For example, IBM stock may experience a run if its price increases from \$158.85 to \$158.86 to \$158.87 in a continuous sequence. Once the price declines by even one tick, the run ceases. A length of a run is a number of ticks that the trade price moves up or down in sequence. In the IBM example, the first run has a length of 3. When the price increases for two trade ticks in a row, the price is considered to be in a positive run of length 2. Similarly, if the price decreases for five trade ticks in a row, then the price is considered to be in negative run of length 5. Figure 6.11 illustrates the idea.

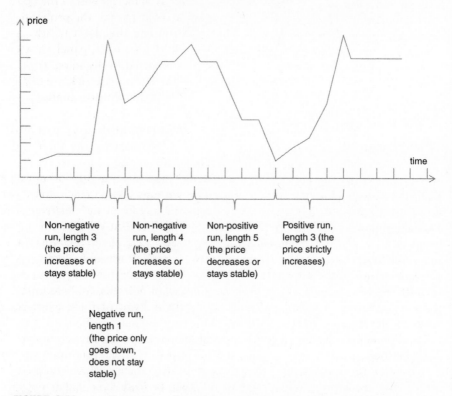

FIGURE 6.11   An illustration of positive, negative, non-positive, and non-negative runs

It is often assumed that price runs follow a so-called random walk, where the probability of staying in the run is independent of the duration or length of the run. Our research shows that the probability of staying in the run actually increases with the duration or length of the run. Ahead of flash crashes, the runs increase in length, resulting in more one-sided trading as well as in irregular trading patterns. Specifically, the runs become unusually long and jut out as data abnormalities. The runs themselves are generated by one-sided order flow, eroding the opposite side of the limit order. Furthermore, certain parameters of runs are highly persistent. As a result, abnormal run activity, as well as the resulting flash crashes, can be predicted as far as a day in advance. Figure 6.12 demonstrates properties of runs computed using tick data on single days in May of 2008, 2010, and 2012. On the horizontal axis, each figure shows the number of periods or lags in the runs that have consecutive returns in the same direction: positive, negative, or zero. On the vertical axis, each figure shows a conditional probability of staying in the run given the number of lags already achieved within the run corresponding to the location on the horizontal axis. That is, the probability of staying in a positive run given that the run has already lasted three consecutive ticks was 3 percent on May 5, 2008 (Figure 6.12, panel a). All data used are for the S&P 500 ETF (SPY), as reported by Reuters. Trade prices that are 20 or more percent away from the latest price tick are considered erroneous and are ignored, as is customary in quantitative analysis of financial data.

Each figure shows that the probability of staying in the run actually increases with the duration of the run. This is particularly true for runs with zero returns: The conditional probability of staying in a zero return run often reaches 99 percent, and such runs may last for 300 or more trade ticks. By comparison, positive and negative runs seldom reach double digits in length, yet a conditional probability of staying in the positive or negative run also increases with the length of the run. In the short term, at lag of two or three or four, the runs are highly unstable: Probability of one positive return following another is only 20 percent. It is more likely for a positive return to be followed by a negative or zero return than by another positive return. In the longer run, say seven or eight nonzero unidirectional returns in length, the probability of staying in the run of them exceeds 50 percent.

As Figure 6.13 shows, such dynamics are undetectable at lower frequencies, say, one-second bars, where the runs appear to follow a random walk.

Figure 6.14 displays the profit obtained by an average positive and negative run. As Figure 6.14 shows, the runs tend to be *back-loaded:* The price change is more pronounced toward the end of the run, possibly due to the limit order book erosion caused by the run.

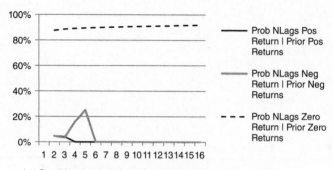

a) Conditional probabilities of continuing in a run measured on
   trade tick data on May 5, 2008

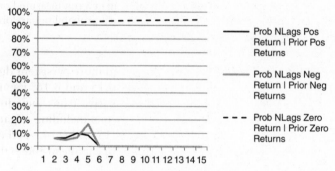

b) Conditional probabilities of continuing in a run measured
   on trade tick data on May 6, 2010

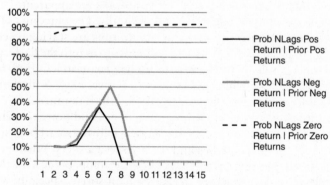

c) Conditional probabilities of continuing in a run measured
   on trade tick data on May 4, 2012

FIGURE 6.12 Empirical conditional probabilities of observing a longer run given the present length of a run

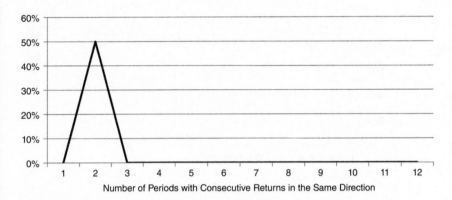

FIGURE 6.13 Conditional probabilities of continuing in a run measured on one-second data on May 6, 2010. Identical conditional probabilities are observed for positive and negative runs at one-second frequencies.

Predictably, then the runs become longer and more persistent due to the inclusion of zero returns, as shown in Figures 6.15 and 6.16. Figures 6.17 and 6.18 show the economic gains of non-negative (runs including positive and zero returns) and non-positive runs (runs including negative and zero price changes) corresponding to Figures 6.15 and 6.16. As the figures demonstrate, positive and negative returns can appear ahead and in the midst of zero returns.

The run phenomenon does not appear to have changed in recent years. Figure 6.19 shows the length of a maximum positive sequence less the length of a maximum negative sequence observed on any given day from October 2009 through October 2012. No structural breaks are apparent.

Next, the runs can be modeled mathematically. The outcomes of models can be compared to realized values to see if the runs are staying on course in the confined "normal" market zone or are drifting off into the flash crash territory. Of course, like the predictions of human heart attacks, the detection of market crashes is probabilistic, and false positives exist. Still, the benefits of understanding the market dangers outweigh the ignorance.

What can investors do when flash crash–ripe conditions are detected in the markets? Hedging becomes a priority, especially for smart beta strategies that bear huge exposure to ETFs and the broader markets. Whether futures or options-based, hedging carries a low cost in comparison with the benefit it provides. It is indeed better to be safe than sorry, especially when the probability of an impending flash crash is high.

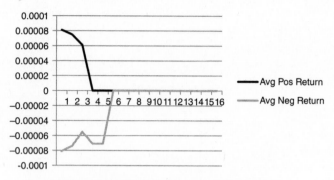

a)   Average gain and loss in positive and negative runs,
        respectively, measured on May 5, 2008

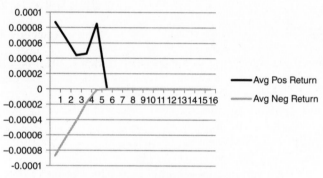

b)   Average gain and loss in positive and negative runs,
        respectively, measured on May 6, 2010

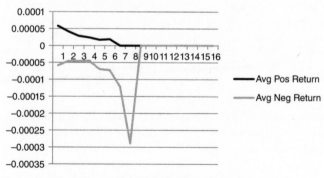

c)   Average gain and loss in positive and negative runs,
        respectively, measured on May 4, 2012

FIGURE 6.14   Average empirical economic gain and loss observed in positive and
negative runs

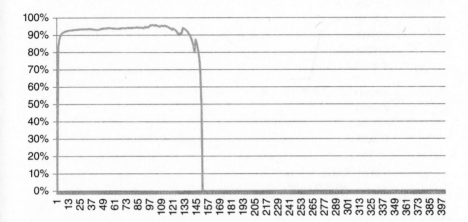

FIGURE 6.15 Conditional probability of observing N lags in a run of non-negative returns, given the run has lasted $N - 1$ lags
Data: Reuters tick data for the S&P 500 ETF (SPY), May 4, 2012.

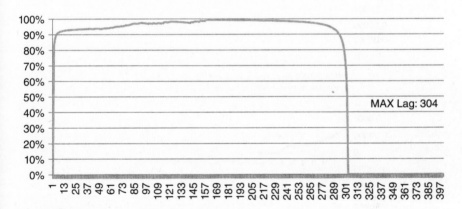

FIGURE 6.16 Conditional probability of observing N lags in a run of non-positive returns, given the run has lasted $N - 1$ lags
Data: Reuters tick data for the S&P 500 ETF (SPY), May 4, 2012.

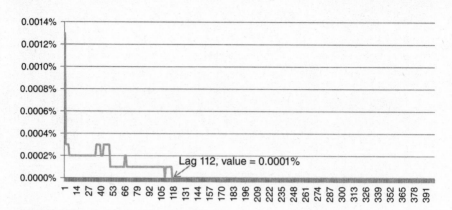

FIGURE 6.17 The average economic value of a non-negative run corresponding to Figure 6.15

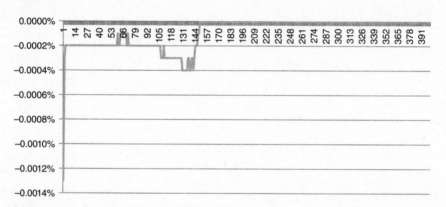

FIGURE 6.18 The average economic value of a non-positive run corresponding to Figure 6.16

ARE HFTs RESPONSIBLE FOR FLASH CRASHES?

Most recent routs in the US financial markets have prompted an outpouring of angst. Detractors of high-frequency trading (HFT) were particularly up in arms about the market downturn, which many of them blamed squarely on manipulation by HFT. Much of the debate about the role of HFT in the events of the August 2015 crash, as well as previous market crashes, was largely based on speculation. The second example for this chapter introduces data-driven evidence about the sequence of events on August 24, 2015, a particularly bad Monday when the US equity markets lost over 4 percent in a single day.

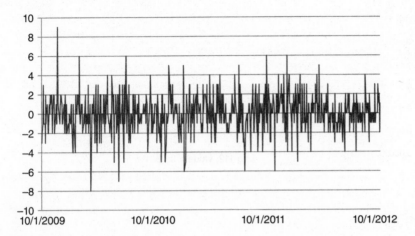

FIGURE 6.19 The difference between the maximum length of a positive run and the maximum length of a negative run observed on a given day

To understand the trading dynamics that led to a precipitous drop in prices on August 24, 2015, we use probabilistic estimates (shown accurate in tests) of aggressive HFT and institutional activity. To detect aggressive HFT and institutional flow, AbleMarkets uses complicated data-intensive computer programs running on hundreds of servers at any one time. The programs use highly granular market data and apply proprietary data science techniques to extract trading profiles of entities behind observed market orders. Since AbleMarkets uses anonymous market data to develop conclusions, the results do not identify particular institutions behind the trades. For instance, the results say with a high degree of confidence that a particular market order was placed by a high-frequency trading firm, but do not point to whether the high-frequency trader in question was, for example, employed by Getco or Virtu. Similarly, the analysis can point to orders placed by large institutions, but does not identify institutions that may include CALPERS or the Harvard University Endowment.

AbleMarkets' analysis of trading on August 24, 2015, shows that while there were bursts of aggressive HFT activity during the sell-off, it was the institutional activity, not the HFT activity, that led and dominated the sell-off. Specifically, the events have appeared to unfold as follows: institutions would sell particular securities, creating acute selling pressure in the markets. Aggressive HFTs would then step in and sell off the market further, but only for a relatively short period of time.

Specifically, on August 24, 2015, aggressive HFT reached 50 percent by volume in several major stocks throughout the day. However, the proportion of aggressive HFTs alternated between HFT buyers and sellers. For instance, the proportion of aggressive HFT sellers in the S&P500 ETF (NYSE:SPY) was 62 percent shortly after the market open. However, proportion of aggressive HFT quickly reversed to spike to 75 percent in aggressive HFT BUY trades in major US equities, such as MMM, at 9:45 AM that same day. Following that, aggressive HFTs further reversed the buy streak and started selling around 10:20 AM on the same day, with aggressive HFT sellers accounting for 53 percent in MMM, for example.

The dominance of aggressive HFT sellers continued through 2:21 PM in equities such as V, GS, and SPY, staying at about 55 percent by volume in these securities. Around 2:30 PM, aggressive HFTs became once again more prominent on the buy side of the limit order book, where they stayed until the market close at about 50 percent of trading volume initiated by market buy orders.

On the same day, August 24, 2015, institutional sellers reached 70 to 90 percent of trading volume at market open and at noon in major US equities such as V, GS, and MMM. In other words, in stocks like V and GS, institutional sellers started the sell-off before HFT sellers by an extensive period of time, as well as an extensive volume of trades.

The results of the analysis make sense intuitively when the nature of HFT strategies is taken into account. By definition, HFT is very short-term in its outlook and does not sustain a prolonged sell-off. Instead, HFT strategies alternate buy and sell (long and short) positions throughout the day. While achieving high-frequency reversals of positions throughout the day, aggressive HFTs tend to be balanced in their buy and sell activity: Market buy orders quickly follow market sells, and vice versa. Aggressive HFTs avoid accumulating large positions, and, as a result, do not tend to be directional on any particular day.

On the other hand, trades of large institutions, such as pension funds, tend to be large (sometimes taking several days to process) and are unidirectional—selling or buying without much alternating. As a result, institutions are capable of impacting the markets much more than do aggressive HFTs.

CONCLUSIONS

Flash crashes are a phenomenon that has been around for years, although the lack of intraday data masked the crashes for years until recently. Crashes in individual securities can be predicted as far as two days in advance by identifying market risk factors that, like clogged arteries in a human, may drive a heart attack in a market.

While the flash crashes in individual instruments are common, they do not necessarily result in a market-wide pandemic. The market-wide flash crashes can be traced to contagions transmitted by ETF trading.

END OF CHAPTER QUESTIONS

1. What is a flash crash? How can it be characterized and measured?
2. Have flash crashes become more pronounced with electronization of trading?
3. What are ETFs?
4. How are ETFs potentially contributing to flash crashes?
5. What is the role of high-frequency traders in flash crashes?

CHAPTER 7

The Analysis of News

—Why are trading floors quiet?

—All the robots are thinking.

News surrounds us. It shouts at us from the television. It pops up at us when we use our computers. It streams across monitors. Now, it tweets at us, too. Nothing is more real time than the news, and nothing carries word of calamities, scandal, failures, and disappointments as fast as the news.

Exposure to real-time risk from the news comes in many forms. The value of understanding news is not only in general event awareness but also in understanding the impact of those events. There is risk in being late to hearing about the news, and there is also the challenge of digesting the news across all of the aspects that matter to your investments. In this chapter, we review news from a risk management point of view to understand how events that carry risk are communicated and analyzed today.

Investors, market makers, traders, and risk managers are watching for news that affects their portfolios of investments. Information is gleaned from earnings announcements, government indexes, and the growing volume of streaming data from the Internet of things (known as IoT). This IoT, discussed in the next chapter, is a vast array of numbers that comes from all of the wireless devices that are collecting and sending information about the movement of goods, the conditions of agriculture, and the weather, to name a few.

But what is news? News is defined as newly received information. In the strictest sense, anything that has arrived prior to here and now is historical data, and no longer information, even though you personally may not have seen it until now.

In the past, financial firms invested only into market data platforms such as Bloomberg, Thomson Reuters, Factset, and others. These platforms collected news and streamed it through their computer systems. Over time, these platforms offered broader services and an increasing numbers of feeds, which we will describe below. Viewing news only from formal news services changed with the Internet and intelligent devices. The introduction of email and social media created a vast amount of information generated by consumers about themselves and their views about everything. A market-place of alternative, often more timely, interesting and predictive data sources has sprung up and is blooming. In fact, the proliferation of alternative data sources is so vast that many financial practitioners are now shunning traditional data providers like Bloomberg altogether and are strictly relying on direct data feeds from data sources. Sourcing news directly from its origin bypasses delays and extra markup costs that inevitably occur whenever the news travels through a news aggregator.

THE DELIVERY OF NEWS

News arrives in a continuous flow, spaced at random intervals. News origins are not always real-time. Some news is delayed or embargoed until a certain pre-determined release time. News aggregators further slow things down, even if only by seconds, when they collect articles, government announcements, and press releases and provide them to the public through mainstream media and Internet-based news services.

News Is Written So Computers Can Read It

Algorithms have been developed over time to recognize specific words and, more recently, to read and understand entire articles. Traditional approaches

to machine reading and comprehension have been based on either manually specified grammar sequences stored in databases or by using a method that transforms language into probabilistic sequences, in the method known as Natural Language Processing (NLP) and discussed in Chapter 8.

The deluge of data makes it really hard for buy-side and sell-side analysts to stay on top of the news affecting their sectors and portfolios. Many traders, however, rely on their internal analyses and are making their trading moves before the announcements. Wouldn't it be great to learn from how they are making their bets?

Understanding the behavior of the markets around announcements is important, and this section shows why. The previous chapter discussed how using the power of analytics can bring clarity on the influence of aggressive HFT on the price of WMT on October 14, 2015, the day when Wal-Mart released news about its upcoming underperformance. While aggressive HFT algorithms were prominent during sell-off of WMT immediately following the announcement, as shown in Figure 7.1, further analysis shows they were not the only force behind the sell-off.

What else was happening at this time? What were institutions doing? When institutional trading activity is considered as a percentage of buy and sell volume recorded in 30-minute intervals, as Figure 7.2 depicts, one can see that the institutional trading in Wal-Mart stock has actually peaked between 10:00 AM and 10:30 AM, at the very onset of the sell-off. At that time,

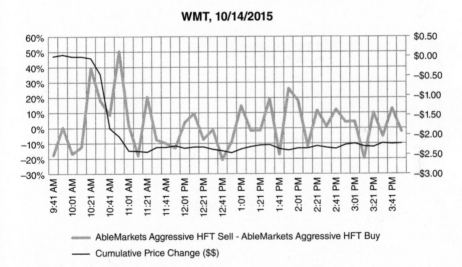

FIGURE 7.1 Aggressive HFT (the difference of aggressive HFT sellers and aggressive HFT buyers), as a percentage of 10-minute volume

the institutional activity comprised 100 percent of trading volume, making the 30 percent of activity previously marked as aggressive HFT activity clearly driven by institutions deploying HFT algorithms in their trading. As Figure 7.3 shows, when considered as a percentage of the total daily volume, institutional trading activity in WMT on October 14, 2015, peaked

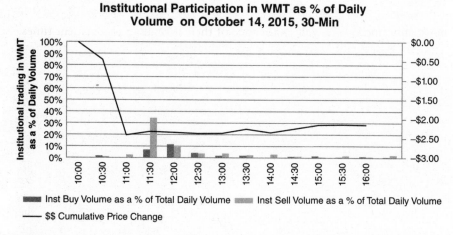

FIGURE 7.2 Institutional investor participation in Wal-Mart (WMT) trading on October 14, 2015, as a percentage of daily volume

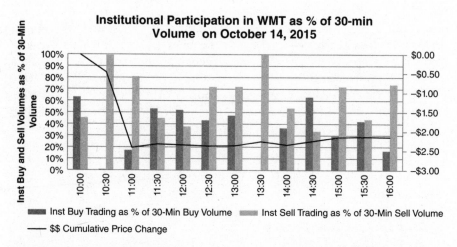

FIGURE 7.3 Institutional investor participation in Wal-Mart (WMT) trading as a percentage of 30-minute volume

from 11:00 AM to 11:30 AM, way after the majority of sell-off was completed. This observation may make market participants believe that it was, in fact, aggressive HFT that was most responsible for the sell-off. However, closer examination of institutional activity paints a different picture.

The Wal-Mart case study followed a very well-documented surprise, but what evidence is there that someone was trading the news early across all stocks?

Analysis appears to imply that people are trading on macroeconomic news announcements well in advance of their formal announcement times. Traders seem to be in the know or are placing their bets about the upcoming news announcements and profit on the news at least $\frac{1}{2}$ hour (30 minutes) ahead of the news announcement, significantly moving the markets and rendering post-announcement trading a true gamble.

According to classical finance, markets are not supposed to move in response to an announcement, as most of the news is priced in prior to the news announcement. Specifically, the news is incorporated into prices through a trading process, with trades carrying information to the market. Traders are acting on their beliefs and "putting their money where their mouths are." It would seem that according to the rational expectations hypothesis, therefore, the markets are operating normally, except that the rational expectations hypothesis was created to work over the days and weeks preceding the event announcement, not minutes.

According to yet another pillar of classical finance, the efficient markets hypothesis (Fama, 1970), the incorporation of news depends on the "universe" of the news: whether the news is public or private. News that is public and is, therefore, known to a large number of traders is incorporated into the markets nearly instantly, while the news that is not widely known tends to seep into the markets slowly. In theory, public announcements, like the ISM Manufacturing Index, are not available for distribution until their precise release time. After the embargo ends, related stocks should experience a clean "step" in price action similar to the one shown in Figure 7.4 for positive news and Figure 7.5 for negative news. Under the efficient markets hypothesis, the price neatly follows the rational expectations hypothesis, fully incorporating all the publicly available news just before and immediately following the news release. With these situations, there are no gradual price transitions.

The efficient market hypothesis, however, allows for selected public news, like the ISM Manufacturing Index value, to be estimated by economists. The economists' thinking, in turn, could gradually filter into pricing through trading, but would not result in a concerted price action. Instead, copious research shows that, whenever public news is released,

FIGURE 7.4 Instantaneous price adjustment in response to positive publicly released news, according to the efficient markets hypothesis

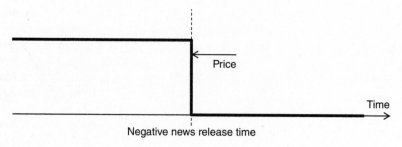

FIGURE 7.5 Instantaneous price adjustment in response to negative news, according to the efficient markets hypothesis

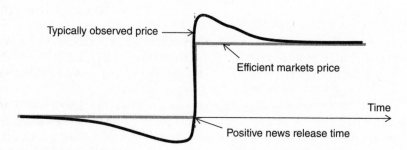

FIGURE 7.6 Actual price adjustment in response to positive publicly released news, according to behavioral studies

the price undershoots just before the news announcement, and overshoots temporarily just after the announcement, as shown in Figures 7.6 and 7.7.

Furthermore, the theory of rational expectations suggests that upcoming news is priced in the markets long before the announcement. One way it may be priced in is by trading on the summary forecasts of a cohort

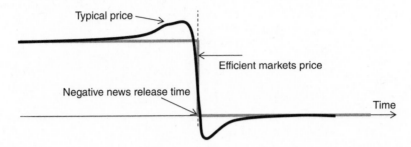

FIGURE 7.7 Actual price adjustment in response to negative news, according to behavioral studies

of economists polled by Bloomberg or other forecasting services ahead of the announcement. The average of these estimates is considered to be a "consensus forecast." Although the consensus forecast might not be perfect, it can be fairly informative. For the ISM Manufacturing Index, for example, the consensus forecast predicted the correct direction of the index (increase or decrease from the prior month) 79 percent of the time from 2010 through 2015, and 83 percent of the time from 2013 through 2015.

Figure 7.8 shows the impact of the ISM Manufacturing Index news releases on the Russell 3000 equities, the most commonly held 3,000 stocks in the US markets. The ISM Manufacturing Index is released once a month on preannounced dates at 10:00 AM by the Institute of Supply Management (ISM). ISM asks over 300 manufacturing firms about their employment, production inventories, new orders, and supplier deliveries, and then creates a composite index reflecting their current manufacturing conditions. An improvement in this index tends to signal better manufacturing conditions, translating into a pick-up in economic growth. Conversely, a decrease in the index potentially signals a flagging economy. Bloomberg considers the ISM Manufacturing Index an important leading indicator.

As Figure 7.8 illustrates, average equity prices on the 3,000 stocks are already moving at the market open, 9:30 AM, a half hour ahead of the upcoming news announcement. By the time the general public receives the news at 10:00 AM, the markets have, on average, moved up by $0.01 per share of the Russell 3000 stocks when the announcement exceeds expectations and down by $0.07 per share of the 3,000 stocks when the news is worse than expected. On average, if you are in the know, you can capture $0.04 per share per news announcement, or $1,440,000 per year if you trade only 1,000 shares of each of the Russell 3000 stocks just once a month. With hundreds of distinct macro announcements released every month (see The Quant Investor Almanac 2011 for details), it becomes easy to build a billion-dollar global macro hedge fund that is consistently profitable.

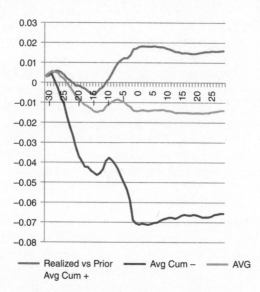

FIGURE 7.8 Realized average price changes for the Russell 3000 stocks in response to (1) higher-than-previous values of the ISM Manufacturing Index (Realized vs Prior Avg Cum +), (2) lower-than-previous values of the ISM Manufacturing Index (Avg Cum −), and (3) all announcements (AVG)

The profits, however, come directly from the pockets of the general investing public who trade after the announcements. As Figure 7.8 shows, the content of the news is completely priced in ahead of news announcements. The markets barely move in response to the news after the news.

Is it possible that the preannouncement trading is not done on the embargoed news, but, instead, is based on superior economic powers of prediction of the upcoming values of the ISM Manufacturing Index? While some economists try to intelligently guess the upcoming ISM Manufacturing Index number, few succeed. Bloomberg compiles and publishes consensus forecasts for the ISM Manufacturing Index by polling well-respected economists and then averaging the respondents' opinions. The reported consensus only has a 42 percent correlation with the realized value.

How does the news leak out ahead of time? The answer likely lies in the antiquated methodology by which the government and other macroeconomic news sources release their updates. Typically agencies distribute the news to journalists and others parties an hour ahead of the news release

under a news embargo. The embargo is an honor system whereby the recipi-
ent of the news is expected to keep the news confidential until the scheduled
news release time.

How can market behavior and that of aggressive HFT be explained in
a sensible manner? Some market participants have blamed aggressive HFTs
for obtaining news and acting on it ahead of its release to the public. While
the assumption of advanced knowledge is tenuous, it is not impossible due to
an outdated concept of news embargo. News embargo emerged in the 1960s
as a solution to the issue of news fairness raised by market participants. To
ensure wide access to news, the figures were to undergo the fullest possible
distribution, which at that time equaled television, radio, and print. To provide adequate time for television and radio broadcast preparation, the news
sources embargoed the news content for one hour, allowing all the news outlets to broadcast in unison, ensuring equal access to all investors. The embargo
system, however, has always been voluntary, and no government penalties of
any sort exist for cases where a reporter decides to inappropriately email the
news to a hedge fund or an HFT friend. Given all the financial incentives, the
often-starving reporters may violate the embargo and share the news with a
hedge fund or trading desk that can trade on the embargoed news.

There is the risk that at least some parties receiving news appear not
to care to observe the embargo. When the rewards of ignoring the embargo
become excessively attractive, all the incentives are there to throw the honor
code out the window.

In the past, placing a single trade took hours or even days, and the Internet as we know it today did not exist. At that time, news embargoes served
an important function: they gave journalists a chance to prepare articles in
order to achieve the widest news coverage possible, enabling all individuals to benefit from the news releases at the same time. Today, however, the
embargoed news distribution not only makes no sense, it is actually disadvantaging regular investors and enabling a clever few to make outsized
profits at everyone else's expense.

Are high-frequency traders (HFTs) involved in this news arbitrage?
According to AbleMarkets Aggressive HFT Index, yes, roughly three-
quarters of the preannouncement trading is due to trades initiated by
aggressive HFTs. However, given the timing of trading (half hour, not
microseconds), the observed aggressive HFT strategies are likely deployed
as order execution/footprint minimization strategies by the entities that
receive the advanced news.

Examining the trading patterns ahead of the ISM Manufacturing Index
and Construction Spending announcement, we find that trading on the
not-yet-publicly released embargoed news or at least placing educated
bets consistently takes place as long as 30 minutes ahead of the news

announcement times. The aggressive HFTs appear to be involved in the pre-announcement trading. In fact, as much as three quarters of the pre-announcement price move appears to be driven by aggressive HFTs.

Of course news moves the markets as discussed previously. Furthermore, according to the rational expectations hypothesis, news is the only thing that moves the markets; everything else is noise. Companies like Bridgewater Associates have built small empires with annual revenues exceeding the GDPs of small countries combined just following, interpreting, and acting upon the news. Not surprisingly, the question of whether news announcements are released in a fair manner remains a hot topic. Even less surprising, the fairness of news releases has surfaced as one of the key concerns associated with high-frequency trading. Specifically, some market participants have accused high-frequency traders of using fast technology to front-run lower-speed traders following major news announcements. This research considers market activity surrounding news events.

Event studies are a classic way to measure the happenings surrounding news announcements. The event study methodology is as established as the science of finance, dating back to the 1930s. An event study compares the impact of the news on market conditions before and after the event, in what's known as an *event window*. The window can be as large or as small as one may like it to be, provided that there are enough data points in the selected window and that the distribution of the dependent variable matches the selected analysis model. Given the short-term behavior of aggressive HFT, we focus on smaller time windows to consider the behavior of aggressive HFTs around a news announcement.

Choosing the event is another matter, no less important than the selection of the event window. One factor to consider is that many news announcements are scheduled outside of regular trading hours. To examine the short-term HFT activity around news announcements, however, we consider news that was (1) released during common market hours, and (2) likely to generate a similar reaction across many financial instruments at once.

One such news is construction spending, computed by the U.S. Census Bureau. It estimates the total value of construction performed in the United States during the previous month, including labor, materials, architecture and engineering costs, overhead, interest, and even taxes. The index covers construction in both public and private sectors. Construction spending is an indicator of economic optimism. The higher the construction spending, the reasoning goes, the more people are investing into long-term projects, the higher is the optimism about the economy's future.

Construction spending announcements often coincide with ISM Manufacturing Index survey figures. The index, now computed by IHS Markit in collaboration with the Institute of Supply Management, is based on the responses to the questionnaires sent out to managers in selected companies. ISM asks over 300 manufacturing firms about their employment, production inventories, new orders, and supplier deliveries, and creates a composite reflecting the current manufacturing conditions. An index increase tends to signal better manufacturing conditions, translating into a pick-up in the economic growth. Conversely, a decrease in the index potentially signals a flagging economy.

Current research analyzes the two events in tandem and uses the latest event study methodology to separate the impacts of the two announcements and the aggressive HFT behavior on the returns.

PREANNOUNCEMENT RISK

On July 1, 2015, the month-to-month change in Construction Spending and ISM Manufacturing Index were reported at 10:00 AM. According to Bloomberg, Construction Spending had increased by 0.8, beating analysts' consensus forecast of a 0.5 increase by 0.3. The simultaneously reported ISM Manufacturing Index value was 53.5, an increase of 0.8 from the value reported in June and a 0.3 improvement over the "consensus forecast," a composite figure aggregating opinions of a range of economists polled by Bloomberg on the matter. The news was good. The economy was observed to be growing, and stocks were expected to go up.

The 10:00 AM announcements were preceded by a 9:45 AM value of Institute for Supply Chain Management (ISM) Manufacturing Index (ISM Manufacturing Index). The 9:45 AM figures were worse than expected and worse than the prior month's figures.

Figure 7.9 shows the minute-by-minute cumulative price response to the news by Agilent Technologies (NYSE:A) recorded on BATS-Z exchange. As Figure 7.9 shows, in the 60-minute time interval prior and immediately following the news announcement, the biggest growth in price occurred nearly a half hour ahead of the news release, just after the market open. The stock price of Agilent appears to be unaffected by the ISM Manufacturing Index values made public at 9:45 AM, 15 minutes prior to the 10:00 AM event.

Figure 7.10 shows the proportion of aggressive HFT activity by volume traded in Agilent around the news announcement, as estimated by AbleMarkets. As Figure 7.10 shows, aggressive HFT buying activity peaked at market open, and again nearly a half hour following the news announcement. Aggressive HFT selling activity was elevated around 10:13 AM, potentially explaining some of the observed post-announcement sell-off in NYSE:A. The aggressive HFT numbers immediately surrounding the event announcement

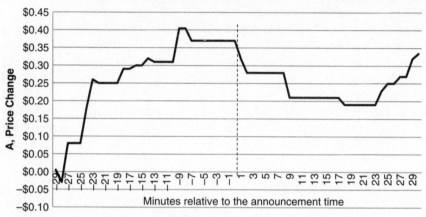

FIGURE 7.9 Cumulative price change of Agilent (NYSE:A) surrounding the 10:00 AM ISM Manufacturing Index announcement recorded in BATS-Z on July 1, 2015

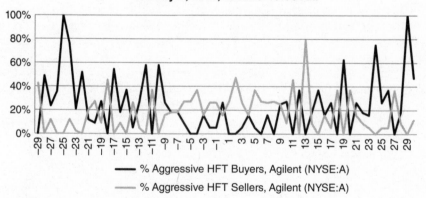

FIGURE 7.10 Participation of aggressive HFT by volume in Agilent (NYSE:A) on July 1, 2015, before and after the ISM Manufacturing Index and Construction Spending figures announcements at 10:00 AM

may have been dampened by the influx of trading volume brought on by other market participants: institutions and retail looking to capitalize on the news.

Is the behavior of the price of A an anomaly? Is the preannouncement gain a random occurrence? To answer this question, we looked at the price response of the entire Russell 3000 index to the same announcement, ISM Manufacturing Index report on July 1, 2015. Using Bats-BYX data, and averaging the cumulative dollar gains and losses of each of the Russell 3000 stocks each minute, we arrive at an even more pronounced preannouncement market movement pattern shown in Figure 7.11. In fact, across all the Russell 3000 stocks, the preannouncement price movement is so pronounced and precise that very little volatility can be observed after the announcement, as Figure 7.12 shows. Figure 7.12 quantifies volatility by measuring the cross-sectional dispersion of returns each minute across all Russell 3000 stocks. As Figure 7.12 shows, volatility indeed declines dramatically following the news announcement.

The minute-by-minute average of the aggressive HFT activity for the entire set of stocks comprising the Russell 3000 surrounding the events of 10:00 AM on July 1, 2015, is equally interesting: the aggressive HFT buyers dominated sellers from 9:45 until the 10:00 AM news announcement, at which point relative proportion of aggressive HFT dropped dramatically from the 20 to 30 percent range to single digits, as shown in Figure 7.13.

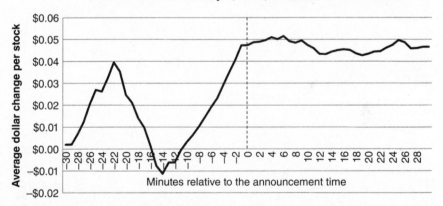

FIGURE 7.11 Average cumulative price change for all the Russell 3000 stocks surrounding the ISM Manufacturing and Construction Spending announcements at 10:00 AM on July 1, 2015

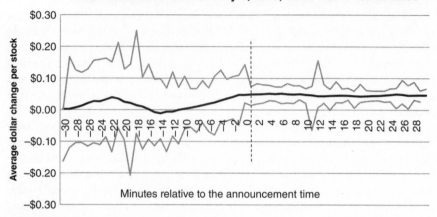

FIGURE 7.12 Average cumulative price change and price change volatility across all the Russell 3000 stocks surrounding Construction Spending announcement at 10:00 AM on July 1, 2015

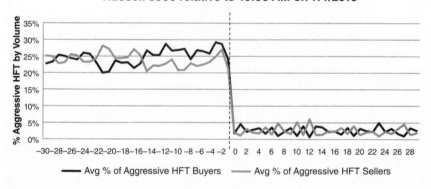

FIGURE 7.13 Participation of aggressive HFT averaged across all Russell 3000 stocks around 10:00 AM news on July 1, 2015

Putting aside aggressive HFT behavior for a moment, let's consider what is wrong with the pictures of Figure 7.11 and Figure 7.12.

As shown in Figures 7.11 and 7.12, market behavior of the Russell 3000 stocks had little to do with the market responses expected under the efficient markets and rational expectations hypotheses. The average price of the

Russell 3000 stocks began to rise 15 minutes prior to the news announcement and barely moved after the news is released at 10:00 AM.

What can be done to ensure fairness in the financial markets? Perhaps catching up with the times and distributing news using social media may do the trick—after all, most traders today are capable of making fundamental stock pricing calls on the basis of the released news figures alone and do not require a reporter's interpretation of the figures. Why not release the news via Twitter or other social media and eliminate the now-ancient embargo process?

Decades-old changes to the news distribution process, however, may take years to complete. In the meantime, investors of all stripes may choose to follow the markets dynamics and observe aggressive HFT behavior in an effort to extract the information about upcoming events directly from the markets. Thus, for example, observing elevated levels of aggressive HFT buyers prior to the 10:00 AM news on July 1, 2015, would suggest that the about-to-be-formally-released news is likely to be positive. With a 15-minute lag prior to the news announcement, such observations do not require high-speed technology, yet deliver powerful predictability and, as a result, profitability.

DATA, METHODOLOGY, AND HYPOTHESES

Deploying an event-study methodology on ISM Manufacturing Index announcements from January 2013 through October 2015, we analyze movements of price, volatility, and aggressive HFT activity around the news release. The results are interesting and surprising, or not so much, depending on whom you ask:

1. The news is "leaking" into the markets well prior to the news announcement.
2. Aggressive HFTs do appear to be trading on the news preannouncements. However,
   a. The aggressive HFTs comprise only a portion of observed trading activity; and
   b. The aggressive HFT activity can be due to institutions using aggressive HFT strategies to trade. While aggressive high-frequency trading activity appears to contribute to preannouncement news incorporation in the markets, it is not the overwhelming factor in the preannouncement trading activity.

How do we know that the news is leaking into the markets well ahead of the proper news announcement time? Consider once again Figure 7.8, which shows the cumulative price move in minutes for the ISM Manufacturing Index before and after the actual time the news is released, averaged over the following two dimensions:

1. All the ISM Manufacturing Index announcements from January 2013 through October 2015
2. All the stocks in the Russell 3000

Figure 7.8 shows three lines:

1. The average cumulative price across all the event announcements and all the Russell 3000 stocks dips mildly ahead of the announcement time (Time 0)
2. The average cumulative price across only those ISM Manufacturing Index news release dates where the announced ISM Manufacturing Index values were higher than those announced in the immediately preceding month (Avg Cum+). This line rises sharply as early as 15 minutes ahead of the announcement (from Time −15).
3. The average cumulative price across only those ISM Manufacturing Index news release dates where the announced ISM Manufacturing Index values were strictly lower than those announced in the immediately preceding month (Avg Cum−). This line begins its steep descent full 30 minutes ahead of the announcement time (at Time −30).

At the time and shortly following the announcement, the markets move little. The lack of movement underscores the dearth of information at the actual news release time (Time 0).

How persistent are the observed price responses across various announcements? What if a single announcement dominates this entire dynamic? Do the rest of the announcements generate a consistent response? To answer this question, we look at the ratio of averages shown in Figure 7.8 to understand the standard deviation of minute-by-minute price responses across different announcements across all the Russell 3000 stocks. Figure 7.14 shows the standard deviations, and Figure 7.15 presents the *t*-ratios: the averages of Figure 7.8 divided by the standard deviations of Figure 7.14.

As Figure 7.14 shows, the variation in price responses is the highest just before the scheduled news announcements, and the lowest following news announcements. However, the variation in the price response also happens to be low about 21 and 8 to 5 minutes *prior* to the proper news announcement

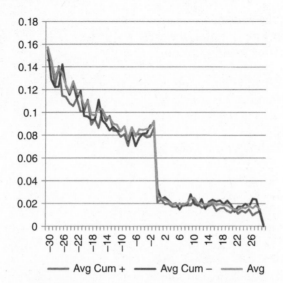

FIGURE 7.14 Standard deviation of average Russell 3000 cumulative price responses surrounding ISM Manufacturing Index announcements. Shown price volatility is measured for cases where the realized news was higher than the prior month's news, lower than the prior month's news and across all the cases.

time, 10:00 AM. The consistency of correct "guesses" of the impending news direction is so high that it is highly unlikely to be purely accidental.

Figure 7.15 displays the *t*-statistics of the cumulative price responses (averages of Figure 7.8 divided by the standard deviations of Figure 7.14). While, as shown in Figure 7.15, the response is much more statistically significant after the news announcement, it still reaches 99.9 percent significance at least 10 minutes prior to the official news announcement time.

What about the Construction Spending announcements that occur at the same times as the ISM Manufacturing Index? Figure 7.16 shows the average price to the realized vs. prior month change in the Construction Spending value. As Figure 7.16 shows, the response to Construction Spending is much more convoluted than it is to the ISM Manufacturing Index, shown in Figure 7.17 and 7.18.

How can anyone possibly trade on the news announcements prior to the news announcements? How would one know what the news value is going

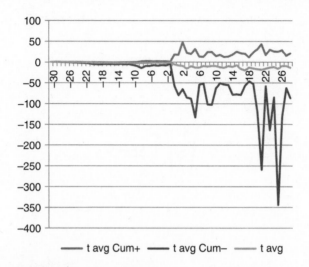

FIGURE 7.15 The *t*-ratios of the cumulative price responses of the Russell 3000 stocks around the ISM Manufacturing Index announcements

to be? An intelligent forecast may certainly be one answer to this question. Bloomberg compiles one set of such forecasts.

How good is Bloomberg's consensus forecast for ISM Manufacturing Index? Research shows that it is not particularly good. From January 2010 to October 2015, the direction of the forecast coincided with the direction of the realized value just 32 out of 73 times. In other words, over 56 percent of time when the forecast said that the ISM Manufacturing Index was going to go up (down) the following month, the released figures actually went in the opposite direction: down (up). From January 2013 through October 2015, that directionally incorrect proportion of forecasts has decreased to 52 percent, with not-even-close forecasts outnumbering somewhat useful ones.

What about the forecasts for Construction Spending announcements? The latter are much better: since January 2010 through October 2015, over 71 percent of time when the forecast said that the Construction Spending was going to go up (down) the following month, the released figures actually went up (down). Since January 2013 through October 2015, that number has actually increased to 74 percent.

Aside from the directional successes and failures, both Construction Spending and Manufacturing indexes exhibit high correlation between differences in realized values and prior values and realized values and forecasts, as Table 7.1 shows. The difference between the realized construction

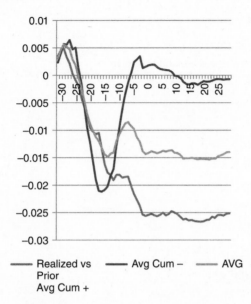

FIGURE 7.16 Average price response of the Russell 3000 stocks to the changes in Construction Spending relative to the prior month's announcements. Many times, the Construction Spending figures remained unchanged relative to their prior values.

values and their prior month values, for example, exhibits 72 percent correlation with the realized index value less its economic consensus forecast. Between the Construction Spending Index and the ISM Manufacturing Index, however, correlations are quite low, as is also shown in Table 7.1. As a result, the news announcements, while overlapping, leave distinct marks on prices at different times.

Is the consensus forecast of Construction Spending driving prices? This does not appear to be the case. Since the consensus forecast is typically released several days ahead of the announcement, the price change would have occurred at that time. Furthermore, no significant changes in prices would be observed in the 30 minutes immediately preceding the news announcement. The latter is not at all the case. Figure 7.19 shows the average price response across all of the Russell 3000 stocks *preceding and following* positive and negative announcement values as compared with the consensus forecast values reported by Bloomberg. As Figure 7.19 shows, when realized Construction Spending is above the forecasted values, the average stock price across all the Russell 3000 stocks actually happens to

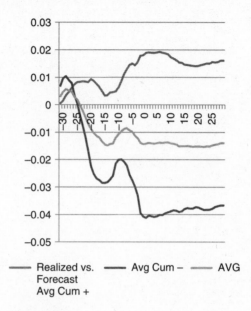

FIGURE 7.17 Average price response across the Russell 3000 stocks in response to (1) realized ISM Manufacturing Index spending exceeding consensus forecast (Avg Cum+), (2) realized ISM Manufacturing Index falling below the consensus forecast for that day (Avg Cum–), and in response to all cases. Data covers January 2013 to October 2015

fall ahead of the news release! On the other hand, when the announced Construction Spending figures are below the consensus forecast, the prices tend to rise ahead of the announcement. The prices stabilize immediately after the news is publicly announced.

Figure 7.20 shows the *t*-ratios of the averages documented in Figure 7.19. As Figure 7.20 illustrates, while the response is much more pronounced after the announcement time, the trading behavior consistent with the realized news release is prevalent up to 20 minutes *before* the scheduled news release time. The evidence suggests that news is indeed leaked or bets are being placed before being made available to all.

How much is this information worth? Suppose one is only trading on the ISM Manufacturing Index. As shown in Figure 7.8, if one were to receive the realized ISM Manufacturing Index value 30 minutes ahead of the announcement time and trade on that information, one would, on average, make 1.5 cents per share ($0.015) on good news—that is,

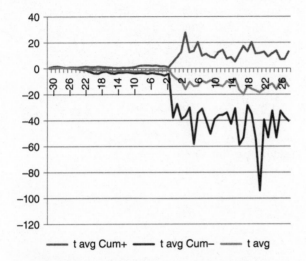

FIGURE 7.18 *t*-ratios of price response of the Russell 3000 stocks to the ISM Manufacturing Index announcements from January 2013 through October 2015 whenever the realized Manufacturing Index exceeded the forecast (t avg Cum+), underachieved the forecast (t avg Cum−), and all cases (t avg)

TABLE 7.1 Correlation of realized values of Construction Spending Index ("Construction") and ISM Manufacturing Index ("Manufacturing") Less Prior Month Values and Less Forecasted Values

Correlation	Construction to Forecast	Construction to Prior	Manufacturing to Forecast	Manufacturing to Prior
Construction to forecast	1	0.721584	0.018799	−0.03117
Construction to prior		1	0.07238	0.017562
Manufacturing to forecast			1	0.88391
Manufacturing to prior				1

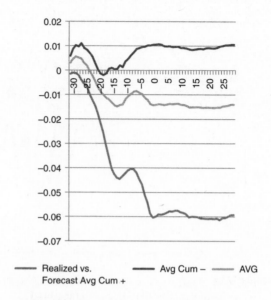

FIGURE 7.19   Cumulative price response of Russell 3000 stocks to the Construction Spending announcement when the realized construction spending exceeds the forecasted value (Avg Cum+), and falls short of the forecasted value (Avg Cum−)

the announcement is better than last month—and 6.5 cent ($0.065) per share on bad news. Trading just 100 shares in each of the Russell 3000 stocks 30 minutes ahead of the news would thus produce, on average, in excess of $12,000 per announcement, not accounting for transaction costs. Trading the same on the Interactive Brokers, where each round-trip trade costs $2.00, our embargoed-information trader would still clear $6,000 per announcement, trading just 100 shares a half hour prior to the news scheduled release. Given the half-hour window allowed for trading, the strategy can be easily scaled, to, say, at least 1,000 shares, easily becoming a meaningful incentive to any journalist!

Fast forward to 2016, and the embargo system is no longer cutting it. One can trade faster than one generates a trading idea, computers can process news as soon as it hits the news wires, and the "level-playing-field" idea behind the original news embargo system no longer makes sense. If anything, the system allows trading on the news to the chosen few, chosen by their ability to procure the embargoed news ahead of the masses. How is this fair?

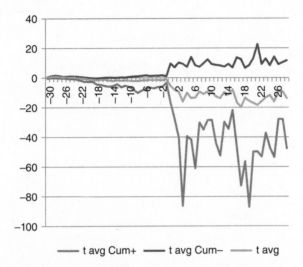

FIGURE 7.20 Statistical significance of cumulative price responses of Russell 3000 stocks measured around Construction Spending announcements when realized Construction Spending figures exceed forecasted values (t avg Cum +), fall short of the forecasted values (t avg Cum−), and all cases

Who is trading on the embargoed news? While it is hard for a bystander to point the finger at the exact trader in the anonymous markets, we can separate categories of traders active before and after the announcements.

One observation from using the AbleMarkets Aggressive HFT Index is the ability to track the behavior of aggressive HFT around the news releases. Aggressive HFT is of particular interest as it has often been associated with advanced trading on news in the popular press.

Figures 7.21 and 7.22 document the behavior of aggressive HFT buyers and sellers, respectively, averaged across the Russell 3000 stocks and all ISM Manufacturing Index announcements from January 2013 through October 2015. As the figures show, behavior of aggressive HFT buyers and sellers is the same whether the realized figures are higher or lower than those of the prior month. The balanced nature of the aggressive HFT activity and higher volumes ahead of higher-than-previous announcements may explain this phenomenon. Aggressive HFTs hold positions for a very short term, and faced with the potentially higher-than-normal flow ahead of positive announcements, the aggressive HFT activity goes up. In Construction Spending announcements, the separation of aggressive HFT buyers and sellers is

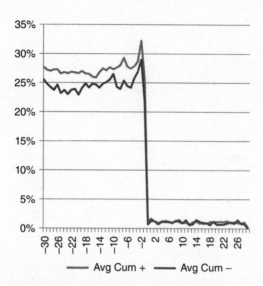

FIGURE 7.21 Behavior of aggressive HFT *buyers* around the ISM Manufacturing Index Announcements in instances when the realized news was higher (Avg Cum+) and lower (Avg Cum−) than the previous month's value

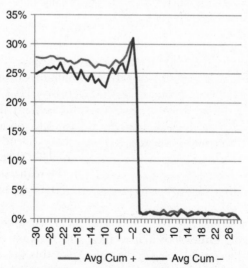

FIGURE 7.22 Behavior of aggressive HFT *sellers* around the ISM Manufacturing Index announcements in instances when the realized news was higher (Avg Cum+) and lower (Avg Cum−) than the previous month's value

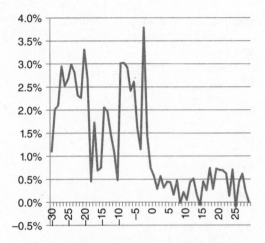

FIGURE 7.23   The difference between aggressive
HFT buyer participation when the realized
Construction Spending Index exceeds the
forecast and that when the realized value falls
short of the forecast

much clearer. When the soon-to-be-released value of Construction Spending is higher (lower) than the forecast, the aggressive HFT Buyers (Sellers) are more prominent than when the realized value is lower (higher) than the forecast, as shown Figures 7.23. In other words, selected aggressive HFTs appear to receive and act on advanced Construction Spending news, if not the ISM Manufacturing Index values. However, given that the cumulative price of Russell 3000 stocks moves opposite to the realized value ahead of the news release, the "in-the-know" aggressive HFTs appear to be trading to their disadvantage.

Figure 7.23 shows aggressive HFT *buyer* participation around events where the realized value was higher than the forecast and lower than the forecast. As Figure 7.23 shows, in cases like this the aggressive HFT buyers are seen to account for a larger proportion of trading activity *after* the proper event announcement time. As seen in Figure 7.23, aggressive HFT accounts for about 1 percent more of trading activity after a higher-than-forecasted figures release than lower-than-forecasted figures release. Aggressive HFT buyers, however, account for a considerably *higher* participation before the announcement time when the announced news is higher than the forecast. This finding is consistent with the price movement ahead of news whereby the released figures are higher than the forecasted ones. It appears that aggressive HFTs are at least partially responsible for the consistent price drop/rise ahead of news whereby the realized numbers differ from the forecast.

How can this be the case? One hypothesis can be that the entities deploying aggressive HFT around the announcements prepare to maximize their profitability and volume traded on a given macro trade well ahead of the announcement. In the process, they assume that the forecast will come short of the realized value and overaccumulate stocks. Then, when the news is revealed to them or when they make their bets about the announcement, the aggressive HFT strategies sell off excess inventory to align their holdings with the expected post-announcement price, now easily quantifiable under the rational expectations hypothesis. The resulting strategy benefits the participating entities in two ways: (1) maximizes traded capital, and (2) helps avoid detection as the direction of preannouncement trading is reversed vis-à-vis the expected price direction given the announcement.

What are the implications of the aggressive HFT activity for market makers? Aggressive HFT flow is toxic and is best avoided from the market-making perspective. As a result, market makers may significantly improve their profitability around news announcements by explicitly tracking aggressive HFT behavior.

CONCLUSIONS

Whether news is being leaked or traders place their bets in advance, there is predictive value in studying market data in the 30 minutes before a macroeconomic news announcement.

What should investors do to minimize the impact of the news on their portfolios without the same access to the preferentially distributed embargoed information to? Tracking aggressive HFT may help make informed portfolio and market-making decisions when trading around macroeconomic news.

END OF CHAPTER QUESTIONS

1. What is news?
2. How is news distributed?
3. How does news impact markets in theory?
4. How does news impact markets in practice?
5. What are the key risk implications for investors?

CHAPTER 8

Social Media and the Internet of Things

—What is the funniest joke a trading program can make?

—Hello world.

The news that we see, read, and hear was traditionally chosen by editors based on its newsworthiness. Press releases allowed companies to share news that might not make it into a story. Today, the Internet takes over, with everyone, even inanimate objects, capable of broadcasting on the World Wide Web. Sponsored content sits next to news, and blogs by reporters and the public update continuously. The resulting content creates data series that, when processed in real time, can be used to derive valuable insights.

An event like the Brexit vote helps to illustrate the importance of social media and social media analytics to risk management. On June 24, 2016, the United Kingdom voted to withdraw from the European Union by a margin of 52 percent voting to "leave" to 48 percent voting to "remain." While polling leading up to the event was nearly even, polls had moved toward the "remain" camp in the final weeks. Such was the perceived sentiment regarding the outcome that the leaders of the "leave" camp were essentially conceding defeat even before the polls closed. As the votes were counted, the "leave" vote began to emerge, and as the evening wore on and all of the polling stations reported their results, "leave" proved to be the outcome. The following morning, the prime minister resigned and a period of political and economic uncertainty began.

Investment banks had ordered staff to be on notice for such an outcome and traded through the evening. The British pound fell to its lowest point since 1985, the year before financial deregulation saw the city of London emerge to be the financial capital of Europe. Instantly, it was unclear what would be the future for financial firms in a country that would be separate from Europe. What securities could be bought and sold in London? Would foreign staffers be welcome?

With the world watching this event, the instant change in the valuation of currencies and stocks is not surprising. The financial markets quickly assessed this vote as bad news. Additionally, the actions of politicians to quit the scene in the following days added to the uncertainty and to the turmoil in the markets.

What is interesting, however, is how some social media analytics firms were predicting a "leave" vote even in the face of largely "remain" coverage screaming from the media outlets. What was the secret of the prediction? The answer is the frequency of "leave" versus "remain" mentions. Apparently, "leave" news stories, however negative with respect to their subject, appeared much more frequently than "remain" news. Several research studies indicated that the popularity of a particular news item, not the underlying sentiment, is the strongest predictor of future value of the item.

Similarly, research shows that stocks that are mentioned most often on social media are not only likely to experience volatility, but also are about to rise. Why does this make sense? At a certain level, the "all publicity is good publicity" rule holds. According to the classical marketing theory, for a consumer or investor to buy into an asset, several things must take place in the following order: awareness, consideration, purchase, retention, and advocacy. Awareness develops independently of whether the attached sentiment is positive or negative. In fact, marketing research shows that many people, when building awareness, store a neutral sentiment in their brains. In the consideration stage, the prospects are evaluating whether or not to purchase

a product or a stock. At this stage, products that have higher awareness feel familiar, and are more desirable, independent of whether the sentiment that generates this awareness was good or bad. People appear to erase all judgment and only recall whether they have heard about a particular stock or idea before, and not whether what they heard was positive or negative.

In higher-level terms, however, the core answer to the question of why news distribution matters is "psychology," a field that never had a chance in finance until very recently. Until as little as 10 years ago, economists completely ignored the distribution of information and people's perceptions about it, including feelings, emotions, and reactions outside of the cold-hearted positive versus negative number-driven universe. While some research existed in the space of behavioral economics, it was largely considered to be a fringe activity. Available data-processing speeds also mattered: In the more traditional approach where people are making trades based on daily-data, intraday news was usually too short-term to matter. Finally, little data existed to study the actual diffusion of news and opinions—social media was just not as advanced as it is now, and many academic experiments involving people's perception and opinion formation in response to news simply lacked data.

In other disciplines, like electrical engineering and psychology itself, however, information diffusion has been studied for generations. Electrical engineering succeeded in quantifying the actual transmission properties of news and any other information in real and near-real time. Psychology has specialized in human processing of data, in-group versus out-of-group opinion formation and the like. With the data afforded by social media, finance academics are now joining their electrical engineering and psychology colleagues in droves to assess the ultimate holy grail of financial economics: exactly how does news make some market participants place their money on the line to buy or sell?

The psychology of finance now extends well beyond pure trading. Some recent studies show that regulators, political commentators, and even top politicians themselves are considerably influenced by social media, and not always for the better. Some researchers insist that psychology is even the root cause behind financial crises: people under stress are thought to make the markets irrational and, in extreme cases, nonexistent. (Ironically, the same researchers stop short of endorsing robots on the trading floor.)

The important aspect of today's social media "news" is its descriptive properties. Search engines and other databases archive not just the news itself but the source, the context, the reaction of commenters, the impact on the news readers (indexing such as "most viewed" or "trending" are examples), and the proliferation of news through the social network of primary readers—are all meticulously time stamped and organized.

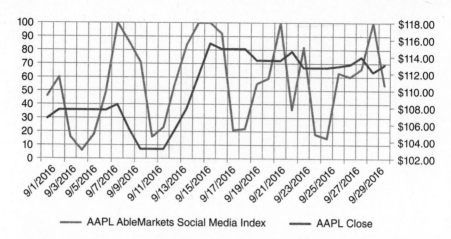

FIGURE 8.1   AAPL in social media leads AAPL closing prices.

AbleMarkets Social Media Index, for example, confirms these findings, as does Ravenpack in pure news. By counting news items ahead of Brexit, and finding that "leave" news items way outstripped "remain" stories, Ravenpack claims to have predicted the Brexit vote. Tracking the real-time mentions of specific financial instruments and keywords across a wide swath of social media, AbleMarkets Social Media Index is reliably predictive of short-term returns and volatility.

AbleMarkets Social Media Index tracks Internet discussions concerning individual financial instruments continuously, and is consistently leading changes in prices. Figure 8.1, for example, is showing the daily AbleMarkets Social Media Index for AAPL and the corresponding daily closing prices for AAPL. As the figure shows, APPL closing prices follow or lag AbleMarkets Social Media Index.

The impact of social media is, of course, palpable intraday in addition to the following day.

What properties are common to price changes that can be anticipated in social media? One property that is particularly pronounced across years of data signals is the stronger effect of social media news on smaller stocks. As multiple researchers point out, smaller stock prices are more likely to display social media reactions. After all, most investors are busy tracking the latest largest cap and SPY developments, leaving smaller stocks to fend for themselves. Thus, a "smaller stock" can be any stock outside of the S&P 100 range, not just a penny stock. As an illustration, Figure 8.2 presents AbleMarkets Social Media Index for VMware, Inc. (NYSE: VMW), and the increased predictability of price peaks is immediately apparent.

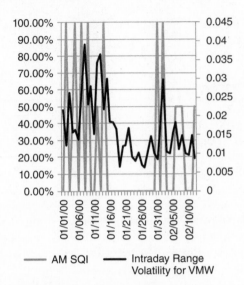

FIGURE 8.2 Normalized social media conversations, as measured by AbleMarkets Social Media Quotient (left axis) vs. same-day intraday range volatility for VMware (ticker VMW)

Some research goes further and weighs the social media spectrum by the subject matter credibility of the commentator. Computers score social media users, web sources, and blog publishers on the selected topic in a superficial performance attribution analysis. They ask questions like "how well did each commenter predict past developments?" This methodology allows researchers to identify the more likely sources of data. Thus, for instance, AbleMarkets has deselected Twitter from its source pool altogether in 2013 as it became a noisy source with little predictive value as a whole.

Can Twitter users be segmented into the better-informed and the chattering class? The tricky part of Twitter is its openness to programmatic interfaces. In other words, it is reasonably easy to create a software robot that will pluck content from the Internet and post it on Twitter. Why would one choose to do that without close supervision? Anecdotal evidence suggests that Twitter's human followers appreciate feeds with more voluminous and timely content, and they spend little time analyzing the quality and relevance of more distant posts. As a result, when analyzing Twitter, it is the machines that tend to fall into a trap. If you assume that all content is created by the same person (and not another robot randomly posting cursory-related items on one's twitter feed), the machines end up assigning arbitrary scores to Twitter participants.

SOCIAL MEDIA AND NEWS

The first iPhone was launched on June 29, 2007, and the world hasn't been the same since. The speed and convenience with which we now process information and communicate has created a new sense of urgency to understand and participate in further unbridled conversations, collectively known as social media.

Still, even social-media-savvy traders and investors cannot read and analyze hundreds of news items that may be simultaneously produced for a multitude of financial instruments across the markets. A category of sentiment analytics sprung up to help investors deal with the onslaught of information. Essentially, computers count the number of positive and negative words occurring in a news article or a social media post. In posts related to financial markets, positive words include "happy" words like *increase, expansion*, and *profit*. Negative words comprise terms like *losses, declining*, and *recession*, among many others. Companies like Ravenpack scan through entire dictionaries, classifying words into "positive," "negative," and "neutral" categories. The total sentiment is calculated as a score, awarding points to positive words and subtracting points whenever negative words are encountered. When the number of positive words in an article exceeds the number of negative words, the article is deemed to have a positive sentiment. When the opposite holds, the sentiment is considered to be negative. In addition to figuring out whether a given news story contains good or bad news, Ravenpack finds a place for the story in its vast classification database. Does the article contain references to "AAPL," the stock-market ticker for shares of Apple, Inc.? If yes, the Apple bin gets an added entry. Does the article talk about "macroeconomics"? If so, the macroeconomics column is updated to reflect the news addition. SENSE-News is another service that collects and semantically filters fundamental information about companies. SENSENews also looks at sentiment around the data and isolates 16 different investment criteria around the stocks it monitors.

Social media further affects the way people and machines read news. For example, machine processing of a streaming Dow Jones feed is interesting but may not be enough to qualify the reporter's understanding of the matter. That's where social media comes in. Scanning the website where the same Dow Jones article was published, and particularly zeroing in on the comments attached by often-anonymous users following the article, one may deduce a so-called *agreement score*. An agreement score is an independent crowd-sourced data point that indicates to what extent readers really value the content of the piece. Often, the comments turn out more insightful than the article itself—and the agreement score sheds light onto the reality of the article subject.

In the Internet-enabled world, all readers can express how they feel. Doing so is possible with abbreviations (LOL = laugh out loud) and "emoticons"—the cutesy little yellow faces often far from smiling, just to name a couple. However, many of these sources of human feelings may be misleading. LOL alone may refer to opposite emotions: happiness and sarcastic hostility. How do computers distinguish how people feel when they post?

Internet Sentiment: How Fintech Decides How You Are Feeling with Natural-Language Processing

The innovation causing computers to read text generates reams of unstructured data. And with the data, a question for researchers: if you could choose, which of the following options would you prefer?

1. Perform a large-scale analysis that involves reams and reams of data.
2. Type in a single question into a specialized search engine and let the engine do the analysis for you.

If you are like most people spoiled by the modern conveniences of Google, you would probably prefer option #2. The ability to understand a natural-language question and convert it into machine-readable instructions for an analysis is a field onto itself, and is known as natural language processing. This new discipline is at the heart of businesses like Kensho, backed by Google and Goldman Sachs.

Natural language processing (NLP) is not just limited to queries. Indeed, most of the advances of NLP are applied in the space of processing news articles, social media posts, and the like.

How does NLP work? The methodology can resemble sentiment analytics, but with its own quirks. Instead of maintaining tables separating positive words from negative words, NLP may instead maintain tables discriminating between positive and negative phrases. A phrase can be defined as a sequence of two or more words.

In addition, NLP researchers often assign probabilities that specific phrases will occur in natural language. When a phrase is used frequently than normal in a given piece of text, this alone may serve as a positive or negative indication of sentiment. NLP may similarly assign probabilities to the words following a specific phrase, and deduce sentiment based on what actually transpires. The study of NLP is complex and well developed in the field of Computer Science.

How does NLP work in practice? Most scientists begin the language-parsing process by removing punctuation and words like *the*. Twitter-like hashtags, searchable keywords preceded by "#" that are now popular on other social media like LinkedIn and Facebook, are converted to normal words with the hashtag removed. Next, all remaining characters are moved to lowercase for consistency, and so-called *terms*—technical items in natural language processing—are born.

Processing terms is no easy task. First, to reduce computer confusion, the words are "cleaned up"—most often reduced to the 7,315 words contained in the complete modified Harvard IV-4 dictionary. The remainder of text is often discarded. Some biases may result from this pruning operation alone. For instance, some financial slang, such as BOT and SLD which are old-school trading acronyms for bought and sold, do not make it through the Harvard filter, among many others.

Next, some researchers choose to perform *stemming*—a procedure whereby all remaining words are reduced to their stem. Stemming may or may not work, depending on the end application. Separating positive and negative words often removes prefixes necessary for understanding the sentiment like "de-," "un-," "pro-," and so on. For example, stemming delivers equal-probability positive/negative estimates for words like *communication* (normally, positive) and *ex-communicated* (negative sentiment).

The words, taken in sequence, are next subjected to Latent Semantic Analysis (LSA)—a principal component analysis of sentences that determines the most relevant terms in the data pool. The idea behind the technique is that the text about a particular subject contains a large number of synonyms of the subject itself. The output "needles in the hay" form the basis for classification of the given opinion piece. In addition, *clustering* techniques can subsequently be used to find related articles, messages, or tweets to map a comprehensive media sentiment across various media channels.

Finally, the machines arrive at the final classification of sentiment, and here the algos follow one of two paths preferred by their human masters: "supervised" or "unsupervised" learning. Supervised learning really refers to learning by the book—the machines are provided dictionaries of positive and negative words, against which the outputs of LSA and clustering are screened. The unsupervised learning lets machines run wild in their own universe, delivering clusters of key data outputs. While the process may seem elaborate, it may take as little as a few microseconds from raw data to finished output, given proper machine configuration.

Are machines making bulletproof decisions on the news? Not always. A classic counterexample to artificial intelligence is a 2008 case of the following nature. An individual looks up an article in the *Orlando Sentinel* in the middle of the night, at 1:36 AM on Sunday, September 7, 2008. The article, written six years prior in 2002, detailed that United Airlines may file for bankruptcy. Surprisingly, the old article made the "most viewed" list at the *Orlando Sentinel*, and was picked up by Google as a trending story. Next, a Bloomberg reporter in search of content looks up the Google trend index, ignores the article's publication date, and instead writes a current article about the imminent bankruptcy of United Airlines. Markets open, and the United Airlines stock plunges 76 percent (!) before recovering by the end of the trading day, when the news was disentangled and straightened out. Of course, in this story, it was really a person, not a machine, making the final mistake. However, the computer-generated risks of similar nature exist.

Where does social media evolve from here? The technology is already here to track not just what you type, but how you type it as well. The current frontier in sentiment analytics is parsing what you type in your reader comments. Basic, very fast, and accessible technologies like HTML5 already allow website designers to track and record how fast you type (a potential indicator of the strength of your emotions), how and where you move your computer mouse on screen, where you click, and so on. While you may take the information you read onscreen for granted, there is a price to pay in giving up your personal feelings and related data, and the price will only become more expensive day by day, as more and more data will be gathered and analyzed by the websites you visit.

Government Data

Social media helps make macroeconomic figures that much more accessible. Why should a researcher wait for the summary of the latest trends observed by the government compiled monthly by a team of government staffers? Why can't financial researchers themselves access the granular data as it becomes available to the government?

New York City is one of the first cities in the world to open much of the data it archives to the public. Available at https://nycopendata.socrata.com, the data contain over 1,600 time series, including noise complaints, taxi service, parking tickets, and more. What good is this information to someone whose job is to deduce the state of the economy? Take parking tickets, for example. While an individual ticket might not signify much, the aggregate changes in parking tickets may serve as an indicator of the economic health of New York City. More parking tickets may reflect the increases in parking shortages, which, in turn, is indicative of more demand for parking spaces, more consumer demand, and, ultimately, higher consumer confidence levels. Naturally, creativity, data analysis skills, and understanding of economics are required to translate seemingly obscure data into actionable economics signals.

Take trash, for instance. It has long been known that one man's trash is another man's treasure, but in the age of big data, the statement takes on a new meaning. It can be shown that NYC trash, and Manhattan's trash in particular, can be indicative of the impending economic changes. Thus, an increase in Manhattan's trash reliably predicts a decline in the S&P 500 as far as three months later. The predictive power may be due to corporate downsizing: trash generated by liquidating offices may only translate into the S&P 500 prices three months later. Whatever the relationship, it is statistically significant and can be used to generate profitability. At least one multibillion-dollar hedge fund has a group devoted to analyzing and processing NYC data to generate incremental returns!

Timeliness of Data Analysis

The key to successfully using any sort of data is timely analysis. Take the NYC trash data, for example. Who reaps the rewards from the information? Usually, it is the person who obtains the data first and is the most capable of deriving conclusions from it.

With real-time tasks come real-time risks. Government data, for instance, are notoriously prone to revisions and updates. Social media data may be subject to Internet outages, malicious hacks, and other activity that puts a dent into objective data handling. Even the Internet of things data may become corrupted: what if the chip-reading sensors fail?

How does one manage risks like that? The answers may boil down to:

1. Redundancies
2. Increased data sampling pools
3. Averaging

Redundancy refers to multiple copies, often of literally everything from data sources, databases, power, to processors. Redundancy helps deal with temporary outages by transferring the load temporarily to an alternate solution, while the primary (failing) solution is awaiting recovery. If and when a key node in the data acquisition and processing chain should fail, the system enters a "fail-over" mode whereby the rest of the units engage and take over the load. The fail-over essentially defines what has become known as a cloud with all the complexity abstracted to the user.

Increasing the sources of data helps with redundancy. Suppose you harvest all of your data from the NYC website and the NYC mayor decides to unilaterally shut the data website down, tearing your business to shreds. Planning for situations like this involves robust number of parallel data sources that can be used together to determine a given outcome. Then, should one of the data sources disappear, the business will not stop, but will continue with other data inputs.

To further minimize the risk of disappearing data sources, multiple related data inputs can be treated as independent samples and ultimately combined into an average. Techniques vary from using rudimentary arithmetic averages to more sophisticated weighted versions. The resulting average will sustain the production of your analysis and diffuse the impact of the missing source should one of the underlying sources disappear.

Some readers may roll their eyes at the mention of averages. However, averaging and the underlying sampling are gaining increased attention in today's world where the amount of available data is outrageous. Take Twitter studies, for instance. Many researchers writing about Twitter's significance don't analyze every single tweet, as Twitter messages are called. Instead, they select 10 to 20 percent of the message universe, sampled in a way that is representative of the Twitter's true much larger universe. Done correctly, this technique helps derive meaningful inferences from mountains of data in a fast and productive manner.

THE INTERNET OF THINGS

Some 30 years ago, the Internet barely existed. People communicated using telephones and whirring fax machines, and the latter were so common that Manhattan ran out of 212 area code numbers. Since then, the Internet became not just widely available, but also a necessity for many. Forget millennials—you can see modern two-year-olds demanding to use iPhones from their parents!

As a result, the Internet has changed the way people do things, including how they trade, receive, and process news, and even game the system. This section discusses the resulting fintech disruptions.

Some social media is tailored to finance. Investors share their perspectives on certain chat sites that are dedicated to them. Chat rooms on Bloomberg, Twitter, or on websites created a new source of information and perspective on the reactions of traders to news. Social media evolved as well to having sites that polled investor sentiment and do so more and more frequently. Twitter created an ongoing stream of posts that could label and categorize names of companies.

Still, the world is filled with meaningful data that falls outside of traditional investment analysis. For instance, pricing information on comparable products is a big factor in detailed fundamental analysis, but such data was typically not readily available until recently. With the expansion of fintech, companies like ThinkNum deliver competitive intelligence by visiting thousands of retail websites at once, compiling product and pricing information. The information is then aggregated and converted into pricing and supply and demand benchmarks, and is used by investment professionals to gauge relative advantage of particular firms.

The process of accessing the websites electronically and recording the content of what humans normally see even has its own technical term: *scraping*. Of course, the scraped web interfaces are not completely oblivious to the advantage that scrapers receive from the posted data. The web interface providers, in turn, take measures to restrict scraping by identifying machine or repeat behavior. This cat-and-mouse game is complex, and successful scraping requires oodles of effort to deploy.

Tracking Shipments, Fleets, and Supplies in Real Time

The intelligence relevant to investment analysis is not limited to entries posted on the Internet. Many of the key figures, like supply and demand numbers traditionally assessed through polls and surveys, can now be reliably aggregated from the merchandise itself.

Take, for example, universal product codes (UPCs) we are completely accustomed to—bar codes attached to virtually everything we buy, and scan at the cash register for easy processing. By now, many items shipped or stored also contain their own radio-frequency identifiers (RFIDs). An RFID is a "smart" UPC. Each RFID is a tiny electronic device that, when in the range of a radio-frequency reader, reflects to the reader its unique identifier information. Most RFIDs are passive devices, in that they do not require their own energy source. Instead, the devices are activated by the energy transmitted by the RFID readers. Much of this technology was invented for the purposes of being undetectable in spying devices during the Cold War. Since they typically don't contain a power source, RFIDs emit no heat until activated by the RFID reader, and are, therefore, undetectable by conventional device scanners under most circumstances. Without a power source makes these devices long-lived, potentially lasting indefinitely, and costless to maintain—there is no need to replace batteries or provide air conditioning. Aside from accidental breakage, the modern RFIDs are weather- and tampering-proof, and are manufactured on a large scale.

RFIDs are not a rare species. Every time you buy new clothes or walk through a modern US pharmacy, you encounter RFIDs embedded in boxes of most items as deterrents to theft (the devices are activated by the scanners at the exit to the store and set off the alarms, unless previously deactivated at the cash register). While the devices are commonplace, it's the emerging ability to collect and to use this information that is innovative.

The best part of RFIDs is that the information they contain, as well as their geospatial coordinates, can be continuously scanned and stored. This information can be subsequently mined for various applications: Amazon uses RFIDs to optimize its warehouse shelf stocking, farms track livestock movements, and fleets follow the locations of their containers.

For financial professionals, all of these databases translate into information-driven profits. The data on warehouse movements can be distilled into relative demand figures for IBM products versus those of Intel, for example. The quantities and movement of livestock allow for more accurate commodity futures pricing. Shipping container movements not only predict the financial health of shipping companies but also of fuel demand and a host of auxiliary products and services.

And the RFIDs are only bound to proliferate further, creating vast pools of information on moving cargo, cars, and other objects.

In addition, RFIDs and similar sensors allow us to build smart devices that continuously report to us their condition. For instance, a bridge built with smart cement (cement with embedded chips) can inform us of important cracks and other structural problems, before any major problems occur. For financial analysis, this translates into a new universe of previously unattainable data helping determine valuation of cement companies and the like.

The Internet of things (IoT) is only getting started. According to industry analysis, only 8 percent of businesses are using more than a quarter of the IoT data they generate. The opportunity for revenue growth from IoT is tremendous—consumers expect their smartphones to do more in an IoT-enabled world and are ready to pay for it; development tools for IoT are continuously streamlined and simplified, and regulation is coming of age to prevent IoT abuses.

Internet of Things Adoption

What IoT devices are coming online in the near future? How about 300 million utility meters, 150 million cars, 1 million vineyard acres, to start?[1]

---

[1]Verizon, Oxford Economics, "State of the Market: Internet of Things 2016," http://www.verizon.com/about/our-company/state-of-the-market-internet-of-things.

The upcoming widespread adoption of IoT across all consumer segments is anticipated due the following five trends in the markets:

1. Smartphone expectations
2. Businesses using more data
3. Regulatory facilitation of IoT
4. Advanced network connectivity
5. Better network security

Many people today live and die by their phone—buzzing text messages, video calls, and a slew of other features. Phone companies compete with one another on the latest gleaming app waiting to induce millions of consumers to ditch their existing device in search of the newest, shiniest item. As such, phone users expect their phones to deliver increasingly more of everything: Turn on the heat in the house, please, and don't forget to water the plants when the soil is dry—are just a few of the basic examples of what is now possible to do remotely over the phone. The benefits generated by devices such as home automation are tremendous, and industries like advertising can use them to create not just targeted ads but targeted lifestyle solutions. Financial companies may, in turn, use the data to better understand consumer trends, predict supply and demand, and forecast the prospects of industries.

Similarly, businesses are prompted to examine the data they generate and take better care of the information. Many businesses are now studying how they can use their own data. From reorganizing shelves to selecting appropriate floor surfaces to tailoring lighting in their employee environments, businesses are able to incrementally improve performance and drive profitability using IoT. Also, IoT helps businesses better understand the usage of their products and build ever more sophisticated offerings.

Tracking user information with IoT, of course, is something that needs to be strictly regulated. Where do we draw a line on privacy in an environment where IoT information is emanating from countless user devices? As regulation of IoT evolves, it is bound to clarify and facilitate all aspects of IoT.

Network connectivity is projected to evolve to support more data, faster, more reliably, and at a lower cost and energy requirements. Already, the buzz is all about 5G—the fifth generation of cell phone technology that promises to deliver interconnected self-driving cars, robots for multiple uses, as well as virtual reality on your phone.

Finally, security is continuously evolving to deliver protection to billions of device users across the globe. The more secure the devices, the more trust businesses and consumers will place into operating them, and the more useful the data output will be.

IoT is on the rise, and it is here to stay. While the beginnings of IoT were largely supported by early adopters, by now IoT is a recognized force across industries and enterprise scales. And business-oriented IoT is apparently growing much faster than IoT for consumers—after all, the gain to business productivity can be large-scale and simply phenomenal, while the people's adoption of IoT may take a while and be much more incremental in scope and value. Of course, financial companies have noticed and are already processing IoT data in search of an investment edge.

How does someone acquire the Internet of things data? There are numerous ways to do so. First, new technology allows for the direct identification of every single shipment and every piece of merchandise. Thanks to bar codes, every mailed item can be tracked online. The data about the origin of an item and the customer who buys it can be also sold to third-party data distributors, enabling end users to analyze and derive inferences about various aspects of the economy way ahead of formal monthly and quarterly indicators. Also, consumer-tracking data are backed directly by consumer orders and dollars, and not just by consumer opinions given to cold-calling survey operators. As a result, observations of consumer purchases (what consumers actually do) are much more credible than what they say.

Other firms collect and sell data displayed on the Internet. In our age of electronic commerce, pretty much every firm has a website that displays its mode of operation, product descriptions, and, often, prices. This information can be collected and used for competitive analysis, and in finance, for fundamental analysis and cash projections for each entity. Complex computer programs are built to "scrape" and distill the information in a fast and efficient manner.

Such analysis is hardly new: In the past, consulting companies chartered planes to fly over factories and count the number of shipping containers as an indicator of supply and demand generated by a particular manufacturer. Today, such analysis can be performed at a fraction of a cost by analyzing satellite imagery with image-recognition software, often involving neural networks.

CONCLUSIONS

Social media and the Internet of things disrupt the traditional model of how information is disseminated. The news about supply and demand of individual businesses or commodities, for instance, is no longer confined to quarterly reports, expensive consulting surveys, and newspaper articles. Instead, the news is generated continuously with smart devices and people. Computers process the news in real time or near real time and incorporate it into the markets. Whoever does not possess this new class of information risks being left behind.

END OF CHAPTER QUESTIONS

1. How is social media changing the financial landscape?
2. What is a news sentiment? How is it determined?
3. What is the Internet of things?
4. Which industries produce Internet of things content?
5. What risks do investors face with social media and the Internet of things?

CHAPTER 9

Market Volatility in the Age of Fintech

—Why does a risk control bot have a reputation as a terminator?

—It terminates trading bots.

Minimizing volatility is important to investment managers focused on capital preservation. After all, lower volatility helps protect capital and improve the key portfolio performance metric, the Sharpe ratio. This ratio, average annualized return divided by annualized volatility, becomes acceptable in the 1.8 range. The higher the Sharpe ratio, the better, and the sky is the limit. Some high-frequency trading funds produce Sharpe ratios as high as 20. Even very small positive returns can produce large Sharpe ratios that attract investors, but only if the volatility of the portfolio is tiny.

Volatility can also be considered a stand-alone phenomenon, something most investors seek to limit. Indeed, investors often talk about minimizing their "exposure" to the markets for individual asset classes, sectors, and across financial instruments in their portfolios (correlation exposure or dispersion exposure). Such volatility-related exposure management is topical across the entire fintech spectrum. Cross-border payment companies need to limit their exposure to exchange rate fluctuations. Real-time insurance outfits need to engage volatility stabilizers to protect their assets against the same shocks as those that may affect their clients.

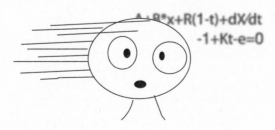

$A+B^*x+R(1-t)+dX/dt$

$-1+Kt-e=0$

Traditional businesses also need to worry about their volatility exposure in the age of rapid "you snooze, you lose" dynamics. Flash crashes, news, and social media, among other issues, affect portfolios in real time, and old-fashioned hedging techniques and passive diversification are not always sufficient to protect portfolio managers from instant problems. Tracking real-time risk can also help thousands of businesses reduce their regulatory capital requirements by upgrading their risk tier. Banks, in particular, can significantly improve their balance sheets if they take care of volatility in their holdings in real-time and near-real-time space. Loan portfolio managers and even the Fed can substantially benefit from a firm grip on intraday volatility. Valuations of corporate bonds and their private-sector equivalents are subject to marketwide, industrywide, and company-cohort-related fluctuations. Entities like the Federal Reserve lend banks money securitized by their equity holdings, which are directly affected by real-time risk. As this chapter shows, even the longest-term buy-and-hold portfolio managers gain from understanding real-time risk in their portfolios. After all, real-time risks directly translate into long-term risk, which makes its way into risk premia, portfolio inter-security correlations, and subsequent diversification solutions.

Most investors are trying to minimize volatility, if not in absolute terms, then in terms of volatility related to the returns. Minimizing volatility is a challenging task. In a nutshell, to minimize volatility, one needs to take three steps:

1. Identify the conditions that result in high volatility.
2. Correctly predict when the conditions identified in step 1 are about to occur in the near future.
3. Select an action for managing this volatility. The appropriate actions may include trimming riskier portfolio holdings, or counterbalancing the offending instruments with offsetting or protective financial instruments, such as futures or options.

Much of the research of the 1980s and 1990s focused on managing volatility with a single approach for all market conditions. By designing all-weather securities that can be bought once and held passively until the securities' expiration (as is the case with futures and options), the new breed of financial engineers advanced portfolio frontiers, and also generated much excitement. For example, collar options protected against too much downward as well as upward movement in portfolio value. Other exotic derivatives helped manage changes in interest rates, oil prices, and things like weather changes in Florida to mitigate the resulting swings in orange juice.

With time, many of the all-weather securities proved to be imperfect, failing to protect their owners' portfolios when it mattered most, typically in extreme market conditions. Does anyone remember Enron? Many smaller investment firms toppled like dominoes in the market crises of the early 2000, and seemingly unending lawsuits followed. Those who bought exotic securities sued issuers and underwriters of options for misleading them about one aspect of the package or another. The bottom line is that all-weather strategies did not hold water against extreme events.

For a while, people tried to address the issue by deploying theories about extreme events and modeling the unlikely *black swans*. However, modeling proved to be too difficult and unrealistic, and the extreme events too rare and unusual to be forecasted with ease. New solutions have to be found and deployed.

In a pretty simple form, premium data came to play since the late 2000s. As a complete surprise to some, premium or "uncommon" data sources have emerged carrying previously unthinkable information. Highly granular and real-time information found its way onto sophisticated portfolio managers' desktops: from the data about the cars shipped from factories to dealerships collected by companies like ThinkNum.com, to the composition of orders placed online for particular products by ReturnPath.com, to the number of high-frequency traders operating in the markets by AbleMarkets.com.

This front-line information, collected and channeled directly from the source to portfolio managers, has been made possible by the evolution in technology. The Internet has enabled software programmers to scan previously disorganized data sources to draw value through synthesizing information into meaningful inferences, directly predictive of near-term market conditions. The technological advances in computing themselves have enabled firms to deliver the data in a super-fast (often, real-time), reliable, and, above all, inexpensive fashion.

How does this uncommon data help to manage portfolio volatility? Acquiring the data is only the first step in the process. Next comes the understanding of how and how far in advance the particular data are able to detect the onset of certain market conditions, and the most appropriate financial engineering approaches are selected for each market condition. Then, when the reliability of prediction is firmly established, the streaming data are deployed to raise warnings about one market condition or another, and the previously chosen volatility mitigation method is quickly deployed to safeguard one's portfolio.

Welcome to the new data-driven world. Whether data-enhanced portfolio management is revolutionary or evolutionary, it is no longer optional, but mandatory for sound portfolio management.

TOO MUCH DATA, TOO LITTLE TIME—WELCOME, PREDICTIVE ANALYTICS

Most investors would like to understand the drivers of performance of their portfolios in order to incrementally improve their allocation decisions. One way to identify what is truly behind their portfolios' returns is to compare the performance of portfolios vis-à-vis benchmarks.

In the past, available benchmarks were few and far between, easily manageable in one Excel spreadsheet. In the last decade, the number of data sources a responsible portfolio manager needs to take into account have multiplied dramatically, requiring databases and dedicated staff to manage the data and to analyze it in a reasonable time. An alternative to buying and processing more and more data for traditional regression and attribution models is to delegate the data aggregation and storage powers to a new industry, predictive analytics.

Predictive analytics comprise advanced big data models. They allow scientists to create algorithms capable of answering questions far more complex than traditional regressions or segmentation frameworks. These algorithms cut through the nontrivial task of making sense of mountains of fundamental data by providing an index that answers a question. Advances in data science allow real-time processing of a massive, previously unthinkable, amount of data. For instance, many investors and traders charged with execution want to avoid trading when aggressive high-frequency algorithms are present. Companies like AbleMarkets now tease out aggressive HFT from streaming data and show in real time when to speed up trading and when to slow it down. Such technology, unthinkable just a decade ago, is now not only feasible but available to all to use.

Predictive analytics transform data into insight. Portfolio managers use performance attribution to explain why a portfolio's performance differed from the benchmark. This review of historical trading attempts to distinguish which of the two factors of portfolio performance, superior stock selection or superior market timing, is the source of the portfolio's overall performance.

However, the past is not necessarily an indicator of the future. Looking at a static benchmark does not necessarily capture the full picture of what is happening in the markets. AbleMarkets uses an approach of continuously reviewing the markets for indications that there is an opportunity to trade, whether because of changes in sentiment or because some aspect of a market's microstructure that is highly predictive of either price movement or changes in volatility. The analysis generates an index and these indexes help to guide trading decisions.

Research on volatility is well-positioned for fintech advances. At the time this book was written, the equity space alone boasted 9,000+ underlying financial instruments, each with 100+ open options contracts with considerable movement in some options' order books. As a representative statistic, the size of a binary file summarizing option activity in the US markets for just one exchange and one trading day often exceeds 100 GB of computer storage space. To put this number into perspective, consider that sophisticated Apple laptops come with just 250 GB of hard-drive storage.

A risk-management platform called ICEBERG, designed by Professor Marco Avellaneda of NYU and approved for risk capital calculations by the SEC and OCC, takes data for the entire universe of financial instruments and processes it at lightning speed to derive correct volatility curves in a matter of minutes. This operation still takes most contemporary practitioners days and months to produce using previous methods. The resulting data can be used to successfully predict volatility over the medium timespans, allowing portfolio managers, risk managers, and execution traders to hedge their positions in a scientific, cost-effective way.

What is so different about Avellaneda's methodology? In part, it is intelligent data sampling, discussed elsewhere in this book. Utilizing the latest digital imaging techniques, Avellaneda is able to reduce the computational times to their minima, while still preserving the integrity of inferences. Advanced mathematics in the form of principal component analysis (PCA) and, finally, Monte Carlo simulation come in later. Taken altogether, and deployed in a cloud, the method reduces week long processes into mere seconds, all while delivering higher accuracy and predictability.

WANT TO LESSEN VOLATILITY OF FINANCIAL MARKETS? EXPRESS YOUR THOUGHTS ONLINE!

In the last year or so, stock prices have been moving drastically up and down, a phenomenon known as *market volatility*. The latest research from AbleMarkets shows that investors can help reduce intraday volatility by collectively expressing their opinions about a stock's imminent direction on social media. By speaking up online, investors appear to speed up the formation of market consensus and the resulting price adjustment, minimizing price volatility in the process.

Social media continuously updates our collective knowledge of financial markets. As discussed in Chapter 8, investors posting online about their thoughts and experiences with a particular publicly traded firm may encourage others to consider investing into the stock of that company. Latest research shows that the aggregate volume of social media commentary may make an impact not just on the price but also on the volatility of a particular stock. This section summarizes the results of analysis using the AbleMarkets Social Media Index, an aggregate of Internet mentions of companies on a variety of platforms. The index, running since 2009, deploys a complicated custom-built technology to continuously poll a vast proprietary universe of social media sites. Twitter is expressly not part of that universe of websites.

As the analysis shows, overall, increased social media activity related to a particular company during a 24-hour period on a given trading day leads to higher stock volatility on that day. However, more social media activity *during* market hours results in *lower* volatility of discussed stocks. This phenomenon may be a product of social media's efficiency in distributing news and the news' subsequent incorporation into stock prices. Increasing social media discussion about a particular company seems to result in the consensus being reached faster. Social media discussions from 4 PM ET until 4 AM ET, however, are highly predictive of the next trading day's volatility.

Research shows that when people discuss their beliefs online, they make their previously private information public, stabilizing the markets. The phenomenon is consistent with academic theories of finance. One of the theories, the efficient market hypothesis, was first posited by Eugene Fama of University of Chicago in the 1970s, long before the Internet existed as we know it today. According to Fama's thinking, if everyone's knowledge and beliefs were available for everyone else to see, prices would reach steady levels almost immediately following any news.

Can one individual's contributions to social media really calm down the markets? As with all social media, strength is in the numbers—the more that people decide to share their thoughts, the faster the market will reach a consensus of the appropriate price level.

MARKET MICROSTRUCTURE IS THE NEW FACTOR IN PORTFOLIO OPTIMIZATION

Understanding market microstructure is traditionally thought to aid execution traders and market makers, the two types of intraday financial practitioners continuously interfacing the markets. The market's microstructure is not usually considered to be a variable in long-term portfolio optimization. However, the latest research shows that long-only managers ignore the market microstructure effects at the expense of their clients' portfolios.

Adding market microstructure as a factor into the methodology of rebalancing a portfolio improves the Sharpe ratio for any long-only portfolio.

As discussed in Chapter 3, in broad terms, the science of market microstructure examines in minute detail the evolution of the orders and matches that occur in exchanges' limit order books. A limit order book is a central marketplace for any given financial instrument—a stock, futures contract, bond, foreign exchange rate, or an option. Limit order books have been shown to be universally superior tools to match buy and sell orders in finance. The order matching process that occurs in each limit order book is somewhat similar to the matching of produce and customers at a grocery store:

1. The grocers desiring fixed prices place their merchandise on shelves of the store. In financial lingo, the fixed-priced wait-for-customer merchandise displays are known as limit orders.
2. The customers who want merchandise right away and at the best available price pick the merchandise off the shelves. The right-away customers use what in finance is known as market orders to accomplish their purpose.
3. Exchanges ring up (match) the orders, making the transaction official.

Market microstructure deals with the all aspects of order shelving (who gets the best display space?), customer arrivals (when do most customers arrive? which customers have the biggest budgets?), and similar issues. In the process, market microstructure incorporates topics like high-frequency trading and runaway algorithms.

Most of the market microstructure activity is sticky. Typically, dynamics persist from one day to the next, even though in the very short term variability can be significant. As a result, phenomena such as volatility and risks associated with microstructure lend themselves well to extrapolation in the near future on the scale of days and weeks.

Market microstructure does little to predict long-term returns, but it works in predicting intraday risks. Long-term portfolio management concerns itself with increasing returns of investments while minimizing risks. By accounting for the market microstructure risk, long-only portfolio managers can reduce volatility and significantly improve the performance of their portfolios. For example, by adjusting the relative weights in their portfolios by the proportion of aggressive HFTs present in the markets, portfolio managers can optimize portfolio performance.

In addition to the risks associated with HFT, understanding market microstructure can help predict flash crashes days ahead, minimize slippage when placing trades, and, of course, predict short-term price movements in the markets. All of these features help improve portfolio performance even for the largest-scale pension funds and hedge funds.

Why hasn't market microstructure become important sooner? First, the data required for market microstructure analysis used to be scarce. Few organizations archived tick-by-tick data beyond the 21-day time frame mandated by the regulators. Second, computing was too slow and too expensive to make market microstructure analyses economical. Third, transaction costs used to be hundreds of times higher just a decade ago, making gains from market microstructure comparatively negligible. Today, in the markets with razor-thin profits, every penny and even basis point (1 percent of 1 percent) count.

Of course, market microstructure analysis is not trivial and requires an extensive understanding of issues underlying modern market dynamics. Also, markets do not stand still. Innovations in order routing, exchange and other trading venue configurations, and pre-trade and post-trade risk analytics affect market microstructure and many associated models. Staying on top of modern innovation in the markets is much more than a simple job. However, incorporating the market microstructure analytics into financial decisions is no longer an option but a requirement for sound portfolio management.

YES, YOU CAN PREDICT $T + 1$ VOLATILITY

One can predict volatility at least one day ahead ($T + 1$ basis) by examining the microstructure elements that have been shown to make financial instruments prone to extreme volatility. Three dimensions that are uncorrelated aspects of market microstructure include:

1. Market "jitteriness" for a single financial instrument—a.k.a., market runs in technical lingo
2. Propensity for downward volatility for a single financial instrument
3. Likelihood of a market-wide pandemic

Both the market jitteriness dimension and the market's intrinsic volatility predict $T + 1$ volatility. Taken together, the two dimensions deliver insight on whether specific equities are prone to crashes.

For instance, AbleMarkets' marketwide crash predictor can be based on aggregating market microstructure-driven volatility parameters into a marketwide indicator. The index delivers considerable predictive power for intraday crashes, also known as flash crashes. Table 9.1 shows performance of the $T + 1$ index values versus realized daily (Low − Open)/Open return for the SPDR S&P ETF (NYSE: SPY).

The market microstructure effects captured by this index build up gradually leading up to a crash. As a result, it detects flash crash conditions up to several days in advance, and allows clients to liquidate large positions ahead of the crash, if desired.

TABLE 9.1 AbleMarkets Flash Crash Index, Predictability of T+1 Downward Volatility

AbleMarkets EFCI threshold	Mean NYSE:SPY (Low-Open)/Open	Std Dev NYSE:SPY (Low-Open)/Open	Count
>0.05	−0.0043	0.0041	155
>0.25	−0.0044	0.0041	151
>0.5	−0.0050	0.0046	61
>0.6	−0.0059	0.0052	27
>0.7	−0.0110	0.0052	5
>0.8	−0.0174	N/A	1

Table 9.1 shows its performance out-of-sample $T + 1$ performance for the second half of 2014. As Table 9.1 illustrates, the Index is highly sensitive to impending crashes, and produced an especially high crash warning (0.84) one day ahead the infamous crash of October 15, 2014.

It can be used to trade volatility, hedge exposure ahead of marketwide crashes, and improve intraday execution. Here is a summary of use cases:

1. *Trading volatility.* When indexes predict high volatility the following trading day, a trader may choose to buy a straddle on the underlying asset. Conversely, when indexes predict low volatility, a trader may choose to buy an option butterfly on the underlying asset.
2. *Hedging market exposure.* When AbleMarkets predicts a high probability of a marketwide flash crash the following trading day, a portfolio manager may choose to hedge his portfolio's exposure to the broader markets by, for example, buying out-of-the-money put options on the S&P 500 and its ETFs.
3. *Improve intraday execution.* When indexes predict high volatility in an individual asset, an execution trader may choose to use a more passive execution algorithm to capture better prices via limit orders. When the AbleMarkets marketwide index predicts a marketwide crash, the execution trader with a mandate to sell an instrument may choose to speed up his execution algo to avoid selling in a potential crash later in the day. This nets about 30 percent per annum extra out of sample in AbleMarkets studies.

MARKET MICROSTRUCTURE AS A FACTOR? YOU BET.

As most portfolio managers are well aware, the valuation of financial instruments no longer depends on single-factor models, such as Dodd-Graham NPV valuation. While aspiring Warren Buffetts of the world may have an occasional win, the markets have grown to be too complex to depend on simple cash-flow projections. In equities, for example, decade-old studies have shown that when the market as a whole goes up, some stocks may go up according to the Dodd-Graham valuation forecasts, while others may go down. However, when markets drop, many investors choose to cut their losses by liquidating their holdings, forcing all stocks with good and bad financial projections down the market drain.

How can portfolio managers navigate such treacherous waters? A popular way that has been a trend on the street for years is to layer screens or signals of disparate well-performing valuation techniques in order to develop precise, well-timed signals about financial instruments' impending moves.

As an investor, you feel it, you know it: Some stocks tend to have more intraday volatility than other stocks. Some stocks are specifically more prone to flash crashes than others. Some stocks have higher aggressive high-frequency trading (HFT) participation than other stocks. At this point in financial innovation, no savvy portfolio manager can afford to ignore intraday risk, and, instead, must make it an integral part of his portfolio selection model.

Why do intraday dynamics need to enter portfolio selection models? Can't portfolio managers simply ride out the intraday ups and downs in their pursuit of longer-term goals? The answer is yes, but at a considerable cost. As the latest AbleMarkets.com research indicates, aggressive HFT participation and flash crashes are "sticky" and change slowly from one month to the next, not to mention from one day to another. Understanding which securities are prone to flash crashes can help avoid unnecessary stop losses. Avoiding financial instruments with high aggressive HFT participation can save double-digit percentage costs in execution.

Why do metrics like aggressive HFT and flash crash probabilities persist in given stocks? The answer can be found in modern market microstructure. The microstructure phenomena such as aggressive HFT participation are directly linked to the automation of financial markets. As trading becomes increasingly electronic, many financial market participants build proprietary computer programs to obtain a cutting edge in the markets. The programs are time-consuming and costly to build, and successive iterations take months and even years. As a result, the intraday dynamics remain stable over long time horizons and may differ significantly from one security to the next.

Why would market participants choose to build and run programs for some financial instruments, but not others? The answer has three parts:

1. Cost of historical data
2. Cost of interpreting historical data
3. Processing power restrictions

Building a profitable trading algorithm requires a considerable investment in highly granular, and, as a result, voluminous data. Data can be very expensive to buy and also to store. Major data companies sell historical data for tens and hundreds of thousands of dollars. Just one day of highly granular data containing individual orders from a major exchange takes up 5 GB of space—the data storage space that can hold more than 1,000 high-resolution digital photos. Given the data costs, trading developers may choose to acquire data for only a selected set of securities, paving the way to persistent discrepancies in microstructure among various financial instruments.

Making sense of data is perhaps the most expensive part of the process. New data-based ideas are hard to come by, and capable data scientists are in high demand and command premium compensation. Even the seemingly basic tasks of retrieving the data and structuring it in a computer database can be an expensive process requiring numerous hours of computer programming. The disparity of data standards among various data providers and financial products make the basic tasks of reading file names very complex.

Even when the data are acquired, properly stored, opened, and turned into successful models, the majority of data-related costs may still lie ahead. To ascertain model performance, the model needs to run on at least one year (most often, two years) of historical data, requiring advanced computer power. Once the backtests are completed and the models are verified to work (80 percent of models will fail), the costs are just about to ramp up. In trading "production" environment, the vast volumes of streaming data need to be received, captured, processed, stored, and turned into trading communication. To capture the full range of data, one needs to invest not just into advanced computer processing power, or hardware, but also into advanced network architecture and data centers, as well as physical network equipment such as fast network switches and physical communication like microwave networks.

As a result, once a working electronic trading approach has been developed and deployed, it can be extremely costly to change. As long as the systems remain profitable, they are typically left online. This, in turn, leads to great persistence in market microstructure in each individual financial instrument. The microstructure dynamics, however, may differ considerably from one financial instrument to the next.

For example, as AbleMarkets.com research shows, in the equities space, Google Inc. Class A stock (NASDAQ:GOOGL) had the highest participation of aggressive HFTs among all the S&P 500 stocks in 2014. Switching investment activity from GOOGL to GOOG, Class C shares of the same company, lowers aggressive HFT participation by 1 percent of volume, reducing trading costs. Similarly, avoiding securities with high flash crash risk can deliver considerable performance improvement. Understanding market microstructure risks is no longer a matter of curiosity, but that of sound portfolio management.

A myriad of solutions for dealing with the aggressive HFTs have been proposed to date. Regulators have been called on to ban HFT from the markets altogether. New exchanges have sprung up with the aim to exclude HFTs from their ranks. None of these approaches give investors any ability to experience the upside of HFT while tuning out its downside.

In response, the AbleMarkets Aggressive HFT Index activity in real time and near real time was developed. Iteratively researched over the past eight years, the computationally intensive methodology for estimating aggressive HFT participation examines every movement of market data and delivers estimates of the percentage of volume driven by HFT orders in any electronically traded financial instrument: equities, commodity futures, foreign exchange, and options. Armed with this information on HFT participation, traditional portfolio managers, low-frequency quant strategists, and regular investors can hedge their exposure to aggressive HFT.

The research shows that a simple daily procedure for adjusting the portfolio weights of various financial instruments comprising one's portfolio significantly increases portfolio returns and reduces portfolio volatility. The process can be remarkably simple: Increase the holdings of securities where the proportion of aggressive HFT has decreased, and vice versa.

How does HFT hedging work in practice? For long-only portfolios, the simplest aggressive HFT hedging strategy works as follows:

1. Obtain the previous day's AbleMarkets Aggressive HFT Index or all the securities in your portfolio. We will denote this number as *AHFT*.
2. Compute the existing percent allocation, also known as *weight*, of each security in your portfolio by value. For example, if the total holding of AAPL in your portfolio is $20,000 and the total dollar value of your portfolio is $100,000, then the weight of AAPL in your portfolio is 20 percent.
3. Multiply all the weights computed in 2 by the following factor: $(1/AHFT)$.
4. For all the securities in your portfolio, find the sum of all weights $(1/AHFT)$:
$SAHFT = (1/AHFT1) + (1/AHFT2) + \cdots + (1/AHFTN)$, where N is the total number of securities in your portfolio.
5. Divide the weight of every security by $SAHFT$ obtained in step 4 above.

The resulting strategy could not be simpler and delivers sizable returns for portfolios of any composition. As our recent research indicates, for the long-only S&P 500, this simple strategy delivers about 1 percent extra unlevered return and 0.1 improvement in the Sharpe ratio. When the portfolio is sizable, such gains amount to a considerable increase in return. Furthermore, the strategy works in all markets: moving up or down, calm and volatile, making the Index an indispensable tool in every investor's portfolio.

Best of all, it allows investors to contain the impact of aggressive HFT on their portfolio with minimal disruption to their current way of doing business: no switching exchanges or adjusting for new regulations is required. How much is the peace of mind worth to you to contain the impact of aggressive HFT algos on your portfolio holdings?

CASE STUDY: IMPROVING EXECUTION IN CURRENCIES

Aggressive high-frequency trading in equities generates plenty of press. However, aggressive HFT in currencies is also on the rise and deserves attention. This case study considers the impact of aggressive HFTs on short-term price changes in GBP/USD, and how execution traders can utilize aggressive HFT data to improve timing of block execution.

The bursts of aggressive HFTs' market orders temporarily wipe out limit orders, resulting in three prominent outcomes:

1. Increasing the bid-ask bounce and, subsequently, realized volatility
2. Increasing slippage via increases in the bid-ask spread
3. Bidding up short-term execution prices

Tracking aggressive HFT activity allows execution traders to significantly improve their current execution methodology. Traders charged with the acquisition of a specific currency pair over a short horizon may dramatically improve their performance by detecting an onset of aggressive HFT buying activity, usually leading to price increases, and speeding up execution in the short-term. Similarly, execution traders commissioned to sell blocks of a given currency will find improvements in execution from executing larger slices of blocks at the first sign of a rise of aggressive HFT sellers.

The vanilla strategy executes the same size of trade once every minute. The enhanced strategy tracks a 20-minute moving average of the difference between the aggressive HFT buyers and aggressive HFT sellers. When the 20-minute moving average of the HFT buying activity exceeds HFT selling activity by at least 10 percent, the buying strategy buys three-minutes' worth of the currency volume, and executes nothing in the following two minutes. From November 18, 2015, through November 27 alone, the enhanced strategy was triggered 256 times, on average buying at 0.3 pips lower than the benchmark (mid or ask) each time over the eight-day period. The corresponding sell strategy performed even better, on average selling at 0.53 pips above the benchmark each trading period out of 294 instances during the eight days. Buying with the enhanced strategy reduced purchasing cost by nearly 80 pips over eight days, and selling with the enhanced strategy delivered prices nearly 175 pips higher than benchmark execution.

The results hold up for various currencies and extended time periods, making the aggressive HFT an indispensable item in an execution trader's tool bag. Due to its nature, the aggressive HFT can be used to enhance both low-touch and high-touch execution, delivering value to execution traders' clients and much-deserved profitability to execution traders themselves.

FOR LONGER-TERM INVESTORS, INCORPORATE MICROSTRUCTURE INTO THE REBALANCING DECISION

Long-term buy-and-hold investors would improve their 2015 portfolio allocation decisions by increasing allocations to stocks frequented by aggressive high-frequency traders (HFTs), according to AbleMarkets research. An illustration is a value-weighted $100 million buy-and-hold portfolio of the S&P 500 stocks formed at the end of December 2014 and held through December 2015 without any activity. This portfolio would have generated $4.6 million, a 4.6 percent return. The same portfolio where holdings were increased in proportion with aggressive HFT participation delivered $4.9 million, or a $300,000 improvement.

The allocations were once again completely passive: the aggressive-HFT-adjusted weights were selected in December 2014, according to the average values of aggressive HFT reported by the AbleMarkets Aggressive HFT Index, and left unchanged for one year.

Aggressive HFT algorithms generate considerable volatility, as shown by many studies. Most of the volatility is a direct result of the aggressive HFTs' mode of execution, namely market orders. A concentrated stream of market orders erode liquidity, widening the bid-ask spread and inducing the so-called bid-ask bounce, increasing volatility. More volatile stocks are more risky, and in the long term, require higher risk premium to compensate long-term long-only investors for holding the risk. Hence, long-term long-only investors in stocks preferred by aggressive HFT reap the extra return award.

What about portfolio risk? It turns out that the stocks favored by the aggressive HFT strategies have higher stock-specific risk and lower market risk than their peers. Stock-specific, or idiosyncratic, risk is relatively easy to diversify away in a portfolio. At the same time, the market risk, commonly known as beta, is often harder to diversify, and its relatively low occurrence among the stocks favored by aggressive HFT is welcome by institutional portfolio managers. On average, for every 1 percent increase in aggressive HFT participation among the Russell 3000 stocks, the beta decreases by 0.4 percent.

Since all HFTs are profit-maximizing agents, and since it takes months, if not years, to build successful trading systems, HFTs will naturally gravitate toward the stocks where their profitability is reliably higher. When a HFT strategy in a particular stock is profitable, it is likely a result of the stock's idiosyncratic propensity to predictably respond to news. Profitable HFT systems, once built, tend to hang around for a long time, as the operating costs of the systems are low. Even when profitability eventually begins to decline, it does so gradually and can keep the systems afloat for months. Therefore, long-term investors can be assured of the considerable longevity of their strategies, even though the underlying nature of the strategy is very short-term.

Buy-and-hold investors should enhance their core strategy by including a rebalancing adjustment based on aggressive HFT participation.

CONCLUSIONS

Traditional portfolio diversification in the age of ETFs does not work as well as when it was devised in the 1950s. Microstructure is a new frontier helping investment managers make quality decisions about their portfolio allocation strategies that result in minimal volatility and better overall performance.

END OF CHAPTER QUESTIONS

1. What are the recent changes in market volatility?
2. What are the causes of changing volatility characteristics?
3. How can investors mitigate the changes in volatility profiles?
4. How can long-term investors benefit from market microstructure in their portfolio allocation?
5. What are other uses of market microstructure, and how does it relate to volatility?

CHAPTER 10

Why Venture Capitalists Are Betting on Fintech to Manage Risks

The innovations in real-time risk surveillance and management present us with opportunities that were previously unthinkable. As a broker-dealer, you can understand factors behind your customers' performance in real time. As an investor, you can pick and choose broker dealers and avoid being pigeonholed based on your performance. Recent advances in transaction cost analytics deliver a powerful set of real-time and near-real-time risk metrics and analyses.

Fintech companies are changing business as usual for many established financial services companies. Firms like Money.net are threatening to undermine the decades-long dominance of Bloomberg. Companies like Virtu are electronically making markets. Disruptors like Kensho are automating financial research by enabling natural-language Google-style queries to replace the traditional way that research is done with immediate online access to information any analyst needs. Online lending platforms are coming out of the woodwork, directly competing with 100-year-old banks. Money transfer firms are taking on established wire operations. All sorts of traditional financial intermediation, trading, and even research are threatened by technology upstarts.

There is no doubt that the financial disruption is driven by technology: automation, often prohibitively expensive some 30 years ago, is now common and cheap. People are now wired to the global Internet through their ever-present devices. For businesses with large workforces and established operations, the new layout of the industry presents a particular challenge—how do individuals reimagine their universe to address the nimbler, faster competition with a lower cost base?

Enterprises are turning to startups to help accelerate their growth. The Internet of things is a case in point. In 2015, enterprise IoT startup companies outpaced funding for consumer startup companies by 75 percent. Verizon's experts say that enterprise IoT startup companies will raise two to three more times in capital in 2016 compared to their consumer IoT counterparts.

"The view has been that IoT is a mashup of complex technologies used only by early adopters," said Mike Lanman, senior vice president IoT and Enterprise Products at Verizon. "In the past year, we've seen compelling examples of how IoT is being deployed by a wide-range of enterprises, entrepreneurs, municipalities and developers to address relevant business, consumer and public needs. Meanwhile, consumers are more willing to try new technologies and apps that introduce a better way of life. The end result will not only give rise to thousands of new use cases over the next two years, but will also create an accelerated pipeline for innovation and a new economy."[1]

What are the incumbents to do? The most tempting solution is to follow suit. Kensho happens to be backed by Goldman Sachs and Google and benefits at least indirectly from Google's expertise in this area. Some established platforms are seeking to imitate Kensho, and are initiating costly projects to bring natural-language processing to their shops as well.

---

[1] "State of the Market: Internet of Things 2016," Verizon study.

Can an incumbent build a comparable system in a matter of months? The answer is likely no: Google has invested billions into its technology over the past decades. For most incumbents, it is difficult to even poach someone from Google: Google's employees tend to be paid handsomely, and often a match in compensation and benefits is prohibitively costly.

Other, similar, examples abound in other areas. Banks are seeking to hastily build out instantaneous lending businesses that often poorly manage risk, not to mention cannibalize their existing successful lending operations. Trading desks are looking to radically change the way they do business, uprooting successful elements in the process and risking the entire operation.

Instead of haphazard in-house replication attempts mired in red tape of compliance and meetings, established firms may choose instead to perform selective investments and acquisitions coupled with workflow reengineering. Several top-tier banks, including JP Morgan and Citi, have already embarked on such a path with much success.

As much as the term "workflow" may sound like a throwback, it actually has a special resonance in the age of automation, big data, and everything Internet. Much of the business today within large corporations happens to be a repetitive task, as much as superstar performers would like to disagree. Disentangling and streamlining business processes, aided with the selective acquisition of functions, is an exercise that is bound to both reduce costs and enhance business edginess without sacrificing competitive position. Plenty of startups provide unique features that bolt on or streamline businesses once they are acquired. They can help established businesses operate leaner, faster, and more profitably. Most importantly, this strategy will save established firms a risky and often massive expense on in-house research and development in catching up with the likes of Google and its tribe.

OPPORTUNITIES FOR DISRUPTION ARE PRESENT, AND THEY MAY NOT BE WHAT THEY SEEM

What's likely to disrupt the way financial services are done? How does one spot the opportunities? Whether you are in an existing business looking over your shoulder to stave off potential competition or an entrepreneur looking for new opportunities, the answer to the question of "What's the next big thing?" may well be worth a billion dollars. In today's world of startups, billion-dollar valuations are not impossible dreams, but pretty reasonable assumptions.

To get to a billion-dollar valuation, of course, the startup needs to have a large market for the product or service. Finding a large-enough distribution channel that pays a considerable premium in aggregate is tricky. According to recent research, most startups die following a second round of funding due to their inability to convince prospective customers to buy their wares.

Still, many billion-dollar products address needs that are not what they seem at the first glance, and many products develop "hooks" rather than identifying latent customer needs by chance. Take Bloomberg, for instance, a company that is (or used to be) the dominant powerhouse of data distribution on Wall Street. At a first blush, its core service was convenient data delivery.

Founded in 1981, in the age where computers were astronomically expensive, Bloomberg first succeeded by leasing custom monitors dedicated to all things financial. At the time, Bloomberg was essentially Wall Street's operating system, like today's Windows or Linux. As email emerged, Bloomberg introduced the @bloomberg.net email address for all its customers. Those emails quickly became coveted tokens of success and separated the haves and have-nots in the banking pecking order. When real-time messaging came online, Bloomberg messaging became a virtual negotiation facility for billion-dollar issues, over-the-counter trades, and other deals. While data was still an important component of Bloomberg business, the hefty price tags Bloomberg commanded ($4,000+ per user per month, while its closes competitor, Reuters, provided a basic setup at just $300 per month) was possible due to its emotional appeal among the financial set. Integrating the latest technology and building a strong user community has certainly worked well for Bloomberg for a long time.

Not surprisingly, then, the most disruptive competitors seeking to oust Bloomberg happened to be two companies: Money.net, focused on data distribution and trading, and Symphony, a secure messaging service with chat and other community applications designed for business. While not the only businesses in the space, the two firms appear to be the most established and advanced at the moment. Symphony has been backed and used by Goldman Sachs, and Money.net is helmed by an ex-Bloomberg executive who arrived with customers in tow.

What enabled Money.net and Symphony to dent Bloomberg's hold over the financial services sector? Several factors come to mind:

1. *Aging looks.* Bloomberg never really bothered to keep up with the evolution of the "look-and-feel" standards. Its platforms, while comfortably familiar to the old-timers, reeked of the 1980s. To the young and uninitiated, Bloombergs just started to look ancient.
2. *Lack of oversight.* The conflict of interest scandal in which it came to light that Bloomberg's reporters were mining traders' Bloomberg chatrooms for confidential information to produce breaking content angered

and alienated clients like Goldman Sachs, who quickly piled money into Symphony development.

3. *Arrogance.* Bloomberg's folks began to feel overly cocky. With their amazing midtown NYC headquarters and a founder turned NYC mayor and a rumored presidential candidate, the organization rested in its laurels and simply let the rearview window on its competition fog up.

Other players in the space, however, exist and prosper. New startups like Quandl and others offer data services similar to those of Bloomberg and Reuters, yet at a fraction of the incumbents' cost. New technologies are bringing unparalleled and previously unthinkable potential. The ability to figure out how to deploy technology to satisfy the customers' latest needs will separate tomorrow's winners and losers.

DATA AND ANALYTICS IN FINTECH

What Is Driving the Increase in Available Data?

In the past, data storage and data processing were too slow and too complex for any reasonable business application. As a result, much of the market data was simply destroyed. Modern computing power, storage, and transmission now allow companies to store and review limitless amounts of market data. Further, analysts are now also looking to IoT for insight. These include all information from applications like tolls, weather stations, freight ship tracking systems, iPhone usage, and more.

Not only has the supply of data grown, but the types of people using all of the data are changing, too. The traditional roles of exchanges, brokers, and data providers are overlapping each other as their business models change, and they are all trying to position themselves as a value-added partner to the trader by providing some form of analysis platform. Since asset managers don't have time to explore all of the new data sets themselves, they reward vendors who can provide useful ways to analyze data.

Companies like AbleMarkets make it easier for analysts to make use of large data sets by doing the hard work to develop algorithms that analyze the data and inform the analyst of insight when the algorithm finds it. AbleMarkets generates indexes that are like ETFs in real time.

Are Feeds Replacing Platforms?

As the amount of data grows, asset managers are placing a more strategic emphasis on data. This makes the reliance on Bloomberg or Reuters more than a simple outsourcing decision. Large asset managers are considering whether structured platforms fit with their need for a broader and deeper library of data feeds.

Reuters, for example, offers clients the ability to use its platform or to receive data feeds directly. The value of a Reuters or a Bloomberg becomes more questionable with new players like Quandl offering data feeds at very low prices. Quandl considers its open platform to be a "democratization of data." By bringing all numerical data into one place and building a smart index and interface, Quandl opens up quantitative information to everyone. Quandl claims to offer 4 million financial and economic time series for free.

Many asset managers prefer to receive data feeds directly. When a specialist like AbleMarkets works with an asset manager, the frequency of downloading data becomes important, and having to work through a third-party platform often just creates latency issues.

As the volume of data expands and is offered more rapidly, the portfolio manager needs to take advantage of new ways to harness data without doing all of the analysis. Predictive analytics is one answer emerging in the marketplace.

What happens when an alpha-generating data source is purchased by a certain number of large hedge funds? Doesn't the alpha of the data source decline, rendering the data source worthless? Not so fast. It turns out that in most cases, the data become a must-have for all investors.

What is must-have data? Must-have data are the reference data that every modern portfolio manager, execution trader, and risk manager should own. Today's examples of must-have data sources include daily data access to all asset classes, streaming high-frequency data for financial instruments of choice, interest rate and volatility curves, streaming news, social media summary, market participant analysis, and much more.

FINTECH AS AN ASSET CLASS

In the current low-interest rate environment, hedge funds and other investors looking for yield are increasingly turning to fintech as an asset class. Merchant banks have become increasingly attuned to the opportunities in the sector. SenaHill leads the way by specializing in fintech, not only do they represent entrepreneurs for raising capital, selling companies, and taking them public but they also have an accelerator that leverages a network of former fintech operators who play a role driving growth in portfolio companies.

The current valuation for fintech companies varies, depending on their subindustry. According to Raymond James, the enterprise value of a fintech

TABLE 10.1 Raymond James Estimates of Enterprise Value Premia over Revenues for Fintech Businesses (USD in millions)

Sector	Enterprise Value/Revenue			Enterprise Value/EBITDA			Long-term EPS Growth
	LTM	2016E	2017E	LTM	2016E	2017E	
Liquidity Venues	9.6×	9.2×	8.8×	15.4×	14.7×	13.6×	11.3%
Information Services	4.7×	4.5×	4.4×	15.8×	14.1×	12.6×	12.4%
Payments	4.4×	3.3×	3.0×	14.5×	12.0×	10.9×	14.7%
Bank Technology	4.9×	4.2×	4.0×	14.7×	12.2×	11.2×	12.8%
Trading Technology	1.3×	1.3×	1.2×	12.8×	12.3×	11.0×	13.9%
Outsourced Solutions	1.9×	1.9×	1.7×	10.1×	9.4×	8.4×	12.8%
Benefits/Payroll	6.1×	5.3×	4.9×	18.7×	16.0×	13.9×	20.0%
Real Estate/ Mortgage Services	1.5×	1.3×	1.2×	9.6×	8.9×	8.1×	14.4%
Financial SaaS	6.3×	5.7×	5.0×	21.1×	16.3×	15.4×	22.5%
Investment Technology	3.4×	3.1×	2.8×	16.0×	12.9×	11.0×	13.7%
Marketing Services	1.8×	1.4×	1.3×	14.2×	16.6×	9.3×	15.3%
Insurance Technology	2.9×	2.8×	2.4×	15.5×	12.7×	15.7×	11.1%
Overall Median	3.9×	3.2×	2.9×	15.1×	22.1×	11.1×	13.8%

Source: Raymond James Investment Banking, *FinTech Monthly* (September 2016), Available at https://www.raymondjames.com/corporations_institutions/investment_banking/pdfs/fin_tech_monthly.pdf

firm as a function of revenues can be a multiple of 1 for trading technologies and 10 for liquidity venues, as Table 10.1 shows. Last quarter annualized (LQA) revenues or even last trailing month annualized (LTM) revenues may be used as a benchmark.

As Table 10.1 documents, liquidity venues such as exchanges and dark pools command the highest multiple of revenues in the group: nearly 10×. When measured relative to earnings before interest, taxes, depreciation, and amortization (EBITDA), however, enterprise value carries the highest multiple for financial software as a service companies (SaaS).

WHERE DO YOU FIND FINTECH?

Where do you find your dream fintech company, whether to invest into or join in? Fin-techies tend to congregate at fintech meetups. A meetup is a quite formal gathering, a mini-conference even, complete with sandwiches and refreshments. These meetings are venues to learn what entrepreneurs are working on and the priorities of investors. Beer tends to be the alcohol of choice; the more obscure the brewery, the better. Fintech is obvious in all: presentations, participants, and end-of-event discussions. A few common fintech themes:

1. *Fintech dress code is not a myth.* To dress fintech is a reality, even a paradigm. The "most sophisticated" fintech participants dressed in the following unisex fashion from down up: (1) expensive shoes, (2) skinny jeans or other dark snug and form-fitting pants, (3) a navy blazer, and (4) a white shirt. According to some participants, such ensemble screams fintech and casts one in a role of the industry insider. Other, more laid-back fin-techies opt for a fleece vest, often inscribed with their firm's logo, atop a collared shirt.
2. *Fintech is not just for kids.* Fintech kids are certainly cool and well-versed in the latest business or computer technologies. Still, the most successful fintech businesses are run by 40-something geezers who have cut their teeth again and again and have enough experience under their designer belts to avoid the most basic pitfalls.
3. *The "new normal" fintech startups can be 12+ years old and still considered to be startups.* Take Money.net, for instance, an up-and-coming disruptor of Bloomberg. In reality, it took Money.net 12+ some years to reach this point. Unlike the original .com wave of the late 1990s that IPO-ed in four years or less, the modern fintech businesses go public in "their teens," if at all.
4. *Fintech is a state of mind.* Lots of formerly "normal" Wall Street types have now drunk the Kool-Aid, seen the light, and converted into the fintech purveyors, whether from the point of view of investing, employment or all of the above. And come to think of it, what other industry in New York is growing at a comparable pace?

FINTECH SUCCESS FACTORS

They say the hardest part of any startup business is to book its first client. AbleMarkets' index tracking aggressive high-frequency trading (HFT) activity on Quandl (http://www.quandl.com/data/ABLE) booked its first client the first day it went live. What is behind the success of this premium new offering? Here are five key success factors for new and reinvented businesses alike:

1. *Uniqueness.* A first-to-market advantage is definitely palpable. While HFT as a market category has been around for a while, AbleMarkets is the first firm to figure out how to statistically identify high-frequency strategies in the exchange data. The index pinpoints even the most sophisticated HFTs, those deploying the latest techniques to camouflage themselves in raw exchange data. With the demand for this information at an all-time high, providing the first solution satisfying the demand is a big competitive advantage.

2. *Applicability.* This is the "so what" question that destroys so many unique startup offerings. Some startup statistics report that as many as 66 percent of all startups close after their second round of funding due to their inability to find customers that validate the use cases for their product. What does one do with the Aggressive HFT Index? As the research indicates, the Index is not only informative about the relative proportion of aggressive HFT in different stocks, but it is also immensely beneficial for portfolio optimization strategies for pension funds and other portfolio managers who reallocate their positions just monthly or even quarterly. Paying attention and incorporating the Index into one's investment decision-making process not only reduces portfolio risk, but it also increases returns. This is a very valuable benefit in today's markets where many finance professionals feel that the aggressive HFTs are eating at least part of their lunch.

3. *Exactness.* Does a product exactly address the problem? In the case of the AbleMarkets Aggressive HFT Index, the answer is yes. Even though a variety of solutions have been previously proposed by top thinkers, including some esoteric academic exercises, for how to adjust to the presence of high-frequency traders, AbleMarkets Aggressive HFT Index takes the problem and solves it in its entirety. This has been made possible only through a careful and thorough study of what the problem actually entailed and related issues.

4. *Proven expertise.* Having an expert in the field on the team is a great benefit. AbleMarkets benefits from the know-how expertise of co-founders who have been studying the field for years and has even a few books on the subject.

5. *Partnerships.* A startup network is part of the business strength. AbleMarkets' decision to partner with Quandl (quandl.com) is mutually

beneficial and complementary. Quandl is a modern data platform that provides seamless capabilities for data delivery, something that AbleMarkets is leveraging in data distribution.

Client development is a hard task that is made considerably easier when a startup strategy incorporates the above five factors.

THE INVESTMENT CASE FOR FINTECH

Through the chapters of this book, we've described many of the risks from the move toward real time. These risks originate in the changes buffeting financial services. The acceleration of technology, the burden of regulation, and the desire to use more and more data faster and faster all create an opportunity for innovators to build new companies that solve pressing problems.

Alpha

A class of fintech companies aim to help investment professionals develop an edge that improves their performance. Analyzing the news or incorporating data from IoT are examples of ways that new technologies can deliver information that was not accessible before.

Using this data as part of trading strategies is not new. Factor models and the use of nonfinancial data have been around for a long time. The opportunity is that more uncommon data sets are now available, in part enabled by predictive analytics.

Predictive analytics is the area of data science that uses large data sets of uncommon information to predict behavior based on analytical technique that go well past regression analyses. Innovation in this area is partly focused on how to use unstructured data to inform decisions for investors or any business manager.

Regulation

A group of companies have sprung up to work on making the regulatory burden easier to manage. The term regtech has emerged to shine a spotlight on the distinct value proposition that these firms have. Some of the ideas driving regtech include making the forms and documentation required by government and regulators part of a platform. Others are creating workflows that enable many people working in different functions to collaborate and to assemble the information required in a thoughtful manner that leverage time-savings workflows.

Capital Management

Financial institutions, especially brokerages, post capital during the securities settlement process and also reserve capital based on their regulatory requirements. The interest in blockchain and fintech ideas that accelerate/ streamline the process of fulfilling a trade or that de-risk their business help financial institutions to reduce their need to hoard cash.

Some of the advances in the analytics of volatility help companies better manage their risks and reduce the amount of cash that they need to keep on hand.

Execution

Many fintech companies have built platforms that help financial institutions with the way their trades are executed. This isn't the decision about what to buy or sell. The firms work on the challenges relating to getting the best price at the lowest cost once the trade decision is made. High-frequency trading technologies, including REDIPlus and the AbleMarkets Aggressive HFT Index, are examples of methodologies that innovate how to place trades and improve the quality of execution.

In the past, fintech innovation in this space focused on obtaining market data, placing trades, building order-entry tools, and speeding up execution. Innovation continues on these topics, and more recently big data and advanced analytics have become the focal point of innovation. As trading platforms and the operational processes that support them become more advanced, it becomes possible to use expanded data sets. Much of this book is dedicated to data and analysis because the advances from innovation in this area move more and more activity toward real time.

Managing the risks related to these advances is important. Risk managers need to have tools that protect traders and financial institutions from exposures that manifest themselves in real time.

Volatility

Understanding volatility is critical to every risk manager and investor alike. The innovations described in this book advance insight into the causes of volatility and the ability to watch out for rapid changes in volatility.

As trading become more rapid, using traditional approaches to assessing volatility become less meaningful.

HOW DO FINTECH FIRMS MAKE MONEY?

Investors into fintech companies can pick and choose the types of innovation just described. But how do these fintech companies make money? What value propositions have proven to be successful? Three groupings summarize the opportunity:

- Data and analytics
- Workflow
- Trading platforms

Data and analytics companies have developed methodologies for acquiring, storing, and processing large amounts of data. These big data solutions generate value for companies focused on both the infrastructure and the software. These firms are scalable and often operate on a SaaS basis earning monthly subscriptions to use the intellectual content.

Workflow companies are focused on automation and standardization. A lot of the effort in fintech addresses the reality that banks have remained largely manual over the years with very large supporting workforces. By automating forms, centralizing regulatory information, to name a few examples, many of the manual processes become digital.

Trading platforms are also the core product for a group of fintech companies. By offering clients better execution, cheaper trading, or market data that was not accessible before these companies have prospered at the expense of full-service brokerages.

These business models share a common thread. They are scalable businesses that bring advances in technology to financial services. They facilitate controlled environments where risk taking is matched with risk monitoring in an environment of increasing automation, digitization, and real-time trading.

FINTECH AND REGULATION

And the regulators are helping along the way, often unwittingly. The new regulations from MiFID II, for example, dictate sweeping changes. All brokerages are required to demonstrate best execution and provide full disclosure and transparency on the following items: price, transaction costs, speed of execution, likelihood of execution, trading venue selection, and so on. To a traditional broker-dealer, implementing these requirements is a maze of complexities, and fintech upstarts in the space seem like a good option.

Another regulator, US Commodity Futures Trading Commission, is also struggling with its own financial data-related troubles. To enable comprehensive surveillance of the US markets, the CFTC has pondered creating a unified database with clean, orderly columns that can be populated by various parties. The challenges of fitting the data into a set of databases are many and cost a serious amount of money, not just to regulators but to all who fall under the regulators' jurisdiction. Some banks, for instance, employ teams of people, often one per product, whose sole task is to work out a plan to neatly store data to match the regulators' requirements. However, the idea that all of the data should fit neatly into a two-dimensional table can be considered prehistoric in the modern computer age.

The bridge between the regulators' dreams and data realities of the big Wall Street players can be fintech. Fintech companies focusing on data science regularly turn volumes of un-unified, unformatted, simply called *unstructured* data into meaningful inferences. The analysis of unstructured data can be as simple or as complex as one would like to make it. Random matrix analysis, for instance, helps researchers find dependencies, inferences, and clusters of insights worth knowing in seemingly random, poorly organized, barely populated data sets. The findings, in addition to answering key questions of who, how, and when, proved to be a goldmine for companies like Google, uncovering marketable patterns.

Settlement is another aspect of finance where fintech adoption is badly needed. Under the current data gathering and management regime, trades take three days to custody and settle—an eternity in the big data world. At the time this book was written, an industry initiative was working to reduce the settlement cycle to two days. The push to speed up settlement is driven by the very firms that are presently threatened with disruption by blockchain, a nascent, yet winning way to manage settlement risk in real time. In the not-so-distant future, fintech blockchain technology looks like a winning piece of the settlement puzzle across the globe.

And the list goes on. Chicago Mercantile Exchange, hungry for fintech exchange innovations, recently acquired the Best Alternative Trading Systems (BATS) group of equity exchanges. Thomson Reuters acquired REDI. CBOE acquired LIVEVOL.

The pace of innovation is accelerating in the financial services industry and the accompanying risks are best tackled with new technologies pioneered by startups.

CONCLUSIONS

Once upon a time, or, more precisely, just some 20 years ago, *data* was a term reserved for magnetic tapes and numerous governance committees, engaged in weekly discussions on the best ways to name data fields in order to accommodate the universe of financial products. Fast forward to today, and (surprise!) many financial firms still engage in the same practices. Extensive data governance committees spar over what is the optimal way to write out a name of a listed option and how that should differ from the requirements of a custom over-the-counter derivative.

Fintech is positioned to solve such challenges. Big data initiatives are typically too costly and too risky for governments and large companies to start up. Red tape and multilayer compliance processes tend to be the graveyards of even the best unproven initiatives. Fintech startups, therefore, present promising test environments—low-risk innovation labs for high-velocity ideas.

> *Life is inherently risky. There is only one big risk you should avoid at all costs, and that is the risk of doing nothing.*
>
> *– Denis Waitley*

END OF CHAPTER QUESTIONS

1. What are the common valuation methodologies for fintech companies?
2. What are the multiples?
3. What are the success factors of fintech firms?
4. How do most fintech companies make money?
5. What is a common driver of fintech adoption?

Irene Aldridge

Irene Aldridge is President and Head of Research at AbleMarkets, a Big Data for Capital Markets company. She is a recognized expert on market microstructure and high-frequency trading with over 20 years of experience on Wall Street. Prior to founding AbleMarkets, Irene was a quantitative portfolio manager and quant trader. Previously, Irene held senior and executive roles in quant risk management, large system integration, software and hardware architecture, and enterprise Internet security. She began her career as a software developer.

Irene holds a BE in Electrical Engineering from Cooper Union in New York, MS in Financial Engineering from Columbia University in New York, MBA from INSEAD in Fontainebleau, France, and has studied in two PhD programs: Operations Research at Columbia University (ABD) and Finance (ABD). She has been a member of the CFTC sub-committee on HFT since 2011.

Irene is the author of *High-Frequency Trading: A Practical Guide to Algorithmic Strategies and Trading Systems* (Wiley 2009, 2013, translated into Chinese) and multiple academic studies published in peer-reviewed journals. Irene is also a columnist for Huffington Post and often appears on television in expert capacity. Irene serves on the Board of Directors of Carnegie Hill Neighbors in NYC.

Steve Krawciw
Steve is CEO and Head of Business Development of AbleMarkets. Steve is a veteran of financial services with over 20 years of experience in industry strategy, financial product development, launch, business development, integration, and operations. Steve has developed channel relationships with quantitative portfolio managers, electronic execution traders, and risk managers within prominent organizations. Prior to AbleMarkets, Steve launched over \$4 billion in products at Credit Suisse, and led business strategy, spanning financial improvements, corporate reorganizations and acquisitions, restructuring, and process improvements at CIBC asset management, McKinsey & Co., and Monitor Group.

Steve frequently speaks and publishes on the topics of predictive analytics, real-time risk, and innovation in the Capital Markets.

Steve holds an MBA (Finance) from Wharton and a BComm from the University of Calgary. Steve is a Trustee of the Southampton Historical Museums and enjoys long-distance running, skiing, tennis, and other racquet sports.

Index

AbleMarkets, 3, 6, 10, 16, 17, 35, 55, 56, 86–91, 93, 96, 98, 113, 114, 116, 117, 125, 131, 137, 139, 151, 158, 159, 173–176, 178–182, 184, 191, 192, 194–197

Accelerator, 192

Access to Data See access to information

Access to Information, 9, 32, 36, 48, 61, 109, 137, 154, 163, 188, 192, 196, 198

Account number, 37, 53, 60

Achilles' heel in models, 24

Acquiring data, 6, 164, 169, 173, 181, 198

Acuity Trading, 6

Adding liquidity See liquidity addition

Adverse selection, 61, 66, 85

Aflac, Inc. (NYSE: AFL), 114

Aggressive HFT activity, 3, 56, 67, 89–96, 99, 125–126, 132, 139, 141, 143, 151, 153–154, 182, 183

Aggressive HFT Index, 87–89, 96–98, 133, 137, 151–153, 163, 174, 178, 182–184, 194, 195, 197

Aggressive High-Frequency Trading, 16, 17, 56, 61–65, 84, 86–102, 125, 126, 131–133, 137–143, 151–154, 174, 177, 180–185, 194, 195, 197

Agilent Technologies, Inc. (NYSE: A), 139, 140

Agreement score, 161

Agriculture, 129

AHFT see Aggressive High-Frequency Trading

Aldridge, Irene, 86, 201

Alere, Inc. (NYSE: ALR), 114

Algo see Algorithm

Algorithm, 6, 10, 14–16, 18, 23, 34, 35, 39, 41, 44, 46, 55, 70, 86–88, 91, 99, 101, 105, 110, 113, 130–132, 162, 174, 177, 179, 181, 183, 184, 191

All-weather securities, 172, 173

Alpha DEC, 28, 29

Alpha decay, 86, 192

Alphabet, Inc. (formerly, Google), 3, 7, 8, 14, 16, 17, 19, 27, 71–76, 80, 90, 96, 161, 163, 181, 188, 189, 199

Alternative data sources, 130

Alternative Trading Systems (ATS), 18, 29, 41, 43–46, 53–54, 57, 199

Altman, Edward, 4, 16

Amazon.com, Inc. (NASDAQ: AMZN), 3, 7, 8, 27, 90, 167

American Express Company (NYSE: AXP), 93, 115

American Pharoah, 21

American Stock Exchange (AMEX), 42

Ametek, Inc. (NYSE: AME), 114

AMEX see American Stock Exchange

Android, 13

Anonymity in markets, 31, 32, 42, 44, 54, 56, 60, 80, 86, 90, 125, 151

Anticipatory hedging, 61, 86

Apache Corporation (NYSE: APA), 114

App, 11–16, 27, 35, 36, 59, 168, 188

Apple MacBook Air, 27

Apple watch, 11, 12, 13, 197

Apple, Inc. (NASDAQ: AAPL), 3, 7, 8, 11–14, 27, 158, 160, 175, 183

Aqua, 43

Arbitrage, 49, 61, 63, 64, 84, 94, 109, 137

Around-the-clock trading, 11

Artificial Intelligence, 163

Ask (offer), 26, 46, 47–49, 66, 184

Australian dollar, 101, 102, 115, 116

Automated Trading Desk (ATD), 69

Automation, 1, 4, 6–8, 24, 29, 30, 34, 39, 51, 84, 101, 168, 180, 188, 189, 198

Avellaneda, Marco, 175

Baby boom generation, 17

Backtest, 181

Baidu, Inc., 34

Ban on ETFs, 112, 113

Ban on HFT, 182

Bank Mobile, 13
Bank of America Corp., 114
Bank of International Settlements, 61
Bank of New York Mellon (NYSE: BK), 114
Bank Technology, 193
BankMobile, 13
Bar codes, 166, 169
Barclays, 2, 43, 44
Basel III regulation, 19
BATS, 42, 49, 50, 68, 70, 71, 81,
    139–141, 199
Behavioral, 69, 134, 135, 157
Benchmark, 113, 174, 184, 193
Benzinga, 11
Betterment, 17
Bhattacharya, Ayan, 112
Bid-ask bounce, 62, 65, 89, 183, 184
Bid-ask spread, 62, 89, 90, 96, 183, 184
BillGuard, 13
Bitcoin, 15, 31, 32
Black swans, 173
Block trading, 44, 46, 70, 80, 183
Blockchain, 15, 30–34, 39, 45, 62, 197, 199
BlockCross, 43
Blog, 19, 155, 159
Bloomberg, 1, 11, 45, 92, 93, 129, 130, 135,
    136, 139, 146, 147, 163, 165, 188,
    190–192, 194
Board of Trade City of Chicago, 42
Boeing Co. (NYSE: BA), 95
Bonds, 9, 30, 41, 45, 83, 98, 104, 106, 107,
    172, 177
Boston Scientific Corporation (NYSE:
    BSX), 114
BOX Options Exchange LLC, 42
Brazilian Real, 115, 116
Brexit, 155,156, 158
Bridgewater Associates, 138
Bristol-Myers-Squibb Co. (NYSE:
    BMY), 114
British pound sterling, 55, 101, 102, 116,
    155, 183
Brokers, 2, 15, 17, 36, 41, 46, 48, 53–56,
    59–63, 80, 86, 106, 150, 187, 191
Buy-and-hold, 172, 184, 185
BuzzFeed News, 8
Byte, 27

Cables, data transmission, 36, 39
Canadian dollar, 101, 102, 115, 116
Capital Asset Pricing Model (CAPM), 22

Caterpillar, Inc. (NYSE: CAT), 95
Centurylink Inc. (NYSE: CTL), 114
Charles Schwab, 53
Chesapeake Energy Corporation (NYSE:
    CHK), 114
Chevron Corporation (NYSE: CVX), 95
Chicago Board Options Exchange,
    Incorporated (CBOE), 42, 199
Chicago Mercantile Exchange (CME), 11,
    41, 61, 199
Chicago Stock Exchange, Inc., 42
China, 28, 33
China International Capital Corp., 34
Chinese yuan, 115, 116
Chronicle, 12
Circle, 33
Cisco Systems, Inc. (NASDAQ: CSCO), 95
Citadel LLC, 1
Citi, 12, 43, 69, 189
Citi Cross, 43
Citibank see Citigroup, Inc.
Cleaning data, 22, 162
Cliffs Natural Resources, Inc. (NYSE:
    CLF), 114
Cloud, 7, 9, 14–16, 27, 164, 175
Clustering, 18, 162, 199
Cobalt International Energy, Inc. (NYSE:
    CIE), 114
Coca-Cola Co., The (NYSE: KO), 95
Cody Willard, Chairman of Scutify, 11
Collateral valuation, 97
Colocation (colo), 38, 39
Column-oriented databases, 25, 26
Commodities, 41, 53, 54, 90, 94, 99, 101,
    107, 113–115, 117, 167, 169, 182
Commodity Futures Trading Commission
    (CFTC), 53, 199
Computer chips, 28
Conference Board, 3
Construction Spending Index, 138, 147, 153
Corporate bonds, 172
Cross-asset, 91, 110, 113, 115, 171
Crossfinder, 43
CROSSSTREAM XSTM, 43
Crowdfunding, 6
Crowdsourced, 161
Crude Oil, 90, 99, 100, 101, 115, 116
Cummins, Inc. (NYSE: CMI), 114
Currencies, 31–33, 41, 94, 101, 102,
    114–117, 156, 183, 184
Custodians, 33

CVS Health Corp. (NYSE: CVS), 114
Cyberattacks, 34

DAB Bank, 13
Daily close prices, 18, 45, 51, 55, 97, 158
Dan Raju, CEO of Tradier, 14
Danaher Corporation (NYSE: DHR), 114
Dark pools, 8, 29, 41–57, 60, 63, 66,
    68–70, 72, 78, 97, 193, 194
Data analysis see Data analytics
Data analytics, 4, 6, 7, 9, 15–19, 23, 26, 39,
    96, 119, 131, 155, 156, 159–161,
    163–165, 169, 174, 178, 191, 192,
    196–198, 202
Data feeds, 62, 129, 130, 159, 191, 192
Data mining, 16, 190
Data Science, 21, 22, 24, 35, 125, 174, 196,
    199
Data Scientists, 21, 23, 32, 33, 162, 174, 181
Databases, 15, 17, 22, 25, 26, 32, 33, 45,
    67, 68, 131, 157, 160, 164, 167, 174,
    181, 199
Dealerweb, 43
Decision tree, 18
Decline in the costs of computer technology,
    14
Deep learning, 18
Deere & Co. (NYSE: DE), 114
Delta Air Lines (NYSE: DAL), 114
Denis Waitley (quote), 200
Derivatives, 18, 27, 46, 61, 86, 107, 109,
    110, 172, 200
Deutsche Borse, 106, 108
Disrupting financial services, 1, 3, 9, 19,
    165, 183, 188–190, 199
Disrupting information dissemination, 169
Disrupting market stability, 19
Dodd-Graham, 179, 180
Dow Jones Industrial Index (DJIA), 104,
    105, 115, 116

E I Du Pont De Nemours and Co (NYSE:
    DD), 95
E*Trade, 12
Earnings Announcements, 52, 129
EBS, 63
Eigenvalue Decomposition see Principal
    Component Analysis
Electronic Communication Network (ECN),
    53, 60

Electronic trading, 59, 61, 96, 102, 109,
    181, 182
Eli Lilly and Co (NYSE: LLY), 114
Emerging markets, 107, 115
Encryption, 37
Enron, 173
Entry barrier, 29
Equities, 27, 41–43, 46, 47, 49, 50, 53, 55,
    56, 61, 80, 90, 93, 94, 96, 98, 99, 101,
    107, 109, 112–117, 124, 126, 135,
    172, 175, 178, 180–183, 199
ETF Ban, 112, 113
ETF turnover, 108
Euro Currency, 94, 102, 113–117
European Union, 155
Event studies, 138, 139, 143
Everbright Securities Co., 34
Exchanges, 1, 3, 8, 18, 19, 27, 19, 31–33,
    35, 37, 39, 41–51, 53–55, 60–65,
    67–72, 75, 78, 80, 86, 87, 94, 97, 98,
    101, 102, 106, 108, 110, 113, 139, 171,
    175, 177, 178, 181–183, 191, 195, 199
Exchange-traded funds (ETFs), 6, 18, 23, 29,
    41, 53, 93, 94, 105–113, 119, 123,
    126, 127, 178
Execution, 6, 10, 15, 18, 29, 31, 33, 41, 44,
    46–50, 52–57, 59–61, 63–74, 76–81,
    85, 87, 88, 90, 92, 97, 98, 101, 137,
    174–176, 179, 180, 183, 184, 192,
    197–199.
Exxon Mobil Corporation (NYSE: XOM),
    95

Facebook, 162
Factset, 129
Fake news, 10
Fama, Eugene, 133, 176
Federal Deposit Insurance Corporation
    (FDIC), 108
Federal Reserve, 172
Fidelity National Information Servics Inc
    (NYSE: FIS), 12, 114
Fill (order execution), 48, 61, 67, 80
Financial crisis, 25, 157, 173
Financial Industry Regulatory Authority
    (FINRA), 44, 53
Financial Information Exchange (FIX), 35,
    70
Financial services industry, 3, 7, 56
Fintech acquisitions, 6, 8, 69, 189, 199, 202
Fintech themes, 194

Fixed income, 101, 106, 113
Flash crash, 45, 97, 103–127, 172, 177–182
Flash Crash Index, 179
Flickering quotes, 66, 67, 76–81
Forecasts, 16, 23, 29, 92, 134–6 139,
    146–151, 153, 154, 168, 173, 180
Foreign exchange, 33, 41, 47, 53, 61–63,
    94, 101, 102, 106, 177, 182
Forest Laboratories Inc. (NYSE: FRX), 114
Funding Circle, 5
Futures, 11, 41, 42, 53, 54, 84, 104, 107,
    121, 167, 172, 177, 182, 199

General Electric Company (NYSE: GE), 95
Getco, 22, 125
Goldman Sachs, 7, 115, 161, 188, 180, 191
Google Wallet, 8
Google, Inc. see Alphabet, Inc.
Graham Holdings Company (NYSE: GHC),
    88

Hacking, 34, 61, 164
Harvard University Endowment, 125
Hasbro, Inc. (NYSE: HAS), 158
Hedging, 61, 85, 86, 121, 172, 179, 182
HFT Ban, 182
Hidden limit orders, 66, 68–73, 76–81
High-frequency trading, 3, 6, 16–18, 29, 30,
    51, 56, 61, 63–65, 67, 70, 78, 81,
    83–102, 124–127, 131–133, 137–143,
    151–154, 171, 173, 174, 177,
    180–185, 194, 195, 197
Home Depot, Inc. (NYSE: HD), 95

IBM (NYSE: IBM), 49, 54, 59, 61, 63, 64,
    84, 85, 95, 104, 105, 118, 167
ICAP, 63
Iceberg orders, 48, 68
IDG Capital Partners, 34
IHS MarkIt, 138
Image recognition, 169
Immediate or cancel orders (IOC), 70
Implied Vol, 100
Information asymmetry, 61, 80, 84, 96
Information embargo, 96, 130, 133, 136,
    137, 143, 150, 151, 154
Information leakage, 27, 38, 80, 136, 148,
    154
Information spillover theory, 107
INSTINCT X MLIX, 43

Instinet Continuous Block Crossing System
    (CBX), 43
INSTINET CROSSING XIST, 43
Institute for Supply Chain Management
    (ISM), 139
Institutional activity, 113- 116, 125,
    131–133,
Institutional Activity Index, 114
Institutional investors, 6, 8, 17, 44, 46, 66,
    67, 80, 81, 90, 97, 101, 113–117, 125,
    126, 131–133, 185
Insurance, 3, 31, 34, 62, 171, 193
Interactive Brokers (IB), 43, 54,
Inter-Continental Exchange (ICE), 41, 70
Interest rates, 16, 19, 84, 172, 192
Internet of things (IoT), 167–169, 188, 191,
    196
Intraday margining, 21
Investment account, 12, 14, 15, 30, 37, 41,
    53, 54, 60, 61
Investment advisory industry, 2
Investment management industry, 17
Investor beliefs, 9, 10, 133, 176
Investor Due Diligence, 97
ISE Mercury, 94
iShares MSCI socially responsible ETF
    (NYSE: DSI), 106
ISM Manufacturing Index, 133, 135, 136,
    139–146, 148, 149, 152

Jamie Dimon, CEO of JP Morgan Chase, 3
Japanese yen, 101, 102, 114–116
Johnson & Johnson (NYSE: JNJ), 95, 114,
    115
JP Morgan (NYSE: JPM), 1, 3, 43, 53, 95,
    189

KCG MATCHIT, 43
KDB, 26
Kensho, 7, 161, 188
Kickstarter, 6
Knight Capital Group (KCG), 34, 43, 53, 84
Know Your Customer (KYC), 31, 32
Korean won, 116
KX Systems, 26

Language parsing, 162
Last Quarter Annualized (LQA), 193
Latent Semantic Analysis, 162
Legal Entity Indentifier (LEI), 62

Lehman Brothers, 62
Lending Club, 8
Level ATS, 43
Level III Data, 71
Light Pool, 43
LightStream, 6
Limit order addition, 67, 68, 70–75, 77, 78, 79, 81
Limit order adjustment See limit order revision
Limit order cancellations, 46–48, 51, 65–79, 81
Limit order revision, 75,
Limit-order book, 44, 46, 47, 49, 55, 57, 59, 62, 65, 66, 68, 69, 72–74, 77–81, 84–85, 89, 90, 108, 116, 117, 119, 126, 175, 177
Linux, 190
Liquidity, 46, 47, 50, 51, 54, 59, 61–67, 69, 76, 78, 80, 81, 84, 87, 89, 90, 97, 110, 118, 184, 193
Liquidity addition, 65, 89
Liquidity erosion, 97, 118, 119, 184
Liquidity taker fees, 51
Liquidnet, 43
Liquifi, 43
Livevol, 199
Luminex Trading and Analytics, 43

Machine-collected, 10
Machine-generated, 79
Machine-learning, 10
Machine-readable, 161
Macro, 8, 109, 110, 113, 135, 154
Macroeconomic, 133, 136, 154, 160, 163
Malicious behavior, 41, 69
Manipulation, 17, 21, 52, 124
MapReduce, 16
MAR, 114
Marco Avellaneda, 175
Market inefficiencies, 96, 109
Market maker, 6, 18, 51, 53, 60, 64–67, 84–86, 96, 107, 129, 154, 176
Market order, 48, 70
Market timeliness, 32
Markit, 138
MCD, 95, 114, 115
MCObject, 26
Meetup, 194
Merchant bank, 192
Merck & Co. (NYSE: MRK), 114

MERRILL LYNCH (ATS-1), 43
Message (s), 8, 9, 36–38, 68, 70–79, 165, 168
Message traffic, 36, 75, 76, 77
Metric(s), 21, 56, 88, 97, 171, 180, 187,
Mexican peso, 115, 116
Microseconds, 22, 63, 91, 92, 137, 162
Microsoft (NYSE:MSFT), 114
Microsoft Azure, 27
Microstructure, 57, 98, 99, 174, 176, 177, 178, 179, 180, 181, 182, 184, 185, 201
Microwave communication towers, 36
Mid-price, 48
MiFiD II, 19, 56, 198
Millenials, 7, 11, 17, 165
Millennial Disruption Index (MDI), 7
MILLENNIUM NYFX, 43
Mint, 13
Mitigating, 30, 173
Mobile, 8, 9, 10, 11, 14
Model(s), 2, 4, 8, 9, 17–19, 22–25, 52, 70, 96, 107, 113, 121, 138, 169, 174, 178–181, 191, 196, 198
Momentum, 7, 17, 36
MoneyWiz, 12
Monte Carlo simulation, 16, 29, 175
Motif Investing, 6
MS POOL (ATS-4) MSPL, 43
MSCI, 106
Municipal bonds, 9
Mutual funds, 27, 106

Nasdaq, 38, 41, 42, 62, 70, 96
NASDAQ BX, Inc., 42
NASDAQ OMX, 42, 50
National, 19, 41, 42, 49, 50, 53, 63, 64
National Best Bid Best Offer, 49, 50, 51, 53, 54, 57, 63, 64, 68, 98
National Futures Association (NFA), 53
National Securiries Exchanges, 41, 42
Nationwide, 7, 80
Natural gas, 90, 113, 115–117
Natural Language Processing (NLP, 131, 161, 162
Natural liquidity, 66
Natural-language, 161, 188
National Best Bid/Offer (NBBO), 49, 50, 51, 53, 54, 57, 63, 64, 68, 98
Near real-time, 21, 30, 157, 172, 187
Negotiation, 15, 31, 78, 190
NEM, 114

Network architecture, 181
Network(s), 9, 11, 31, 34–38, 53, 59, 67, 157, 168, 169, 181, 192, 195
Neural, 18, 169
Neutral sentiment, 156, 160
New York Stock Exchange, 41, 42, 63
News, 3, 8–10, 19, 22, 35, 38, 41, 45, 47, 51, 52, 63, 64, 84, 92, 93, 95, 96, 99, 103, 129–172, 176, 185, 192, 19
News Absorption, 93
News aggregators, 130
News analysis, 129–158, 160, 196
News announcement, 47, 52, 90, 92–96, 129–131, 133–154
NewsHedge, 12
Newspaper, 18, 45, 51, 170
NKE, 95
Node (blockchain), 33, 164
No-flicker, 79
Nonfarm payroll, 92, 93
Normal exchange, 50
Normalized, 88, 159
NQLX LLC, 42
NYSE, 26, 42, 50, 53, 63, 70, 88, 93, 94, 95, 106, 108, 109, 110, 111, 112, 114, 115, 126, 139, 140, 158, 178, 179
NYSE Arca, Inc., 42, 53, 108

Offer see Ask
Office of Financial Research (OFR), 62
Official news announcement time, 133, 138, 143, 145, 148, 153, 154
One-sided trading activity, 117, 119
Online channels, 4, 10, 17, 18, 19, 167, 169, 173, 175, 176, 181, 188, 190
Operating model, 2, 8
Operation, 4, 15, 27, 29, 34, 80, 162, 169, 175, 188, 189
Operation costs, 36, 185
Opinion formation, 9, 10, 22, 136, 139, 157, 162, 169, 175
Opportunistic liquidity, 66
Opposing orders, 59, 62, 89
Option(s), 27, 41, 42, 53, 61, 84, 86, 110, 121, 161, 175, 177–179, 182, 199, 200
Options Clearing Corporation (OCC), 175
Order flow, 37, 53, 54, 66, 71, 86, 101, 119, 125, 151, 154
Order Management System (OMS), 59
Order matching, 45, 50, 53, 65, 66, 68, 72, 73, 78, 79, 177

Order(s), 5, 10, 15, 22, 27, 31–37, 42–94, 97, 108, 114–119, 125, 126, 137, 139, 156, 169, 173–183, 190, 200
Orlando Sentinel, 163
Outbound message packets, 37
Out-of-sample, 179
Out-of-the-money, 179
Outsourcing, 14, 191
Overhead, 2, 138
Overlay, 55
Overreliance on machine learning, 23
Oversampling, 23
Oversight, 190
Over-The-Counter (OTC), 15, 190, 200
Ownership transfers with Blockchain, 33

Packet, 36
Patterns, 55, 56, 99, 118, 119, 137, 199
Performance attribution, 159, 174
Phishing see Pinging
Pinging, 66, 69, 77–81
Platforms, 1, 2, 3, 6, 7, 9, 14, 129, 176, 188, 190, 191, 192, 197, 198
Portfolio, 6, 11, 17, 18, 19, 27, 35, 52, 66, 91, 92, 97, 101, 106, 107, 110, 154, 171, 172, 173, 174, 175, 176, 177, 178, 179, 180, 182, 183, 184, 185, 192, 195, 201, 202
Portfolio allocation, 6, 91, 92, 97, 174, 182, 184, 185
Portfolio weightings, 91, 92, 165, 177, 182, 184
Portfolio weights adjustment, 177, 182, 185
Post-trade analytics, 19, 178
PowerShares WilderHill, 106
Predictive, 17, 22, 23, 30, 89, 96, 97, 101, 130, 154, 158, 159, 164, 173, 174, 176, 178, 192, 196, 202
Predictive analytics, 17, 96, 97, 192, 196, 202
Predictive technology, 17
Price, 8, 17, 27, 28, 46, 47, 48, 49, 50, 52, 53, 55, 56, 59, 60, 61, 62, 63, 65, 66, 67, 68, 69, 71, 74, 75, 76, 84, 85, 87, 88, 89, 93, 94, 96, 100, 103, 104, 109, 110, 113, 116, 118, 119, 121, 131, 132, 133, 134, 135, 136, 138, 139, 140, 141, 142, 143, 144, 145, 146, 147, 148, 149, 150, 151, 153, 154, 158, 163, 174, 175, 176, 177, 183, 190, 197, 199
Price adjustment, 134, 135, 175,

Price equilibrium, 25, 109
Price or market movement, 17, 19, 52, 79, 86, 113, 117, 118, 129, 141, 143, 144, 154, 167, 172–177, 182
Principal Component Analysis, 18, 162, 175
Probabilistic, 121, 125, 131
Processing, 6, 13, 14, 16, 18, 19, 28, 41, 49, 57, 78, 81, 84, 87, 131, 157, 160, 161, 162, 164, 166, 169, 174, 180, 181, 188, 191, 198
O'Hara, Maureen, 112, 113
Profitability, 6, 27, 36, 86, 87, 88, 143, 154, 164, 168, 184, 185
Program, 14, 35, 62, 155
Programmatic, 159
Projected, 48, 91, 168
Prop, 24, 56, 84, 94
proportion of high-frequency trading, 6, 67, 68, 69, 87, 90, 94, 95, 97, 98, 101, 114, 115, 126, 139, 140, 141, 146, 153, 177, 182, 184, 195
Proprietary, 24, 36, 70, 114, 125, 176, 180
Providers, 13, 26, 51, 56, 130, 166, 181, 191
Proxies, 113

Quandl, 191, 192, 195, 196
Quant, 3, 18, 24, 25, 59, 135, 182, 201
Quantitative, 4, 21, 52, 53, 119, 192, 201, 202
Quantlab, 22, 86
Queries, 7, 161, 188
Quote, 11, 19, 36, 45, 49, 50, 53, 62–68, 76, 80, 84, 98
Quote dissemination, 36

Radio-frequency identifiers (RFIDs), 166
Random, 19, 26, 37, 45, 119, 130, 141, 159, 199
Random walk, 119
Range-bound, 184
Rapidly decaying alpha, 86
Rational Expectations hypothesis, 133, 134, 138, 142, 154
Ravenpack, 158, 160
Raw data, 22, 162, 195
Raymond James, 192, 193
Real-time, 11, 12, 15, 16, 21, 33, 41, 49, 59, 87, 96, 109, 129, 130, 155, 157, 166, 170, 172, 174, 182, 187, 190, 191, 196, 197, 199

Real-time margin calculation, 15
Rebalancing, 29, 52, 101, 176, 184, 185
Rebates, 50, 53
Reconciliation of trades, 31, 32, 62
REDIPlus, 197
Redundancy, 164, 165
Registered, 41, 42, 44, 104, 116
Regression, 17, 174, 196
Regtech, 196
Regulation, 1, 8, 18, 19, 46, 49, 50, 56, 57, 99, 167, 168, 183, 196, 198
Regulation Alternative Trading Systems (Reg ATS), 18, 46
Regulation National Market Systems (Reg NMS, 2005) 19, 42, 49, 50
Regulators, 46, 47, 56, 61, 62, 98, 157, 178, 182, 196, 198, 199
Regulatory, 7, 8, 19, 35, 41, 53, 168, 172, 196, 197, 198
Regulatory burden, 196
Regulatory capital, 172, 175
Reliability, of measurement, of prediction, 5, 15, 36, 70, 116, 158, 164, 166, 168, 173, 185
Research, 7, 11, 14, 18, 36, 56, 62, 67, 78, 83, 86, 88, 90, 93, 97, 98, 109, 110, 116, 117, 119, 133, 138, 139, 146, 156, 157, 159, 172, 175, 176, 180, 181, 182, 184, 188, 189, 190, 195, 201
Resting liquidity, 47, 66, 72, 73, 74
Retail investors, 6, 8, 14, 15, 29, 43, 141, 166
ReturnPath, 173
Returns, 10, 22, 61, 86, 87, 91, 96, 97, 104, 107, 109, 117, 119–123, 139, 141, 158, 164, 171, 172, 174, 177, 178, 182–184, 195
Reversal, 104, 113, 116, 117
RFID, 166, 167
Risk aversion, 6
Risks, 1, 15, 19, 23, 24, 32, 37, 38, 39, 41, 56, 57, 61, 67, 70, 84, 91, 108, 109, 112, 163, 164, 170, 172, 177, 182, 187, 189, 191, 193, 195, 196, 197, 199
Rite Aid Corporation (NYSE: RAD), 90
RIVERCROSS RCSL, 43
Rockwell Collins, Inc. (NYSE: COL), 114
Round-lot order, 35
Round-trip, 50, 150
Route of an order, 48, 49, 54, 60, 86
Row-oriented, 25, 26

Rows, 17, 22, 25, 32

Run, 29, 47, 49, 65, 79, 118, 119, 120, 121, 123, 124, 125, 162, 180, 181, 194

Runaway algo, 35, 41, 105, 177

Russell 3000, 135, 136, 141, 142, 143, 144, 145, 146, 147, 148, 149, 150, 151, 153, 185

Russian ruble, 115, 116

Sample Data, 23, 47, 71, 179

Sampling, 78, 164, 165, 175

Scalable architecture, 6, 201

Scale, 78, 92, 166, 177

Scenario, 37, 48, 63, 78, 109

Scheduled announcements, 12, 137, 138, 144, 148, 150

Scraping data, 166, 169

Scutify, 11

Securities and Exchange Commission (SEC), 50, 50, 53, 62, 81, 80, 175

Securities, 15, 30, 34, 41, 42, 44, 49, 56, 87, 104, 108, 109, 110, 112, 113, 116, 125, 126, 155, 172, 173, 180, 181, 182, 197

Security information processor (SIP), 19, 49, 53, 62–64, 80, 81

Security information processor (SIP) tape, 7, 53, 62, 80, 81, 189, 200

Selerity, 6

Self-driving car, 168

Sell-off, 95, 112, 113, 114, 115, 116, 117, 125, 126, 131, 133, 139

Senahill, 192

SENSENews, 160

Sensors, 164, 167

Sentiment, 6, 10, 155, 156, 157, 160, 161, 162, 163, 165, 170, 174

Sentiment analytics, 160, 161, 163, 174

Sentiment score, 159, 160, 161

Servers, 34, 39, 125

Settlement, 4, 15, 29–33, 45, 62, 197, 199

Shares, 35, 42, 43, 44, 46, 49, 54, 59, 72, 73, 76, 104, 109, 110, 135, 150, 160, 181

Sharpe ratio, 86, 87, 91, 92, 171, 176, 183

Shorter settlement time, 15, 30

Short-selling, 109

Short-term, 10, 16, 21, 22, 64, 92, 94, 96, 97, 113, 126, 138, 157, 158, 177, 183, 185

SIGMA X SGMA, 43

Signal, 16, 23, 78, 135, 139, 158, 164, 180

Signaling, 80, 81

Silicon Valley, 1, 3, 5, 7, 8, 9, 11, 13, 14, 15, 17, 19

Silver, 90, 104, 115, 116

Single-column tables, 25

Slippage, 177, 183

Smart Beta, 6, 107, 121

Smart cement, 167

Smart Order Routing, 56

Smartwatch, 11, 12, 13

Social media, 1, 9, 10, 11, 16, 34, 84, 129, 143, 155, 156, 157, 158, 159, 160, 161, 162, 163, 164, 165, 167, 169, 170, 172, 175, 176, 192

Social Media accounts, 10

Social media analytics, 9, 155, 156, 159–161, 163, 165

Social Media Index, 10, 158, 176

Software, 12, 16, 83, 159, 169, 173, 193, 198, 201

Software-as-a-Service (SaaS), 7, 193, 198

Southwestern Energy Company (NYSE: SWN), 114

Spark, 16

Speed, 18, 22, 24, 29, 30, 33, 35, 36, 37, 38, 41, 46, 49, 50, 56, 63, 65, 67, 69, 78, 84, 157, 160, 174, 175, 179, 199

Spreads see Bid-Ask spreads

Square, 7

St. Jude Medical, Inc (NYSE: STJ), 114

Stale quotes, 36, 62, 63

Standards, 35, 51, 61, 181, 190

Startups, 2, 3, 5, 8, 13, 17, 29, 188, 189, 190, 191, 194, 195, 199, 200

Stat-arb, 1, 24, 25, 109, 113

State Street Corp (NYSE: STT), 114

Statistical significance, 79, 81, 113, 145, 151, 164, 165, 177

Statistics, 12, 17, 68, 74, 79, 81, 88, 96, 104, 109, 145, 151, 164, 195

Stop losses, 180

Straddle, 179

Strategic role of data, 99, 191

Strategies, trading and investment, 9, 24, 25, 27, 48, 55, 65, 67, 84, 86, 87, 88, 90, 92, 96, 109, 113, 114, 121, 126, 137, 143, 150, 154, 173, 182–185, 189, 195, 196, 201, 202

Streaming data, 3, 160, 173, 174, 181, 192

Structure, 3, 22, 31, 41, 43, 45, 47, 49, 51, 52, 53, 55, 56, 57, 70, 181

Studies (academic, reseach, case study), 7,
16, 68, 77, 80, 91, 101, 133, 134, 135,
138, 139, 156, 157, 162, 165, 179, 180,
183, 184, 195, 201
Suitability, 13, 15, 36, 51
SunTrust Banks, Inc. (NYSE: STI), 6, 13, 114
SUPERX DBAX, 43
Surveillance, 17, 37, 38, 187, 199
Swiss Franc, 101, 102, 115, 116
Symphony, 1, 190, 191
Synthetic ETF, 113

Taking liquidity, 50, 59, 89, 126
Techniques, 17, 18, 69, 125, 162, 165, 172,
175, 180, 195
Technologies, 6, 8, 16, 30, 32, 36, 39, 139,
140, 163, 188, 191, 193, 194, 196,
197, 199
Temporary market phenomena, 59, 93, 109,
113
Terminals, 1, 2, 28, 45
Testing of data, 22, 31, 39, 78, 116, 125, 200
Text, 26, 28, 37, 161, 162, 168
The Two Sigma model, 6
Thematic investing, 6, 12, 106
Theories, 27, 107, 133, 134, 154, 156,
173, 176
ThinkNum, 166, 173
Thomson Reuters, 1, 11, 119, 123, 129,
190, 191, 192, 199
Tick, 22, 47, 49, 65, 118, 119, 120, 123, 178
Time magazine, 13
Timeline of cross-asset institutional activity,
114
Timeliness of Data Analysis, 164
Time-sensitive, 64, 65
Time-series, 26
Time-stamp, 25, 26, 71, 78, 157
Time-weighted, 55
Timing, 51, 55, 137, 174, 183
Tobacco, 106
Tool, 15, 112, 183, 184
Toolkit, 70
Tools, 9, 10, 17, 36, 167, 177, 197
Toxic flow, 154
Toxic liquidity, 51, 66, 67
Trade, 6, 10, 12, 14, 16, 23, 25, 30, 31, 32,
33, 36, 41, 42, 43, 44, 45, 46, 48, 51,
52, 54, 61, 62, 64, 66, 67, 76, 84, 85,
86, 87, 89, 98, 109, 110, 112, 114, 118,

119, 120, 135, 136, 137, 143, 145, 148,
150, 154, 165, 174, 179, 183, 197
Trade negotiation on trading venues, 31, 33
TRADEBOOK, 43
Trade-by-trade reconciliation, 62
Tradier, 14, 15
Trading desks, 24, 36, 69, 137, 189
Transact, 10, 30, 46
Transaction, 4, 10, 15–17, 31–33, 35, 36,
45, 56, 87, 150, 177, 178, 187, 199
Transaction Cost Analytics, 187
Transactional data, 16, 39
Transfer, 4, 15, 33, 34, 35, 36, 188
TransferWise, 4, 10, 15
Transform data, 131, 174
Transformation, 3, 7, 8
Transmission, 36, 37, 39, 48, 63, 70, 127,
157, 166, 191
Transmission Control Protocol (TCP), 36
Transmission Control Protocol / Internet
Protocol (TCP/IP), 36
Transparency, 17, 35, 56, 112, 113, 199
T-ratios, 144, 146, 148, 149
Travelers Companies Inc (NYSE: TRV), 95
Treasuries, 90, 98, 99, 101, 106, 113, 115,
116
Trend, 4, 17, 21, 39, 115, 157, 163, 168, 180
Trends in Technology, 27
Triple Crown, 21
Trulia, 12
T-statistics, 145
Turkish lira, 115, 145
Tweet, 129, 162, 165
Twitter, 6, 10, 143, 159, 160, 165, 176

U.S. Census Bureau, 138
UBS, 43
UK pound sterling see British pound sterling
Ukraine, 34
Uncertainty, 19, 34, 47, 155, 156
Uncommon data, 6, 113, 173, 196
Uncorrelated data, 6, 178
Unemployment rate, 92
Unencrypted, 37, 59
Unformatted data (see unstructured data),
22, 39, 161, 196, 199
Unified database, 199
Union Pacific Corporation (NYSE: UNP),
114
United Airlines see United Continental
Holdings, Inc.

United Continental Holdings, Inc. (NYSE: UAL), 163
United Technologies Corporation (NYSE: UTX), 95
UnitedHealth Group Inc (NYSE: UNH), 95
Universal product codes, 166
Unlevered return, 183
Unregulated, 53, 101
Unstructured data, 199
Unsupervised learning, 162
Upfront premium, 86
US Dollar (USD), 55, 94, 102, 113, 183, 193
Use cases, 9, 10, 12, 17, 19, 25, 27, 31, 32, 57, 61, 64, 65, 69, 70, 78, 80, 86, 88, 90, 91, 102, 110, 125, 129, 165, 167, 168, 174, 177, 179, 188, 191, 192, 195, 196, 197, 198
User Datagram Protocol (UDP), 36
U-shaped pattern., 55

Valuation, 7, 25, 29, 97, 110, 156, 167, 172, 179, 180, 189, 192, 200
Value-weighted, 184
Vanguard, 17
Variations, 88, 96, 97, 101, 144
Vector machines, 18
Venmo, 8
Venture capital, 3, 17, 187–200
Verizon (NYSE: VZ), 95, 167, 188
Video-gaming, impact of, 14, 29,
Virtu, 22, 84, 88, 125, 188
VIVUS, Inc. (NASDAQ: VVUS), 90
VMware, Inc. (NYSE: VMW), 114, 159

Volatility, 10, 17, 21, 48, 51, 52, 62, 65, 86–89, 91, 96–99, 101, 104, 109, 110, 112, 141–145, 156, 158, 159, 171–185, 192, 197, 198
Volatility curves, 175, 192
Volume, 1, 16, 18, 19, 28, 29, 42, 43, 45, 46, 55, 84, 87, 88, 94–96, 98, 99, 101, 102, 106, 110–112, 125, 126, 129, 131, 132, 139, 140–142, 151, 154, 176, 181–183, 192, 199
VWAP, 55, 70

Wait-and-hold strategy, 90
Wal-Mart, 95, 131, 132, 133
Walt Disney Co. (NYSE: DIS), 95
Warren Buffett, 179
Wayne Gretzky (quote), 11
Wealthfront, 17
Weather-based, 129, 166, 172, 191
Web content, 22, 155, 159, 166
Weyerhaeuser Co (NYSE: WY), 114
widening spreads, 47, 62, 89, 184
Workflow, 8, 15, 189, 196–198

XE WDNX, 8 43
Xerox Corp (NYSE: XRX), 114
Xetra exchange, 106, 108

Yield, 96, 192

Zopa, 5
Zynga Inc (NASDAQ: ZNGA), 90